THE PHENOMENON OF POLITICAL MARKETING

THE PHENOMENON OF POLITICAL MARKETING

The Phenomenon of Political Marketing

Nicholas J. O'Shaughnessy

St. Martin's Press   New York

First published in the United States of America in 1990

Printed in Hong Kong

ISBN 0–312–03222–6

Library of Congress Cataloguing in Publication Data
O'Shaughnessy, Nicholas J., 1954–
The phenomenon of political marketing/Nicholas J. O'Shaughnessy.
p. cm.
Includes index.
ISBN 0 312 03222 6: $39.95 (est.)
1. Campaign management. 2. Electioneering. I. Title.
II. Title: Political marketing.
JF2112.C3084   1990
324.7—dc20   89–6387
                                                    CIP

Contents

List of Plates

Acknowledgements

I would like to warmly thank those who helped in the making of this book. Gillian Peele at Oxford was a particular source of inspiration, and Chapter 5 is very largely based on our joint essay 'Money, Mail and Markets' in *Electoral Studies*. I also owe a real debt to Mrs Vera Cole of Loughborough University. Her prodigies of valour with my hieroglyphic script merits high tribute. My thanks also to Mrs Sally Jarratt of the University of Wales who typed my first, ungainly draft.

NICHOLAS J. O'SHAUGHNESSY

The author and publishers are grateful to the following for permission to reproduce copyright material:

New York Times for tables in Chapter 6.
The Economist for extensive quotations in that chapter.

Introduction

Th' applause of list'ning senates to command,
The threats of pain and ruin to despise,
To scatter plenty o'er a smiling land
And read their history in a nation's eyes.

Thomas Gray, *Elegy written in a Country Churchyard*

The process by which the most powerful democracy in the world arrives at its electoral judgements can never be over-studied. The consequences of that choice, for Americans and the world they influence, are too profound. Yet political science, the academic craft whose profession it is to study elections, has adhered to the interpretative traditions it comprehends best: the interrelationships between branches of government, the powers and nature of the presidency, the legislative process, bargaining, and so on. Its focus, in other words, is institutional, and while it acknowledges the role of marketing it is bemused by it, not knowing what precisely it should call the phenomenon.

Indeed, the phenomenon is baffling. How influential is it – merely peripheral to the major determinants of electoral behaviour such as the state of the economy? There is about it a mercurial quality that defies prim categorisation, the elaborate model buildings of intellectual abstraction the matter is coarse, gaudy, booming, garish; mawkish, sensational, bloodshot; to the priesthood of learning, then, profoundly irritating. So they have avoided the matter, or, when they address it, have done so in terms of the most lofty condescension, fluctuating between dismissing it as a sideshow or lapsing into despair at such evidence of the trite follies of their fellow-men.

And yet – what is really so new? Could we have watched a Pericles or a Quintilian, a Cicero or a Demosthenes, charm and stagger their crowds, raise them from the dross of every day to intimations of historic glory, we would have read in their smiles, their protestations, their gestures, the same old tale: there never was an aboriginal innocence. Honour fled when men first congregated. Is there, then, a connection between Reagan's rhetorical sugar lumps, his histrionic

xi

backdrops, and Alexander's addresses and stage-managed episodes: do the pageants of Rome and the pageants of the campaign trail connect in any way? From the first, symbolism and rhetorical gestures were inseparable from the political process.

Even political marketing as a formal process, as distinct from propaganda, is now an old guest, going back at least to Whitaker and Baxter in the nineteen-thirties. But when the last button is dropped into the trashcan, the last banner swept away, will Americans have suffered a serious diminution of the quality of their politics as a result of the arrival of political merchandising techniques? While it is legitimate to view its contemporary excesses with alarm, the ritual mudslinging that so well attests to the anti-heroism of the age, there are limits to what marketing can do. It can certainly define and enhance the message and image. Thankfully, it cannot create them. There is, at least, scope for real political skill, and democracy does have a remarkable power to generate antidotes to the abuses it incubates.

Cambridge, 1989   NICHOLAS O'SHAUGHNESSY

1 Introduction: The Electronic Soapbox

'The people reign in the American political world as the Deity does in the universe. They are the cause and the aim of all things; everything comes from them, and everything is absorbed in them.'

Alexis de Tocqueville, *Democracy in America*

'Political Marketing' – a term we see increasingly in newspapers, a part now of the baggage of conventional orthodoxy – has come into its own with popular recognition that it is a convenient shorthand for something people recognise as central to the operations of their democracy. In 1988 the Presidential campaign confirmed yet again the magnetism of approaches that conceived of politics as a product marketing exercise, with chairmen of major advertising agencies backing top Republican candidates Dole (Gray Advertising) Kemp (BBDO) and Bush (the ex-Chairman of Young and Rubicam).

This book is concerned with political advertising on the paid media and other promotion channels and, to a lesser degree, with free publicity from television news. For this is the fulcrum of the American political process, and its prizes go to those best able to modulate the media. We examine the import of commercial selling techniques to politics and the use of modern technology to communicate candidate, party and programme, arguing that such promotion is demonstrably highly effective and that from this fact flow ominous consequences. In Presidential campaigns, this marketing task will centre on the management of events, speeches and debates, and such esoteric exercises as damage limitation and press control; in lower campaigns purchased media is the focus.

But our conclusions are of the tentative rather than the declamatory kind. The central thesis is that American politics are shaped by the need to market candidates and parties as if they were soap powder, employing techniques taken from the world of business. The consequences, so often negative, are by no means always so, for there is about this entire subject an inherent moral ambivalence.

Many aspects of the political process from the very earliest times could be described as primeval forms of marketing under its most broad-brush definition. We could say indeed that all politics was

1

marketing but this would be tautologous; speech-making and advocacy is promotion of a kind, and so are the venerable political skills of packaging a programme to appeal to a strategic coalition of constituencies. Yet this would be to nag the term to its furthest limits and deprive the concept of its usefulness. For the definition to be functional, it must be tight. It should embrace a bounded category, a point at which conventional politics ends and a distinctive appendage begins.

Yet the term 'political marketing' operates upon several levels. One is mechanical, a description of a set of commercially derived techniques and their application. The other relates to orientation – the consciousness of the marketing concept on the part of politicians and their associates, and the insights and behaviour that flow from this. This is not to claim that politicians always see themselves as performing a marketing activity, for marketing is simply a description of the reality that arises even if they would ostensibly spurn such a label.

Marketing is furthermore a derivative of what people seek in so far as this can be determined. It is not simply the attempt to persuade them to a point of view; therefore the election conducted by the British Labour Party in 1987, though it used media creatively, was not driven by any marketing concept: it was advertising devoid of the larger awareness that marketing brings, otherwise the party would have attended more to the popularity of its 'product', that is, its policies, as well as to its communications. The essence of marketing is reciprocity: 'consumers' themselves bring something to bear on the selling; they are not passive objects and the process is an interactive one.

POLITICS AND MARKETING THEORY

In 1960 the American Marketing Association (AMA) defined marketing as 'the performance of business activities that direct the flow of goods and services from producer to consumer or user'.[1] The subsequent history of the discipline was one of expanding this definition, a history that is important to us since a pre-requisite of this work is to establish the legitimacy of the political marketing concept. Marketing as an academic study originated in the early years of this century, a derivative of applied economics that emphasised the analysis of distribution channels;[2] later it focussed on the increase of sales and then, under the guise of a behavioural science, on buyer or seller systems. Thus by the stage at which the AMA sought a clear definition for it the subject matter seemed clearly established – pricing, market research, sales management, distribution, retailing, advertising, international marketing, purchasing and so on all rested comfortably in the shade of its disciplinary umbrella.

But academics become restless. Other areas of human activity seemed to share analogous processes, but were excluded from their subject's conceptual embrace: for Kotler 'the traditional conception of marketing would relegate this discipline to an increasingly narrow and pedestrian role.'[3] In 1965 a group at the University of Ohio[4] described marketing as not just a business discipline but a social process, and Lazer pronounced that marketing should not remain a mere technology of the firm; Dawson drew attention to the 'social ramifications of marketing activity' and in 1969 Kotler and Levy[5] stressed that the concept should be expanded to embrace non-commercial entities – police, churches and so on. These moves opened up a potentially rich field of study, but they were initially resisted by those who felt it would create conceptual vagueness and dilute the business focus; in other words, by becoming more academic this subject would become less relevant and practical. Carman[6] for example saw the 'exchange of values' as the core marketing definition, so that processes like politics which did not involve this should be rejected; however, 95 per cent of marketing academics believed that their subject should include non-business areas.[7]

So now there could be 'social marketing' or 'political marketing' or the organisation's relations with non-client groups ('consciousness three'). New definitions of the subject concentrated on the idea of the transaction – 'Marketing is specifically concerned with how transactions are created, stimulated, facilitated and valued'[8] – then 'a general idea of exchange rather than the narrower thesis of market transactions',[9] and finally 'actions undertaken by persons to bring about a response in other persons concerning some specific social object'.[10]

While it is possible to achieve definitions so abstract as to be meaningless, there could be no doubt now that the application of marketing to politics was a legitimate field of investigation, at least to marketing academics ('the political strategist, to the extent that he is effective, is a professional marketer').[11] Marketing might legitimately interact with other subjects such as psychology which also studied transactions, though it was distinguished from them because 'only in marketing is the transaction the focal point'.[12] Writers also stressed that such value was defined subjectively from the market's viewpoint: this has important political implications since it would extract from modern statecraft all leadership function, the articulation of unpopular truths and the creation of a novel vision. The approach taken in this book is not however one of rigorously applying marketing theory. We could have used the core litanies and terms at every stage, that is, politics and candidates are 'products', voters are 'customers', going to the polling booth and foregoing alternative pleasures are a 'price', candidate meetings are 'distribution', and so on; but those labels can be taken as understood, and continuously to reiterate them would be to strait-jacket the approach and undermine a sense of the pressure, the fluidity of political processes. Marketing is a soft technology, and our real aim is to stress the extent to which modern campaigns are infused with a marketing awareness articulated with marketing tools, rather than to fit the chimerical nature of elections into a rigid disciplinary framework.

Kotler, in addition to his work in more conventional areas of marketing, did seek to discuss its applications to politics. He spoke of 'legislative marketing', the persuasion of parliamentarians, and also of 'citizen marketing', the influencing of voter behaviour.[13] He admitted that he was applying to an extent new language to old truths – 'campaigning has always had a marketing character', and what was new was not the methods but 'an increased sophistication and acceleration of their use'. The 'candidate concept' forms the orientation of the campaign; voters are given the 'symbolic reassurances' they seek; the candidate is 'positioned' *vis à vis* competition; the campaign must adjust to new events, possible themes must be based on samples of target voters. Kotler quotes Glick:

> The personal handshake, the local fund-raising dinner, the neighbourhood, the rally, the precinct captain, and the car pool to the polls are still very much with us . . . the new campaign has provided a carefully co-ordinated strategic frame within which the traditional activities are carried out in keeping with a Master Plan. It centres on a shift from the candidate-controlled, loosely knit, often haphazard 'play it by ear' approach to that of a precise, centralised 'team' strategy for winning or keeping office.

The ethical implications of political marketing appear to elude Kotler. He quotes Nimmo's 'cynical' view:

In screening potential candidates the mercenaries have given a new dimension to the notion of 'availability'; the marketable candidate is selected on the basis of his brand name, his capacity to trigger an emotional response from the electors, his skill in using mass media, and his ability to 'project'. Analysis of social problems and issues yields to parroting of themes; televised debates between contenders produce meaningless confrontations rather than rational discussion.

Kotler finds fault with the 'moral judgmental' tone adopted, and claims that the marketing of politics will exist anyway whatever the particular methods used. But chosen methods cannot be irrelevant to the ethical argument, and the fact that the marketing concept appears inseparable from modern politics does not mean that we should therefore resign the role of critic. Moreover these methods are seen by some as creating a qualitatively new kind of democracy, and the value of this marketing re-created political culture needs to be assessed. Kotler raises, apparently without concern, a number of concomitants of this political marketing approach. The candidate must 'Formulate a look and behaviour that match the target voters' perceptions and needs' *and* 'Voters are in need of a certain political character at a given time who will champion their hopes and assuage their fears'.[14] Now as technical prescriptions for electoral success these notions are valid, but Kotler appears oblivious to their connection with a particular paradigm of democracy which many would gainsay. Edmund Burke, for example, saw the parliamentarian as in no way a delegate, but as a man chosen for his high abilities to offer them in the service of the state.

There is a broad gulf between these ideas. Burke's is avowedly elitist; the other has been a consistent notion in the history of the American Republic. But the more representative concept of democracy which political marketing sponsors implies the problems of weak leadership, vacillating policy, insubstantial ideas and all the other ills of giving electorates, uninformed and impulsive, the central direction of events – noise without meaning, movement without purpose. To the ultra-democrat however value is measured by mass approval, and wisdom is that which most people hold to be true. But others may see menace in the abandonment of the leadership function by politicians.

Moreover politics is not a product, however useful such a conceptualisation is for campaigning purposes, and the consequences of political choice may be deep and lasting in a sense that consumer choice never can be, for they ultimately determine the kind of society we are: to conceive of politics as a product is to invest it with a banality which does a disservice to idealism and to the citizen's kinship with the state.

MARKETING AND POLITICAL THEORY

In what ways does political marketing contribute to and re-define American democracy, and what of the ethics of the process? The answer to the ethical question depends on the views of democracy we hold, and our assessment of the handiwork of earlier democratic theorists. While we could begin with some idealised conception of democracy and work back from that, we know that such a paragon never existed and never will, for the conditions for its success would demand a nature nobler than humankind.

In the history of political thought, the kind of fragmented group-interest democracy that political marketing today sustains and articulates received mixed reviews. A consequence of political mass marketing seems to be the supersession of broadly-based political associations by single cause groups and other narrowly defined factions. This issue-oriented 'political nation' is distinguished from the older base of political support by greater commitment to narrower issues, and the possession via direct mail of detailed and intimate information, so that the ambiguities of political parties have been discarded by some for the immediate satisfaction of adherence to a specialised lobby.

The effect of merchandised politics is to sharpen faction. This is because emotive political appeals aimed at specific groups and addressing their key aspirations have proven much more effective than general, and therefore necessarily bland, propaganda. The political philosophers of antiquity, Herodotus for example, perceived factions as one of the inevitable errors of democracy, while more recently faction has been viewed as the definitive democratic trait and even a virtue, so that Bentham believed that competing interests would naturally balance each other and Lipset saw the essential test of government as its ability to satisfy individually powerful pressure groups.[15] But Dahl thought that every policy created democratically would merely reflect the agenda of some influential minority, and earlier this century continental writers were even more sceptical, believing the fault of democracy to be its vulnerability to powerful interests. The limitations of the group interest concept of democracy were well put by one Republican in 1968:

> We believe the Democratic candidate is a decent man, trapped between 1932 and Camelot. And at a time when this nation cries for unity, he talks in the sad, old jargon of the hyphenated American – Spanish–American, Black–American ... We must stop talking to Americans as special interest groups and start talking to special interest groups as Americans.[16]

For Plato and political theorists down the ages, a further problem of democracy has also been the poor leadership democratic systems create. The adoption of a marketing orientation by politicians may be seen as producing weaker leadership since it stresses a constant vigilance towards public opinion and the shaping of policy to accord with it. Thucydides feared the emergence of men who flatter the vanity of the mass, while Aristotle saw a need of successful democracy as being a willingness to trust talented men with the management of its affairs (in this he was echoed by Weil in the twentieth century).[17] Edmund Burke reflected that little men are not made great by being popularly chosen, and de Tocqueville was at one with the ancients: 'I attribute the small number of distinguished men in political life to the ever-increasing despotism of the majority of the United States'.[18] John Stuart Mill stressed that under democracy the people do not govern but choose their governors, and feared for the survival of the able individual in public life; all such theorists could only accept an elitist-arbitrated democracy if they accepted it at all, a notion which has been anathema to Americans since the early years of the Republic. But the progress of the marketing concept through American politics has accentuated this preference of democracy for the likeable leader over the strong, the smart phrase over the smart idea, the common over the elegant; it has redefined democracy's criteria further along the paths antiquity most feared since it vaunts appeals to immediate satisfaction and superficial, instantly communicable indices of worth.

A related criticism of the adoption of the political marketing orientation is that it makes politics more fickle and opportunistic. To de Tocqueville, the American constitution seemed to exacerbate the problem: 'The Americans determined that the members of the legislature should be elected by the people directly, and for a very brief term, in order to subject them, not only to the general convictions, but even to the daily passions, of their constituents.'[19] Thus political marketing may on a cynical interpretation be viewed as magnifying the vices inherent in democracy, vices observed by its earliest critics, such as the feckless popular will feared by Herodotus.

However, there are important arguments in defence of the political marketing approach. Through its very stress on disaggregation, its intimate appeals to specific sections of the public rather than the public as a whole, it helps to frustrate the evolution of oppressive majorities. For de Tocqueville, the potential for majoritarianism was the greatest danger in American democracy: 'For myself, when I feel the hand of power lie heavy on my brow, I care but little to know who oppresses me; and I am not the more disposed to pass beneath the yoke because it is held out to me by the arms of a million of men.' He saw the antidote as being corporations of private interests, the very groups which merchandised political communications help develop: 'Governments, therefore, should not be the only active powers: associations ought, in democratic nations, to stand in lieu of those powerful private individuals whom the equality of conditions has swept away.'[20]

Political marketing methods enable such agglomerations to take shape and voice, but not every theorist perceived a danger in the existence of majorities powerful enough to force their will onto other groups. Bentham reposed happy in the greatest good for the greatest number. Political marketing is anti-majoritarian in the long term as the pursuit of fragmentation is its core dynamic. But even here there is ambivalence. For the marketing approach can exacerbate short-term pressures when interests briefly coalesce.

A CRITIQUE OF POLITICAL MARKETING

First, and above all, the need to market candidates, parties and policies – a compulsion partly created by the laxity of legal controls on the use of television – imports a massive monetary imperative into US politics, and that is when the damage begins. In 1986 the cost of a typical Senate run was $3.1 million; in 1984 Jesse Helms had spent $16.5 million on his campaign, Jay Rockefeller $12 million on his, and Mondale $40 million on primaries alone. House and Senate candidates raised $340 million in 1986.

The high costs of merchandised politics are met by politicians who in effect barter legislative favours in return for subsidy; they become mortgaged to high-pressure vested interests. So laws help the benefactor industries and professions, and bills express the legislative ambitions of articulate pressure groups. To label the process 'corrupt', to dismiss its intricacy and nuance in that one word, would be overly simple, although it is difficult to adopt a stance of moral neutrality.

Interest group politics then, and new men. For Americans might also find themselves represented by a new kind of politician. He may be a good communicator (though this is not essential: the technicians can varnish ungainly natural style). The real point is that he will be adept in the skills of attracting money, and this in fact will be his primary task and the central preoccupation of his life both before and during his time in office. Political consultants, the hired guns of the process, are also a consequence since participation demands the leasing of specialised expertise; power goes to consultants who manage the campaigns and therefore accumulate influence, staffers who become decisively involved in policy formation because the statesman is engaged in his public relations battle, and the civil servants. Moreover there has been a filtering down of knowledge of marketing's various tools and technologies; while organisation and strategy are often well comprehended even at the bottom of the system.

Electorates also remain uninformed as to the candidate's credentials in many vital areas of whatever job specification we might imagine for the political task, for there is scant pressure for television analysis and debate when politics is expressed through a barrage of lucrative advertisements. Quite the reverse: for to saturate the audience with yet more politics would be to exhaust their tolerance. The claim is not that advertising is specious but rather that politics are too important a task to be the exclusive property of jingle-writers.

The phenomenon of political marketing has further led to the demise of the volunteer, the heavy cavalry of an earlier political age, for professional consultants have begun to replace them and the volunteers themselves will be found punching data into a computer rather than on the sidewalks. Gone too is the local party boss, commander of loyal legions of organised ethnicity, the block vote, since demographic changes and the advent of political consultants have made him and the patronage he once wielded an irrelevance. Such a new world order would not necessarily be more stable, indeed Dr Goebbels is said to have called for American-style methods of campaigning to elect Hitler as Reich Chancellor. As a result the democratic process may become curiously moribund, for when the body of the contest is fought in the media there may cease to be any meaningful popular participation in the election.

Marketing may also promote a blander kind of politics on exposed and public media, especially television, as candidates shun the sort of ideological imbroglio that their opponents could vilify, and this is particularly important in America with its diversity of races and creeds: strongly to affirm values will be to offend some key voter segment.

Another consequence is an attempt, sometimes crude, sometimes cunning, to cajole voters with the latest techniques. They do not witness a process of sharp debate in which fallacies are exposed, lies confounded, and some sort of approximation to the truth laid bare – instead of the interchange that might be the essence of the democratic system, rival camps shout factional slogans like vendors in a street market. Yet most political theorists, Weil for instance, have viewed debate as being the core of the democratic process, and de Tocqueville saw it as one of the remarkable features of the US democracy: 'An American cannot converse, but he can discuss; and his talk falls into a dissertation. He speaks to you as if he was addressing a meeting.'

An earlier effect of political marketing was to help articulate anew a traditional American constituency, the right, in its rural and small town heartlands, for whom central government and metropolitan values have been sources of deep and enduring resentment. The new approaches enabled them to circumvent the mediating influence of media and liberal lobby to reach prospective supporters directly, speaking the crystal language of non-compromise and pressuring elective officials, and the result has been the accumulation of a political weight which, while insufficient to determine events, has certainly influenced them.

In the United States we see factional propaganda. Like all propaganda it represents in its strident certitudes a refuge from a troubling world: the more troubling that world becomes, the more appealing is such a haven. Propaganda is antithetical to democratic traditions and more associated with revolutionary epochs and totalitarian regimes. Seen in this light the propagandising of the American political process must disturb. Television is especially a propagandistic medium, conveying a visual world requiring no literacy and only superficial attention. In its gleeful imbalance, its contempt for the processes of reason, propaganda is the undermining of the rational centre as it constructs its rococo world of garish images. The deposit it leaves on human minds is often cynicism.

Moreover, while political marketing methods, especially direct mail, may well have mobilised more people into political involvement, it remains involvement of a very passive variety and has rightly been described as 'armchair activism'; there is something curiously anodyne about it and the contrast between the virility of the message and the physical action demanded – a stroke of the pen – is striking. In the past political involvement was a more committed affair, the impact was personal rather than financial so that the 'political nation' thus produced was an active one and loyal, but now we have substituted the politics of rented allegiance. Even the personal touch has been scientifically manufactured by the political consultant.

Perhaps this is part of a general movement to a society of muffled, introverted individualists so it is not surprising that their representative political culture should assume the same identity. With the old cohesion of communities gone, along with the play of personalities that was so characteristic of them, we can hardly blame politics for being coloured by that fact. Politics and culture are an integrity. A frequent concern of democracy's earlier critics was the primacy it gave to individual self-interest and the shrinkage of the public virtues and broader loyalties. Thucydides made this point, and de Tocqueville elaborated: 'In democratic communities each citizen is habitually engaged in the contemplation of a very puny object, namely himself.'[21] Marketing orientated politics will sharpen this feature since it stresses targeted propaganda methods and disaggregated modes of analysing political civilisation: it only seems to envisage political behaviour in terms of individual self-interest.

Business invented these marketing methods; it is continuously refining them and a process of transfusion takes place; arguably wholesale adoption leads to a preoccupation with the short term, especially since the pressures naturally lead to the wish to defend policies vigorously, for continually available data on the state of public opinion and breakdowns of this induce an obsession with its manipulation, and the means are readily at hand. Combating the pressures of the moment diverts attention from long-term planning and strategy.

The need also now arises to fight a perpetual campaign, a concept crafted to a new excellence by Ronald Reagan. The reasons for this are several. First, politicians – even local ones – are subject to media scrutiny. Next, well-financed opponents are ever willing to make a thrust in anticipation of the next campaign. The notion here is that the conduct of office is performed with some of the promotion methods used to gain it: constant appeals over the heads of opponents and interest groups to the broad public, direct mailings and fund solicitations, pollings, personal appearances and so on. Many politicians are now doing this, albeit in a less histrionic way than Reagan, and this is perhaps the logical consequence of media politics, a tax on political energies. The process becomes circular: Americans elect people not to govern but to continue in the election business. Politicians and especially their campaign consultants have come to realise that the electorate's overall impression is the accumulation of small impressions, of individual episodes that merge into a wholeness by election day, so constant public relations success should create a momentum that leads to the right verdict. The consequences of this perpetual campaign are that the politician has to spend much of his time planning and executing it, performing his act before the arc lamps of publicity, and others then assume the power he has forsaken – the shadowy men of the political backrooms, the subterranean toilers in the offices of Washington, the bureaucratic incubi.

The conscious marketing of candidates has therefore transformed American politics. But political marketing has been partly caused by a weak party system, and also contributed to its further demise. Some candidates even avoid showing their party label: many more de-emphasise it; the candidate is no longer dependent on the party for his candidacy and support and can appeal via the paid media direct to the party's registered voters, while large parts of a more volatile electorate are no longer pre-committed to either party. Among the long-term effects are that Congressional discipline will be more erratic since it is subject to eccentric loyalties, making it harder to pass a party's programme intact.

Another criticism of the political mass employment of marketing methods therefore is that they abet the demise of the party. The central functions of the party can now be supplanted by commercial purchase, there is an alternative power source now available to aspirant politicians and while this jettisons the negative things associated with parties it also abolishes the positive contributions they made. For a party programme has a coherence and balance which an agglomeration of assertive single-issue causes never can have; for one thing, under this system the richer causes are likely to have the loudest voice and to be most absolute in their demands. Yet another consequence is that coalitions of support are created with much greater ease than in former times, for the thrust of the new technology is towards segmentation and its results – which new developments mature with time – are that groups can now be solicited as individuals on their key interests and enthusiasms; but the loyalties of such coalitions are also more fickle since they no longer depend on organic linkages to political parties. Parties, being coalitions, were less divisive, having to represent some broad social consensus; they were and are a way of reconciling competing factions and arguably they taught groups in society to moderate demands and to go for the socially agreed solution rather than the optimal one.

And the lore of political marketing has now become international. Other countries experience conditions for its fertile growth, most especially when traditional parties cease to command their old loyalties or when a country attempts democracy after a period of military government as in South America. These ramifications clearly give the subject an importance beyond its influence on the United States – if in this as in other things America can be regarded as a mirror of this world's future, and here the evidence suggests that this is especially the case. The politics of other nations may be affected in similar ways. In the 1987 Korean elections observers noticed the attention given to televised candidate spots and presentation: 'The emphasis on style has done little to elevate the level of serious debate on issues among voters.'[22]

Thus the discussion becomes one about the future conduct of democratic politics, with forebodings of a world order where parties and candidates are merchandised like consumer non-durables. This would surely make for the belittling of the politics of democratic societies and for electorates holding their representatives in contempt; it would be undermining of conventions of argument and media analysis and create a pseudo-glamorous urbanity in the politics of an array of countries as the sugared confections of image, theme and emotion are fed to voters.

A POSITIVE ASPIRATION

The temptation to write polemics is a strong one. Moral sententiousness is satisfying because it affirms our own decency and supplies us with a tangible enemy, and the attractions of rhetorical intoxication are clear. Truth is not as simple: for while the phenomenon of political marketing is disturbing and is sometimes a corrupting influence, important qualifications have to be made and the entire question constitutes a curious exercise in moral ambiguity. For the mature approach would acknowledge benefits derived from the phenomenon of political marketing; it contains benevolent potential and were its employers altruistic they could give salience to worthy if neglected issues. This does not fully counterbalance the negatives and the whole process remains in sum a detraction from rather than addition to the political wholesomeness of democracies. But what is really new? Many of the characteristics of American politics are not actually created by political marketing, rather the practice of salesmanship simply exaggerates trends and characteristics which already existed and political marketing is in some degree the product of them.

Hence the constitution has always been cumbersome by any standard of efficiency; it is merely that now, in McKay's words[23] the pressures on the central institutions are greater while the ability to respond effectively has been weakened. The slowness of congressional decision making is simply made more slow by the perpetual public relations imbroglio. The bureaucracy and the special interests always were the possessors of great power so that political decision making was always piecemeal and fragmented; 'log rolling', for example, where congressmen obtain expenditures by exchanging mutual supports, guarantees muddled policies.

It would be mistaken to dismiss political marketing as an entirely negative process. Through its agency many people have been able to gain a sense of political involvement; it has broadened the franchise of political participation even though such participation is of the recumbent sort: signing cheques and enlisting in the membership roster of the cause. This cannot be bad. Democracy has always numbered the apathy and lack of interest of electorates among its foes, and now at least we see the commitment of some to the great debates. By being involved, people find their desire to feel needed is mollified.

Politics is also opened up to new talent. Such men will probably be rich, possibly through inheritance, more probably through having earned their wealth, and as a result they will be endowed with knowledge about certain areas and issues and possess a level of competence. In many ways they could contribute more to the affairs of the nation than a pedantic party warhorse who, while possessing intimate knowledge of internal party dealing, would not have any large dimension of external experience and sophistication. The diminished power of the party boss and his local machine is not invariably a cause for lament and American politics is less dependent on their idiosyncrasies. On the other hand, such men may have made their money corruptly, and, while wise in the ways of business, they may be naive politically: there is no necessary correlation between commercial shrewdness and political wisdom.

In a sense also political marketing contains its own antidote: electorates weary of the glibness and demand authenticity. Thus in 1988 one could remark that 'Pasty-faced floppy-eared Simon is the antithesis of the slick, packaged candidate, and Axelrod is pitching his authenticity.'[24] Marketing allied to new targeted technology also has potential for conveying a higher calibre of political communication – Dukakis for example spoke to students at 56 colleges for one hour via satellite (price $9000).[25] The 1988 campaign appeared at first to promise regeneration of the campaign debate as voters demanded realism and tests of skill, and by Christmas 1987 there had already been twenty-three debates.[26]

Political marketing was precipitated in part by a tough, interrogative, scandalmongering journalism; and perhaps its cosmetics balance the unease such journalism produces. There is good and bad political marketing: at its worst, it is a caricature, at its best it could be an asset to democracy. Of course there is always the danger of an over-obsession with the role of marketing in politics, and the neglect of traditional politics and its more orthodox interpretations. Nor is 'negative' advertising, regarded by critics as one of the most undesirable features of political marketing, any new invention – witness the 1884 Republican rhyme against Grover Cleveland:[27]

> Ma, ma, where's my pa?
> Gone to the White House, ha, ha, ha!

But, above all, political marketing can be viewed as a means of neutralising the deeply alienated in society. In democracies governments have in fact limited power; in society power is diffused and there are also opinion-forming agencies with considerable informal powers: fashions, ideologies, dogmas, social orthodoxies.

Perhaps also then the chief power of government is a variation of this informal, symbolic power. Government 'markets' statements and gestures which are in a sense the verdict of society, and as a result condition the behaviour of bureaucrats and power holders everywhere and establish normative criteria in the public mind. It is this kind of power which is possibly the strongest. Governments which conceive their work in marketing terms send messages of symbolic reassurance to those who do not feel fully integrated within the social mainstream, either through economic, class, racial or regional factors. By articulating a viewpoint, government gives it the sanction of the state; by backing it up with financial resources it enhances it further; and government action can turn into social orthodoxy what was once merely a minority cause. Such a view of government rests on the disenchanting premise that its financial powers in themselves are constricted in the amount of good they do since bureaucracy and mismanagement take their bite, as do illegitimate beneficiaries.

Of course, such a description is naive: it describes an ideal, and reality is usually far removed from this, yet the notion that the power of government is in large measure symbolic is a useful one. Moreover employment of the perpetual campaign brings such an idea much nearer its fulfilment, since it involves registering the complaints of hostile groups and providing language and gestures of reassurance. Democracy, especially American democracy, is not a changeless artefact. It is in constant flux, but we may reasonably infer that change is swifter under the aegis of political marketing, and that a democracy that is renewed comes into being.

2 Big Lies, Little Lies: The Story of Propaganda

'The public has therefore, among a democratic people, a singular power, which aristocratic nations cannot conceive of; for it does not persuade to certain opinions, but it enforces them and infuses them into the intellect by a sort of enormous pressure of the minds of all upon the reason of each.'

Alexis de Tocqueville, *Democracy in America*

THE RELATIONSHIP OF MARKETING AND PROPAGANDA

Marketing is a technical term that must relate to modern practice and the body of theoretical knowledge it draws from. We define it as being all those behaviours by which the firm relates to its externalities, but in recent years, as we have seen, theory and practice have taken it well beyond this to embrace non-business organisations, and after initial resistance this more elastic conception has been generally accepted. Can it thus be called marketing? We could argue that this is a matter of self-definition: if people call themselves marketers, then they are. But it is also an analytic description of a set of distinct processes and technologies which in commerce are called marketing, and which in recent years has been applied to non-commercial areas where analogous conditions arise.

Consumer marketing certainly has historical antecedents. It may be said to have arisen long before the American economists gave it formal status before the First World War, for advertising, packaging and distribution existed for centuries in a naive form, and urbanisation and machinery simply brought them to new levels of sophistication. However, for the term 'political marketing' to have any descriptive value it must replicate most of the processes involved in consumer marketing – research, advertising, personal selling, product management and so on – and this would make it an almost exclusively post-Second World War phenomenon. What we know as political marketing is in large part derived from commercial practice.

But political 'marketing' also has an ancestry, an alternative pedigree so distinct that it is described by an everyday adjective,

17

'propaganda', for it stands as the culmination of a historical propaganda tradition. How then do we define propaganda? The term is one with flexible borders; it operates on many levels, both crude and subtle. Are religions propagandistic, since they use all the classic techniques of propaganda? Has primary education been propagandistic in content, celebrating myths about a nation's past and simultaneously fortifying current orthodoxies? The very fact that we can refer to education shows how inclusive is the concept of propaganda. A useful clarification may be the suggestion that propaganda must take place in a political context – not necessarily a democratic one, but one where there are elements of an appeal to the popular will.

ANCIENT ANTECEDENTS

The ancestry of propaganda may be identified in the symbols and myths of the Egyptian Pharaohs. Ancient religions and cults were harbingers of later propaganda methods, with their processions and emphasis on symbols, and some of these cults such as the mysteries of Eleusis had political overtones. Particular events, such as Alexander's festival of reconciliation at Susa, were arranged as political propaganda. The schools of rhetoric in Athenian Greece were in a sense propaganda seminaries, since they trained their acolytes in all the arts of verbal persuasion, for whenever it is necessary to persuade large groups of men the need arises for arranged argument and selectivity of facts. The Assemblies of Greece and later Rome offered the chance to employ such formally acquired skills. Many of the great classical authors were also propagandists of an elevated sort – Tacitus and Thucydides for example – and indeed historians through the ages have often acted as apologists for dominant orthodoxies and ruling factions. In fact wherever in history public opinion has been important to rulers – and not necessarily in democratic contexts – some form of propaganda has tended to emerge.

By Roman times we can possibly use the term 'propaganda' with greater legitimacy. Roman propaganda methods comprised 'Harangues to assembled peoples, discussions in streets or public buildings, inscriptions on walls, letters and formulae graven on the pediments of temples or palaces, rites and ceremonies, processions carrying emblems, flags, flowers, symbols of all sorts . . .'[1] The triumphs of Roman generals were in particular propaganda exercises.

The art of rhetoric was never merely verbal, for it also involved physical tutelage as well so that the verbal is underpinned by the non-verbal physical communication. So the eloquent magicians of antiquity sought to manipulate their listeners: how accurately, then, did they anticipate the electronic future, when visual image manufacturing would reign, and the play of smile and grimace, gesture and pose be once again orchestrated by the hired masters of their art.

But a speech, however dramatic, is a fluid event. Effective persuasion needs something more permanent: we retain what we see more easily than what we hear, and thus the invention of printing enhanced the role of propaganda.

EARLY MODERN PROPAGANDA

The invention of printing created the first mass medium; it had the limitation of literacy, and it follows that its power was extended by the literacy campaigns of the nineteenth century.

German woodcuts played a propaganda role in the Lutheran Reformation.[2] Posters and pamphlets were used in times of flux such as the English Civil War period and whenever the sentiments of the masses become important to their rulers, if only to appease the unrest of what an eighteenth-century statesman termed 'our supreme governors, the mob', and the traditional skills of rhetoric now wooed a broader public, amplified by a visual dimension. In that it was striving towards an emotive mass persuasion this has some slight affinity to modern political marketing. And there are resemblances in such populist propaganda down the ages, as it seeks to glorify the great personalities of a cause, and use a strident tone of moral absolutism; it causes apprehension and enmity with frequent 'atrocity' propaganda about the misdeeds of some opponent, invariably caricatured and stripped of their human identity and represented as beasts and so on. Symbolic appeals are frequent, since symbolism is a way of signifying and summarising a cause pictographically.[3] Pellerin's print factory in France, or Remondini in Italy, supplied such illustrations.[4]

But alongside the popular dialogue there developed a strand of elite propaganda, one of less interest to those concerned with historical continuity. Parliamentary speeches and political orations, printed and disseminated, constituted a form of intellectual propaganda, such as Burke's speech to the electors of Bristol.[5] These were loquacious texts studded with Latinate words and references, and by the late eighteenth century the mode had reached almost self-parody, while limitations of franchise and literacy often led to a high standard of propaganda since it was aimed at an elite audience. Such restrictions did not, however, make for a uniformly conservative propaganda, since the bourgeoisie were often excluded from power and were therefore radical (as in the City of London during the Wilkes case).

Newspapers also served, sometimes primarily, as propaganda organs for certain factions. *Le Petit Journal* in nineteenth-century France, or *Simplicissimus* in Germany, were propagandists through the medium of satire.

There is also an obvious relationship between populist propaganda and revolutions. The need is to persuade the volatile, fix and clarify support. In the French Revolution newspapers such as Marat's *Ami du Peuple* flourished, with great theatrical processions, tableaux and ceremonials, pamphlets and Jacobin trained orators.[6] After the French Revolution traditional hierarchical authority was never as assured again, and the revolutions over the next century, along with technological developments in the accurate reproduction of graphics and with colour printing, re-created propaganda. Groups idealised themselves in fabulously ornate engravings. Technologies such as lithography or intaglio engraving sharpened the effectiveness of political art. Paul Revere's print of the Boston Massacre or Goya's Peninsular war etchings 'The Disasters of War',[7] are examples of agitation propaganda. Hogarth's engraving 'The Times, Plate 1', an attack on John Wilkes, is early party propaganda.

AMERICAN PARTY PROPAGANDA

Throughout the nineteenth century important American candidacies were articulated through promotional artefacts. Thus, with Andrew Jackson in 1824, 'A host of devices from hickory poles to campaign songs, ceramic ware, and campaign novelties promoted the hero's powerful reputation'.[8] Today campaign novelties are still an indispensable piece of political marketing paraphernalia and they serve the same function: to popularise and domesticate a candidacy and to root it in common lore and affection. In 1840 William Henry Harrison espoused song, slogan and printed portrait to promote his candidacy, as did Lincoln, who could also add photographic prints. Symbols were important to all the candidates, Henry Clay using that of a raccoon in 1844,[9] and all such devices served to create and sustain image, a task central to American popular democracy from its very beginnings. Most frequent of the nineteenth-century images was that of man of the people, the blunt agrarian from humble beginnings – Jackson, the patrician Henry Clay, Harrison, Lincoln and many others adopted this posture – while another pose was that of heroic military figure – Jackson, Zachary Taylor, Harrison, Grant and Garfield. Honesty was another politician's totem, notably with Lincoln, and populism (William Jennings Bryan) yet another; and generally eminence earned in any walk of life, such as that of 'Pathfinder' Frément, the explorer.[10]

Such postures are more than echoed in today's candidate propaganda: the image compulsion may be communicated electronically, but the Hero, the Common Man and the Honest Man still bustle for America's votes with a timeless animation. For Boorstin political images are simple and ambiguous: 'They serve as devices of short-hand identification, distortion, appeal, and illusion – inevitable elements of medium political persuasion. Like language itself, images create a symbolic universe'.

In addition there was the press, often itself under the control of some powerful political figure or faction, for popular media began early in the United States, and in the early eighteenth century the colonies sustained seven newspapers, while by the end of the eighteenth century there were 180.[11] The nineteenth century saw a coarsening of tone in this vigorous press, and political polarisation. Andrew Jackson for example was supported by sundry sloganeering broadsheets.[12]

Nor were the excesses of negative politics a vice exclusive to the future. During the 1828 campaign there passed between Jackson and J. Q. Adams: 'Accusations of being a would-be emperor, murderer, duellist, and adulterer, among other things; Adams was tagged as a monarchist, procurer, and an effete snob. Jackson's successor Martin Van Buren had to run against charges that he was a corset-wearing dandy and an unscrupulous political schemer'.[13]

LATER PROPAGANDA

Once men had defined politics as a persuasion task, propaganda came into its own and nation-states began to use it not as an occasional but as a permanent resource. Propaganda became more engrossing, for the notion arose that to be effective it also had to be incessant, and established regimes created a base of permanent propaganda. It differed from that which had preceded it by offering not just an issue position but a world view: it went beyond mere advocacy, and its style and its technology made it a closer approximation to what we today know as political marketing.

Propaganda does not have to be fully believed to be effective. This is a common misapprehension. People may lend to propaganda suspension of their disbelief and there is a permissible licence in the dramatisation of their own prejudices, so that with the advent of sound and film propaganda was able to graduate to new levels of menace. People could identify with moving images more intensely than with printed words: sound film communicates a fullness of reality, an immediacy; the tax on reason is lower.

The First World War acted as a catalyst for modern propaganda techniques. Lord Northcliffe established a Ministry of Propaganda in February 1918: records were used in no man's land and even radios were employed. In Russia Kerensky's government sponsored a propaganda service under Denikin,[14] posters were produced daily and screens were used for the projection of photographs. Their most interesting innovation was the maps of political 'meteorology', where colours represented key local and national political and economic variables so that the situation could thus be read instantly and interrelationships observed; subsequently the Bolsheviks adopted this technique.[15] Kerensky's Osvag ministry also trained speakers and sponsored political films; however such propaganda has been faulted for being intellectual in appeal. The Bolsheviks did not make that mistake.

Bolshevik methods were described thus: 'tracts by the million, illustrated newspapers, photographs, placards, shop-window displays, staffs of agitators working in markets, trains, cinemas and all places where crowds were assembled, and travelling propaganda groups. Trotsky, for example, travelled about the country in a special train fitted up as a propaganda office, with a printing-press in one coach . . .'.[16] They promised Utopia with a system that, being hitherto untested, could only be theoretically condemned; and this was a master strategy. It is tempting to perceive their work as an aboriginal expression of political marketing, except that the phrase is too passive and corporate to describe a situation so rabidly political.

TOTALITARIAN PROPAGANDA

In all the post-First World War totalitarian revolutions, propaganda was central: Lenin like Hitler was in essence a propagandist, while Mussolini had been a newspaper editor.[17] Comparisons with contemporary political marketing would yield superficial resemblances but ultimately be misleading: the sponsors of these methods were not parties in our sense, but revolutionary groups. In no sense did they adopt a 'consumer' orientation or borrow techniques from business: they began with the ideology and did not moderate it. Nor, of course, was marketing the description they themselves employed: the marketing approach has its roots in what people themselves say they want; totalitarians would tell them what was good for them. Totalitarian propaganda was insistent and continuous; the person living in such a society would breathe a permanent atmosphere of propaganda.

The aim of the political propagandist is to package the universe in ribbons of trite simplicity, its essence is a call to the average or sub-average, and the Nazis recognised the importance of appeals to raw emotions: 'the greater the mass of the men whom it is desired to reach, the lower must be the intellectual level of propaganda'.[18] The men from ordinary backgrounds who became dictators in the early twentieth century possessed insight into the the apoliticality of most people, and Hitler recognised that 'opinions and actions are determined much more by impressions produced on their senses than by reflection'.[19] One leading SPD organised a controlled experiment with a number of Hesse towns, treating four with new propaganda and using traditional 'rational' methods only in the fifth, where, not surprisingly, the Nazis won.[20]

Good propaganda is often stigmatised as 'Goebbels-like' and through diverse media Goebbels sustained the Third Reich. His diaries illuminate a preoccupation with public response and informed observation,[21] and his contribution was a bastardised form of classic marketing thinking, his antennae – one naturally thinks of an alert insect – picking up every nuance of public mood. Hitler himself was helped into power by tailoring different messages to different groups; he was the creation of every segment's imagination. Nazi propaganda concealed its true intentions, harbouring a hidden agenda; however allegiance was cemented by incorporating people into organisational structures, and through mass participation.

Social cohesion, beguiled by state propaganda and intimidated by state terror, remained until the end. But one cannot of course see propaganda in a vacuum, divorced from political conditions – the Germans were politically immature, and their resentment over the verdicts of 1918 made them ripe targets for every kind of fallacious reasoning, voodoo and magic lantern show. Since these means had never been used before, the population were more credulous: propaganda was working on a conscripted population with centuries of militarism as background.

Hitler himself was a theorist on propaganda, and in 1936 at Nuremberg he attributed his entire success to its workings: 'Propaganda brought us into power, propaganda has since enabled us to remain in power, and propaganda will give us the means of conquering the world'. The Nazis sought to create a total propaganda environment, with films, symbols, myths, a quasi-sacerdotal cult of leader with incantations and rites.[22] Hitlerian propaganda also perceived the importance of climate. Voters were not the only target groups; their children were not ignored and they recognised the power of the perpetual campaign and the ability of modern communications to sustain such a phenomenon, illuminating a relationship we shall see many times again between technology and propaganda.

POLITICAL PROPAGANDA AND POLITICAL MARKETING

Propaganda, then, is conceptually different but vague parallels exist between it and conventional political marketing. Both genres are low in information content: both employ special propagandists, and are able to bypass the mediation of the existing media to reach and motivate targets directly (could there be any connection between this and their ability to sustain an ideological absolutism?).

At what point does political propaganda become political marketing? Propaganda usually exists in the more authoritarian state; it is not related to a commercialised approach to politics; it can attain a level of saturation that is difficult to achieve in a democracy. The phenomenon of political marketing on the other hand arises where:

– There are strong linkages between politics and business, politicians are aware of selling methods and inhabit a densely commercial milieu.

– Advertising agencies and commercial media are employed, and there are stylistic similarities to commercial advertising, as in the use of hired actors.

- There are declining levels of popular participation in politics and therefore a need to dramatise its appeals.
- Geographically and socially mobile societies create a 'value vacuum', and political territory is open with low pre-existing loyalties.
- Large amounts of money are available to be spent on campaigning, and this itself is owing to a constitutional acceptance of the rights of wealth to purchase political power, to the crucial importance of lobbies, and to a tradition of 'pork-barrel' politics.
- Politicians are prepared to modify a stance according to the counsels of research: there is a notion then of electors as political consumers who demand persuasion not dogmatism.

Political marketing is non-authoritative; everyone knows the message and even messengers are hired. Such messages are ever trivial. In societies where it is prevalent no great dignity attaches to the political avocation.

THE RISE OF POLITICAL MARKETING

It would seem that the technology of each medium was first used at an early stage, but that the development of the medium for political purposes was slow since this demanded a revolution in attitudes, in the way politicians and party bosses perceived the task of political persuasion. They would have to learn skills which they regarded as a diminution of their function: for their skills were those of action rather than expression, the talents of the fixer. The film *The Last Hurrah* depicted the defeat of a brilliant old pro, a machine politician, by a stupid, rich tele-candidate: even when it was made people were aware of the coming mode of political communication and it aroused disdain.

Political advertising, purchased, written by hired experts, emanating from a conscious recognition of the power of commercial persuasion and communicated through the major public media of the day, had to await the twentieth century. In 1916 Roosevelt supporters purchased four pages in the *Saturday Evening Post* and other magazines, with copy by the Erickson agency, while Democrat newspaper advertisements demanded that the Republican candidate

(Hughes) articulate his position on the issues. Hughes himself was employing the Batten agency.[23]

These were early intimations of the power of political advertising, for Hughes lost wherever he had not advertised extensively, and by 1917 Congress was debating legislation on political advertising. The ability of purchased communication to short-circuit the press had already been noted: 'The men behind the movement decided to get quick, co-ordinated action through the ungarbled and definite medium of paid advertising'.[24] By 1930 *Advertising Age* could claim that 'A political campaign is largely an advertising campaign', quoting a victorious candidate who had spent ten times more than his defeated opponent.[25] In Presidential campaigns from 1920 onward the winners were generally those who spent most on advertising, though the inference that advertising is therefore decisive is not necessarily true – high expenditure could merely reflect a pre-existing level of popularity expressed in campaign contributions, being a consequence therefore and not a cause.

Hence the involvement of advertising companies and personnel was significant from the nineteen-twenties onward. Campbell Ewald invented the 1924 slogan, 'Keep cool with Coolidge', and in 1936 a partner of Blackett-Semple Hammert organised Republican promotion,[26] but such a role was not achieved without challenge, and there were strong murmurs of disapprobation, usually from the political opponents. In 1940 advertising actually became a campaign issue in consequence of top agency support for Wilkie ('The idea is first to create fear, and then offer a branded antidote').

FILM AND RADIO

It was inevitable that the electronic media, first radio and film and then television, should become the prime mediums for political marketing. Radio was the first electronic political medium, used by Roosevelt in 1936 and Calvin Coolidge even earlier, while Chester Bowles, who had extensive experience with radio in his advertising agency, ran a successful gubernatorial campaign via brief, frequent and well-timed messages.[27] Radio was perhaps F. D. Roosevelt's strongest asset: with it he could short-circuit the press and project a dependable personality, which was important since anti-FDR papers had a circulation eight times higher than those supporting him.[28]

Earlier Al Smith had also used radio to counter bizarre rumours about his Catholicism.

But political marketing in its now familiar format as a visual diatribe must begin in California. Blumenthal has described the first cinema political commercial when MGM produced film aimed against the socialist candidate for California Governor, Upton Sinclair:[29] 'Reporter to old lady in a rocking chair: "Who are you voting for, Mother?" "I'm voting for the Republican, Frank Morrison, because this little home may not be much, but it is all I have in the world. I love my home and I want to protect it". Next, the reporter approached a bedraggled bearded man in a mangy overcoat. "I am voting for Seen-clair", he replied in a stilted foreign accent. "His system worked well in Russia, so vy can't it vork here?" And in another film, "an army of hoboes is depicted hopping off a freight train and whooping it up on arrival in the Golden State. 'Sinclair says he'll take the property of the working people and give it to us', says one of the bums'. Ten million dollars was garnered to fight Sinclair, and 2,000 billboards proclaimed: "If I am elected governor, half the unemployed in the country will hop the first freight to California – Upton Sinclair"'. These films have some affinity to rightist propaganda of a later date and to strands in American culture, for they are permeated with national and class prejudice and apocalyptic consequence: they delineate a sense of alien threat that has often been strong in US politics.

But in California there was no settled political memory. Californians were the first to elect an actor to high office – ex-tap dancer Senator George Murphy. Receptiveness to political marketing is governed by the degree of social homogeneity, and therefore California at this time was ripe for political promotions. The parties were weak and the state fluid under the impact of depression migrants; moreover California's constitutional arrangements made possible referenda on policy issues, thus making campaign managerial skills a saleable asset to business. Thus 'Californian politics became subject to elite political management firms and a parade of ephemeral social movements that were never absorbed by the weak political parties'.[30] California anticipated the future in political marketing because it was in its social structure a mirror of that future, with new industries and no entrenched class system or mature vested interests; hedonistic, curious, it did not reject the past for it was not aware there was one, and it is no accident that Ronald Reagan spent his career there and is a political expression of its ethos.

At this time the most prominent political consulting firm was Whitaker and Baxter, and for over twenty years (1933–55) they won seventy of seventy-five political campaigns they undertook. Whitaker and Baxter were the first consulting firm and the blueprint of all that were to follow; they were ideologically motivated and intimately connected with big business. Originally put on retainer by the power company whose initiative they defeated,[31] it was they who managed the campaign against Sinclair, and generally they offered the complete range of electioneering services, including strategy and advertising. We can call what Whitaker and Baxter did 'marketing', but in a limited sense. They were consciously applying all the methods of commercial persuasion to a target market; they thought strategically; and what they did is identifiably a modern campaign. But in those early years they did not use polling: in no sense did policies emanate from the politicised populace, while in the absence of television they could not achieve the visual impact, and the saturation, of the modern political merchandiser.

But the first television campaigns were in 1950 by Senator Barton (a founder of BBDO) and William Benton (founder of Benton and Bowles agency and successful Democrat candidate for Connecticut) and later Senator Estes Kefauver in California in 1952. The Eisenhower campaign that followed was inspired by Kefauver's campaign and included a telethon, staged conversations and so on. The Eisenhower campaign set up a unit distinct from its advertising agency to make the first Presidential television commercials (at a cost of $1.5 million).[32] By 1955 Democrats were also spending heavily on radio and television advertising, but invariably trailing the Republicans, who in 1964 for example spent twice as much.[33] The new medium favoured the telegenic: television brought Kennedy rapidly from anonymity to fame. With television, political skills had to be updated: thus the actor Robert Montgomery gave Eisenhower lessons in creating a more comfortable television manner.[34]

Another critical development was the active involvement of advertising people during the period in office, and the emerging conception of a perpetual campaign. Consequent on this was, arguably, an increasing disassociation of image from substance. BBDO was retained by the GOP after 1952 and in 1953 it superintended a televised presentation by four cabinet members.[35] In the Nixon cabinet 'on too many occasions, interest in promotion of a program exceeded interest in details of substance,' and unsurprisingly advertising men began to attain senior political positions as their craft advanced centre stage.

Benton and Barton had both been Senators while many Presidents had advertising men close to them (Harding: Lasker; Kennedy: O'Brien; Johnson: Valenti; Carter: Rafshoon; Reagan: Deaver); Nixon, with his five J. Walter Thomson ex-employees, surpassed them all.[36]

However there are those who maintain that the changes have been technical rather than symbolic. David Garth has been quoted thus: 'As if the machines ever turned out high-quality candidates. Imagery is nothing new. Most of it hasn't happened by accident. Manipulation by publishers and bosses is nothing new. It's the style of manipulation that is new, except for the fact that the voter is more informed with the lousy commercials than he was before'.[37] It is disingenuous to neglect the power of the television medium over the traditional forms of persuasion: it has an immediacy and ease of reception, a human interest, and insinuates itself into every home. However it would be very easy to neglect the continuities between past and present campaigns, so his remarks have some validity.

3 Only in America

> 'The colony approximated more and more the novel spectacle of a community homogeneous in all its parts. A democracy, more perfect than antiquity had dared to dream of, started in full size and panoply from the midst of an ancient feudal society.'
>
> Alexis de Tocqueville, *Democracy in America*

THE INFLUENCE OF AMERICAN HISTORY

The American Constitution

Since political marketing is largely an American invention we must look to American history for explanations of the growth of the genre; for many themes touch the American political psyche and political marketing is sometimes their expression. Both early and recent American historical experience define the political culture and values from which contemporary political marketing draws its subject matter.

Conscience and politics are among the reasons why the first colonists departed (the state church was insufficiently protestant, for instance). That gave to America a strongly moralistic note; and it remains important to Americans that their country should embody a moral greatness (hence their shame over Watergate), so such tenets are reflected in political advertising. Moreover the England they left was never a centralised nation state in the manner that, for example, France was under the Bourbon monarchy, and this helps to explain the old antagonism to the state and big government, core national values extolled in political marketing. Such an attitude is sharpened by the fact that before the Continental Congress the United States had no national unity or consciousness: colonies were a series of semi-independent states, each with its own social structure, religious systems and so on. To comprehend all this the new nation state had therefore to be a pluralist society.

The new state was a novel political experiment in a world of antique monarchies: its citizens were individualists. The colonialists brought with them a tradition of political debate and argument.[1] They had their assemblies. They were made political by being part of

30

a highly politicised empire. America has also inherited a Georgian constitution designed by landowners nostalgic for a less centralised past, a sentimental squirearchy, and it was the Americans who looked back to the old-fashioned conception of state as a weak agglomeration of feudatories so that co-ordinated and coherent policy was difficult from the very start, though its defenders would claim that this has also made co-ordinated tyranny impossible. Political marketing exacerbates this situation, since to be effective it must generally stress the more emotive and therefore divisive issues. Such a system puts a premium on political compromise so that the constitution the founders created has influence on everything in this book – their federal organisation was weak, with the locus of power residing in the states: the colonialists, having witnessed abuse of power, aimed to prevent its recrudescence either as a consequence of an elected monarchy or of parliamentary majoritarianism.[2] Those who formed the constitution had a greater fear of the abuse of power than an ability to exercise it.[3]

In consequence the constitution unintentionally provides opportunities for political propagandists to assert themselves. Much marketing for example arises within the context of state elections, since the early architects of the constitution gave the states substantial power, so making the possession of local office attractive, while a constitution framed for perpetual elections inspires a marketed politics as a natural consequence. America's constitutional arrangements also underlie some of the popular political propaganda issues, like that of encroaching bureaucracy, since such evolutions appear to compromise the local independence enshrined in the constitution.

The president of the United States was more than a political leader. He was a national figurehead endowed with a pseudo-monarchical function, and these roles were somewhat contradictory, while unlike a prime minister he had no automatic podium and was therefore naturally impelled towards rhetorical and symbolic forms of communication. The president had to be above all a persuader: his role was ameliorative, that of a constructor of compromises. The Americans built a giant and extracted his teeth.

The Nineteenth Century

In the nineteenth century fresh waves of immigrants mellowed America's Anglo-Saxon ethos into something more genuinely pan-

European, and a society of immigrants well lends itself to the
segmentation approach stressed by the marketing credo and technology, where specific appeals focus on the specific grouping; but such a
society also needs a common national identity to bind people,
whereas marketing strives to disaggregate, in order to achieve a
persuasion stronger than the bland fare necessary for an undifferenti-
ated market.

The immigrant is almost by definition disillusioned with the
opportunities of his home, prepared to accept an alien culture in the
interests of material betterment, so consequently America as a
society of immigrants and free from colonial tutelage was re-created
and sustained by a belief in the possible.[4] Hence the crucial role of
hope as a value in America, and the effectiveness of any propagandising salesman who offers it among his merchandise: political marketers are in the business of providing hope for the sustenance and
extension of material affluence. Earned wealth, since it was regarded
as proof of social merit and attainable by anyone sufficiently determined, was permitted a full role in politics, thus heralding the great
expenditure made in our own time on purchased persuasion. Then
there is the affluence of the United States, creating cohorts of rich
people who will give to causes and thus sustain the costs of electioneering.

Social cohesion, which America appears to have acquired early on,
led to a remarkable homogeneity that eventually created a large role
for the political salesman since automatic class and therefore party
loyalties had never been strong, and became much diminished. The
absence of a landed aristocracy meant that leaders were professional
men, who needed to find and pay for methods of persuasion to
mobilise followers since there were few inherited loyalties, and many
such cash-thirsty politicians were courted by business, for goals – such
as the construction of railroads to facilitate distribution systems –
could be delivered politically.

Party and political propaganda was thus prominent in America
from the early years of the Republic, so its contemporary significance
is hardly surprising. Political marketing began early and became
significant because of

– the lack of patrician elites;
– the internalisation of the free market ideology in general, and the
  marketing concept in particular;
– specific pre-First World War constitutional developments in California;

- the close connection between business and politics;
- the prevalence of 'pork-barrel' politics;
- the need to accommodate diverse interest groups and belief in a politics predicated upon interest groups; the need to integrate diverse types;
- the fact that parties did not have an ideological base and there existed a high degree of ideological homogeneity.

The Republicans, the 'Grand Old Party', were the party of the victorious North in the civil war. The Democrats were the political articulation of the humiliated South and, subsequently, of the new ethnic arrivals in the north – Irish, Italians and others. The South, with its sense of alienation, was a critical factor in subsequent politics and race conflict was often the underlying, unstated factor in many propaganda exchanges – especially concerning welfare – in later history.

Party politics took on a special momentum in the United States since they were sources of substantial patronage. Ideological differences were few; rather, they represented different aggregations of interest, and it follows that when the key functions they performed were superseded the parties began to fall into disrepair, ending the automatic loyalties and opening the way for political pedlars and salesmen. American politics were politics of self-interest and not ideological abstractions, and seeking in politics a direct material reward was an old tradition in America. Only when such notions began to decline, when the ghosts of Boss Tweed and Tammany Hall were exorcised,[5] did political marketing become a really potent force.

Political Marketing and the Challenge of Liberalism

In America's ideology can be discerned a set of vague principles sometimes antithetical to each other, a common, if confused, social mythology. Much of the future debate would centre around different interpretations of the ideology of the American nation state, the idea of self-sufficiency against the ideal of social justice. For American ideology is inherently nebulous: 'We hold these truths to be self-evident, that all men are created equal . . .' But with equality of what – of legal status, or of opportunity or condition? What is meant by the 'inalienable' right to pursue happiness, especially if in its seeking I trespass on the liberties of fellow citizens? The theme of the state – how much power should it have, is it a blessing or a curse – is a major one in the advertisements, mailshots and radio spots of purchased persuasion, a genre which is affected by the old pseudo-anarchy of US tradition.

The New Deal legislation was the harbinger of much that was to come. Its ethos informed, and still informs, the marketing projection of Democratic politics. Economic as well as constitutional fairness became a theme, and the lineal descendant of the New Deal, the Great Society legislation of the nineteen sixties and its derivatives, kindled the great debate between efficiency and equity. Denunciation of the legislation's costs and consequences became a major theme in the political propaganda of the 'new right'.[6]

In earlier days liberals had a clear vision to communicate which well lent itself to media exposition; in contrast conservatives appeared merely obstructionists, for the Democrats had some telegenic candidates and were the beneficiaries of an implicit media support ('I have no party, I'm a Democrat'). It was a period in American life as disturbing in its way as the earlier great tribulations of American history. From it emerged a kind of national consensus which the right was eventually to challenge, a definitive orthodoxy. But the problem was bigger than the politicians – the failings of the Great Society illuminate the limitations of a merely administrative action, for society was shaped by many inputs and the state was only one dimension of the totality, and the solutions politicians offered in their propaganda were so often merely symbolic, panaceas that would not touch the heart of the problem.

Vietnam was for liberals a formative experience, one that impelled many to question the assumptions of their society at a fundamental level, and they forever discern its ghost in the foreign policy initiatives of Republican administrations. For a long time their propaganda looked with nostalgia to the New Deal and Great Society programmes and to the grand coalition of unions, radical and ethnic groups: it retained for some time a dated belief in government spending as the lenitive for all social ill. An alienated liberalism also incubated a variety of other social cause issues.

The belief, the faith, was that change should come from the state. Yet the high hopes engendered by this second American Revolution were let down and, while America experienced a social revolution during these years, as with all revolutions its excesses were savaged by its detractors and turned into counter-propaganda: modern political marketing expresses in part the rising alienation of those on the right who thought themselves marginal to Washington's decision making. Nor was it of a merely regional form: it manifests and broadcasts urban and suburban tensions. Liberalism's vehemence precipitated the growth of the new right; and the right adopted some liberal tactics. The two propagandas fed off each other. The right borrowed the slogans, the simple rage. The liberals on the other hand have annexed the technology and the merchandising methods of the right, since their comparative failure had been not just political failure, the atrophy of theme, it was also a failure of technique, of marketing, one they determined to repair.

Not just change itself but the fact of its central direction were perceived as threats to freedom by many on the right and partisan communications and purchased advertising reflected this concern. All this is rooted in different interpretations of what the American value system, of what it is to be American, really means. The disillusion of political rightists was often understandable. There may have been justice in some of their points: but once the old structures had been dismantled they could not be resurrected. As the sixties went on into the seventies their dreary agenda grew. The civil rights movement and the welfare state, defeat in Vietnam and the declining international prestige of the United States, crime and the permissive society and federal bureaucracy – these were all sources of grievance on the part of the right in its provincial fastnesses, and they provided its marketed subject-matter, the emotional charge to its appeal. The 'new right' was the articulation of a wider disenchantment with social and political experiment: and also the expression of old reaction that had never been even momentarily beguiled by such things. The right were joined by some able disillusioned liberals. Political marketing also articulates a rebellion against the hegemony of the north-east; as a method of persuasion that does not demand large urban concentrations it is the regionalist's own tool: they yearn for a mythological older America of individualism and devolved power, but in their grasp of marketing technology they have been thoroughly futuristic, pursuing their legislative agenda with all the apparatus of modern fund-raising and communications technology, the methods of commercial marketing. Those who felt powerless had one course: through a political system open to money and marketing they could finance a lucid opposition, and in comparison the methods used to mobilise civil rights protests seem antiquated and more attuned to classic propaganda. Seeming Republican dominance owed a great deal to their surer grasp of technology, a grasp precipitated by their junior position: the right gleefully adopted the tone of the youthful arrogant left, even the slogans (such as 'Stop the Babykillers') and its unctuous self-rightousness. But it used much more powerful methods to convey it. The right acquired a vision because of the poverty of state-organised solutions and the naivety of the ideology that underlay them. It had found its influence blocked in all three branches of government, especially the judiciary, and also in the media; it had to discover a new way of influencing and it found it in political marketing, while in direct mail especially the right discovered a way to short-circuit the media and reach its constituency directly.[7]

The best way to elicit change appeared to be in influencing values rather than in the simple tangibilities of a legislative agenda, in building a governing consensus, forming new orthodoxies. Reagan understood this. 'Solutions' really lay in changing the governing values, in shifting the common ground. The beginning of the nineteen eighties seemed to have left the Democrats stranded as a political force, ideologically bankrupt in their inability to sustain a creative and populist alternative to Republic policy, defensive loyalists of a challenged orthodoxy, and the old Democratic consensus had been decisively broken, releasing legions of fickle voters free of traditional party loyalties, a promiscuous host. A more ideological Republican Party lost strength in the north-east but rose in the south-west. As Robert Teeter commented, 'Nonalignment has helped Republicans to win elections, but it hasn't helped them to gain adherents to the party'.[8] The significance of this weakening of parties and the social phenomenon they signified is the scope it creates for merchandised politics.

Then the Democrats began to fight back with the very marketing methods that had defeated them, showing the extent to which they had internalised the new ethos, and this involved taking the political conflict to the centre ground, in other words modulating their 'product' and being alert to the needs of the contemporary political 'consumer'. The essence of political marketing is this, a rootedness in what people are claiming they seek: the Democrats recognised this in being prepared to jettison so much of their old rhetoric. Is, indeed, political marketing ultimately a centralist and neutralising force? For a time it seemed responsible for a drift towards more extreme politics, but the long-term effect may in fact be a moderacy resurrected.

THE INFLUENCE OF AMERICAN CULTURE

America is a market-place. The culture is defined by salesmanship and the citizens inhabit an element of commercial noise, whether they want it or not. America is an electronic bazaar. Americans recognise that there is a marketing dimension to any activity or institution that needs money to sustain it: therefore every aspect of corporate human activity operates in a market-place, however elevated its purpose. Therefore it is natural for politics to be marketed in a society where everything else is. Politics is a material transaction; the currency of votes is changed for the promise of dividends. Such a salesmanship impetus is one aspect of culture created by colonial rebellion and incubated by immigrants, who almost by definition represent the most ambitious members of the home culture (until after the First World War America's population increased by 20 per cent at least, every ten years). However it is reasonable to argue that the political process ought to be something more than mere purchased persuasion, and even that the entire political marketing concept is morally flawed, for in their readiness to grasp marketing technologies people have sometimes neglected fundamental distinctions: the primacy that should attach to debate in a democratic process, and the distinction in ethical value between buying a product and voting for a politician.

Samuel Huntingdon thus summarised the relationship of belief to culture in the United States: 'It is possible to speak of a body of political ideas that constitutes "Americanism" in a sense which one can never speak of "Britishism", "Frenchism", "Germanism" or "Japanesism". Americanism in this sense is comparable to other ideologies or religions. . . . To reject the central ideas of that doctrine is to be un-American. . . . "It has been our fate as a nation", Richard Hofstadter succinctly observed "not to have ideologies but to be one".'[9] We digress here because so many of the most effective specimens of political propaganda play on this American value system, arguing that by voting in a certain way the individual can express it, resurrect it, prevent it being overthrown, gain its benefits for himself and so on. Successful propaganda thus emphasises the key values of a culture. Optimism, for example. Americans are the beneficiaries of positive national myths – that effort, not inheritance or genius, would be the determinant of success. And propaganda therefore plays on the traditional suspicion of government which such individualism has traditionally created. The United States remains an optimistic society – a recent poll revealed that slightly more than half of Americans believed that their children would do better materially than they themselves – and politics is impregnated with the exuberance of American culture.[10] Political propaganda seeks to exploit this optimism, which under Reagan, indeed, became its chief theme.[11] Propaganda is thus a celebration of the national myths, hence the frequent appeals to an ideology of self-help and its elevation to the status of panacea for current ills.

Then there is the lack of historic tradition, with few shadows of old conflicts, for parts of America are 'new' communities in every sense; and weakness of affiliation makes them candidates for persuasion by the methods of political marketing; their loyalties are saleable. Moreover there is the fact of America's geographical immensity: people have to be reached in distant communities, and it is therefore no accident that political marketing is often most influential in the most isolated areas, and that the old ward-healing politics died last in the big cities (Mayor Lindsay using it a great deal).

Constitutional factors also explain the supremacy of marketing in American politics, with the number of elective offices: local assemblies, governorships, school boards, judgeships as well as national offices, and all candidates for such offices have to advertise to establish some kind of public identity. In addition elections under the American system occur regularly. Presidential elections are held every four years and congressional elections every two; each senator has a term of six years and one-third of the Senate is due for election every second year; and so America experiences a perpetual election. There is always one batch of politicians for auction, fresh with newly-minted promises. Size and regularity therefore make for much greater incentive for a merchandised politics. Moreover television is less regulated than in Europe, with more access on more channels, and no limits to individual spending in campaigns.

The magnitude of political marketing in the United States is also attributable to the concentration of devolved power, combined with regional loyalty. As a result, local power in the state Senate can be exhaustive, including for example rights of decision on the death penalty, so that parochial politics are a satisfying option, their prizes more alluring than the more moribund authority conferred by some European local governments. This makes people try harder for those rewards. They are willing to spend more.

Other factors underlying the growth of political marketing include the increasing political fragmentation of the United States. The party

system that inhabits such a constitutional context has become
tated over the past five decades, over one-third of people claim no
political leaning whatsoever and their numbers have been rising, and
there is open season over much of the political territory.[12] Some
candidates do not bother to mention party affiliation in their advertising, and this trend (for which the explanations, including the
disintegration of the veteran urban voting blocks, are manifold)
entails that the candidate ceases to be a mere cipher for his party. He
is voted in on perceptions of his personality and the particular issue
coalitions he manages to assemble, and this contrasts with European
practice, where the character of the candidate is sometimes almost
redundant, so that the localised selling of an individual image
becomes more significant in the absence of national party promotion.

This point is a key one in the rise of political marketing. New
territory is now opened up to exploitation: the efficacy of marketing –
the evidence of this is compelling – is very limited where there are
entrenched pre-existing loyalties. When such loyalties atrophy,
marketing becomes a power tool, so the weakening of the party
encourages and sustains political marketing. Party magnates no
longer control cohorts of territorially based automatic votes: media
and money can pin down the floating electorate, and there is a lack of
legal willingness to restrict them. The party machines have more
bondaged power, there is not the same need for service to gain the
party's approbation; rather, paid media can circumvent the orthodox
channels so that political status is open to the rich outsider. And
politically ambitious businessmen did not want to be excluded from
office by party machines: they therefore sought to use their money to
bypass them. The confusion about our values, the decline in inherited
allegiance, has given rise to a politics of rented allegiance from which
political marketing benefits.

The marketing approach to politics was also facilitated by the
retreat from social involvement and organic social units to the world
of armchair activism. In addition, the scale and intensity of media
scrutiny makes American politicians seek ways of both manipulating
and short-circuiting the media: marketing holds the answers. And
there is a tradition of lavish political campaigning in America which
translates readily into high expenditure on political marketing. This is
itself the result of cultural values, the notion that men are as justified
in using money to persuade as for any other objective, an entrenched
belief in the commercial ethos. And there is the legacy of the old
graft; the system did not expunge it but resurrected it: hireling

precinct captains were replaced by the hired political consultants. Also in the United States there is an honourable tradition of philanthropy and this includes donations to the communication campaigns of political causes: liberal and especially right-wing pressure groups have harnessed this habit with far-reaching effect.

America is a country of vocal groups, whether union or corporate, who have traditionally lobbied and the advent of political marketing has presented opportunities to create debts that will subsequently be returned as a legislative dividend. Historically, this is a key American virtue. With so many different races, nationalities and traditions it has to be, and the notion of give and take, of a generous measure of tolerance, is part of the intellectual furniture of most Americans.

How then do we reconcile this generosity of spirit with the intolerance that political marketing so often seems to incite? It could be claimed that, since political marketing deals primarily in personalities, this is an intolerance towards individuals rather than ideas, while also in a market-place of ideas extremisms will somehow counterbalance each other: there is a centrifugal pull. Marketing, because it makes people more sensitive and aware of others' positions, makes them more tolerant. The United States has worked by seeing itself as a market-place for competing and sometimes antithetical lobbies, and it has recognised that for the cause of social harmony such interests should be permitted to express their cases as they wish, and gain some form of tangible return. American attitudes to politics are also predicated upon the notion of divergent interests which are reconciled to the social order by getting portions of the patronage, and unlike the situation in Europe such interests are only loosely affiliated to the class system. The politician also needs someone to pay the high costs of commercial electoral persuasion, while industry seeks political influence, so that congressmen through the 'pork barrel' process give favourable legislation to industries and support grants to particular areas in exchange for their help.

There are other significant reasons for the primacy of political marketing, located in America's social style and arrangements. American politics have not had any especial dignity attaching to them that would insulate political institutions from the marketing ethos and furnish a spurious sanctity. Traditionally politics have lacked upper-class involvement, in contrast to politics in Europe, and have associations with upwardly mobile immigrant groups, while generally in America there is less concern for the kind of institutional bombast that would scorn the application of business techniques. There is an aggressive perception of business opportunity, even in politics, and here as elsewhere Americans have sought to turn their interests into cash.

American Political Style

American culture has produced a distinctive American political style. On viewing or reading candidate propaganda one is struck by the similarity of personality types and the values they advocate: this is explained by the extent of the middle-class self concept, a broad target market, and by the rightward shift of the Reagan era Democrat Party. Pragmatism is the dominant vein, with few of the exhausting ideological conflicts more characteristic of Europe, and politicians reflect the values of a society where half the work-force is classified as white-collar, where there is 65 per cent home ownership, and where one-third of high school graduates gain a university degree. So political marketing vaunts the middle-class life-style and pays ritual homage to 'family' values. How does this relate to claims that political marketing is sometimes sectarian and divisive? Direct mail, video, radio and other focussed mediums constitute a 'private' media where the candidate can address core supporters rhetorically; television constitutes a 'public' medium in which the candidate strives not to offend members of his coalition. The fact is that there can be strong similarity of style, value and emotional appeal, and differences on issue positions. The Stars and Stripes, or the smiling dark-suited candidate, can be made to signify different things. Also, paradoxically, the fact that today so much is often common ground between candidates can mean that areas of disagreements are disputed more angrily. And the sentimentality of American culture is also deployed by the political marketers, in a (rarely subtle) attempt to orchestrate the deeper emotional responses so that synthetic attempts are made to manufacture Kennedyesque 'charisma', rather like an incompetent medium struggling to create ectoplasm.[13] Thus Senator Hart acted a pastiche of the Kennedy style and the effect was artificial, missing entirely the intellectual essence of JFK. It is a matter of image as well as content: and as elsewhere there are followers and imitators – of the romanticism of J. F. Kennedy, the warmth of Reagan, the mediability of both.

America is a fluid society, transient both socially and geographically, and the impetus towards instant rapport this creates is translated into an easy-going political style. There is no hint of paternalism; American politicians never patronise their listeners, and the aim as with many popular heroes is to appear as a well-manicured version of a familiar type. The curious sameness of American's politicians has often been remarked on but should not necessarily surprise: for as McKay notes, 'some observers make the mistake of inferring a general cultural individualism when noting the undoubted prevalence of economic individualism in the United States', and he goes on to cite examples of popular 'collectivist' thinking – McCarthyism, fundamentalism and so on.[14] To be successful, it may be that you must occupy the centre ground of mass marketing. There are so many sensitive and politically powerful groups capable of being offended that this has often made for a politics of blandness: the bland, as it were, leading the bland.

After the heady days of Richard Nixon there was a concerted attempt to reduce the role of individual wealth; to some extent it succeeded. It is however quite another matter to exclude the operation of small sums from many donors, which collectively form large amounts. Marketing demands money; continued dominance depends on its constant supply, and should a successful way be found of reducing finance the phenomena of political marketing would die. All attempts have failed. A critical ethical issue arises here, wherein many Americans assert that moneys so raised have a legitimate role in political persuasion, that democracy has always been about committed groups seeking to influence the mass, and this is its contemporary expression. Another stumbling-block is the legislatures themselves, for the marketing nexus has become self-perpetuating; the whole process favours incumbents since they have the best access to funds: so congressmen have high political longevity.

NOTES

Marketing and Decline of the Party

It is easy to exaggerate the decline of the parties, for they still command a residual loyalty in most people. The party's weakening pre-dates the phenomenon of political marketing: indeed it is a consequence of that decline and has fuelled further decline. The attrition of its power to deliver block votes, due to demographic and social factors, meant that candidates turned elsewhere for management of vote delivery.

Consultants are especially severe in their dismissal of the party. Napolitan claims: 'I work in lots of campaigns where I don't even know who the Democratic Party Chairmen are'.[15] The decline of the party proved to be especially strong among the young, so that by the nineteen seventies 40 per cent of voters in their twenties were registering as independents, and in California the parties, long weak, became almost a redundancy, with campaigns ebbing and flowing around individual men and issues.

Yet parties were never a purposeless excrescence; they were founded and sustained for particular objectives. In the early days of course they helped to provide welfare in a pre-welfare state; and they enabled diverse interests to be in some degree satisfied through the provision of a common, aggregated platform, and this was particularly important in the United States, with so many disparate groups competing. Decline has had manifold consequences. As we have discussed, candidates can be nominated without needing the assistance of the party, and often they conduct their elections in the same way: 'As a result of the party's atomization the candidate has to build his own organization.'[16] Richard Nixon's CREEP was a classic example of this, since it was a dominant presidential campaign structure that was independent of his party; often now the party is reduced to a consultancy function. McKay makes the serious accusation that 'a Presidential nominating process outside the control of party boosts media created candidates who may be skilful at winning primaries but rarely make good Presidents'. He also claims that the weakening of parties makes for more ideological politics, since the essential element of coalition, with its demand for tolerance, is now missing.

By the nineteen seventies there were 'wild and unpredictable swings in outcomes and vote margins from one election to the next'.[17] Voting was now a minority habit, voter turn-out in the United States was the lowest in twenty-one democratic countries. Seventy million failed to vote in the 1976 Presidential election and we may speculate on the potential for dislocation that lies dormant in this, the largest and alienated party.[18] Ticket splitting (voting for different candidates in the same election) also increased: during the nineteen seventies between two-thirds and three-quarters of independents and Democrats and half of Republicans split tickets at some point.

Ethos of the New Right

It is necessary to consider the 'new right' in great detail, because it is the principal agent behind the modern rise of political marketing, for the right sought a way to short-circuit the alleged liberal bias of the media, and so the story of the modern right begins in its recognition of the manipulative power of television and its status as a legitimising force. The new right has thoroughly comprehended the marketing approach to politics. To change society it is necessary above all to change the prevailing social orthodoxy: to a surprising degree they have achieved this, conspiring to make many liberal positions look dated. Of the many defences of the 'new right', one line in particular recommends itself: that they are a corrective to liberalism, and that in the process some sort of balance emerges.

Crawford lays a special stress on the differences between new rightists and traditional conservatives.[19] The 'new right' is excited by all methods of involving the general public more directly in democratic processes and thrives on referendums and initiative campaigns. The 'new right' vaunts, it idealises, the ordinary man, and it has been described as 'McLuhan- era

marxism'. Traditional conservatives are among the new right's most eloquent critics; for George F. Will it represents 'a radically antipolitical
ideology, decayed Jeffersonianism characterized by a frivolous hostility
toward the state'; it represents 'an anarchy of self-interestedness'.

The roots of the reactionary right lie deep in American history. America
began as a rejection: by the colonialists towards the sponsor power collectively, and then individually by each immigrant towards his own native land, for
in leaving it he became a rebel. The corollary of rejection is affirmation, and
the immigrant idealised his new home and believed that the malign influences
of the past would be exorcised here. Crawford quotes Stephen Tonsor:[20] the
American experience 'was such as to encourage the immigrant to *strip off his
European institutional and cultural past* and to become a new American man
... They created a myth of American novelty and simplicity, virtue and
harmony which is constantly threatened with corruption and confusion from
the forces of high culture and history'. For Tonsor the American is essentially
mobile, a nomad who seeks in movement some visionary, lost Arcadia.

A distinctively American populist style goes back to the very early
nineteenth century. Andrew Jackson was an early hero. Typically these
rightist forces represented a radicalism of minor capitalists. They had
successors in the late nineteenth century. A consistent thread throughout the
history of the 'new right' has been suspicion of large organisations, whether
business, unions or the federal government: it represents a variant of class
politics, emanating not from a peasant or proletarian resentment but from a
class of small but independent smallholders and traders.[21] Their activities are
hence characterised by idiosyncratic and unco-ordinated outburst rather than
the sustained opposition that might characterise proletarian unrest. It was
and is, then, discontent of a peculiarly American type. Such discontent needs
demagogues to lead it and they have come forward: but their work has been
at the level of rhetoric, not organisation – until now – so that in the past such
movements have fizzled out because they lacked a structured framework.
William Jennings Bryan was an early leader. And in the nineteen thirties
emerged some new stars in the reactionary firmament. Huey Long was one,
Father Charles Coughlin was another, projecting his rabble-rousing oratory
via the radio, supplemented with extensive mailing lists. A later hero was
Joseph McCarthy.

The 'new right', conditioned by such a past, has an ethos and a flavour all
of its own. It is virulently opposed to the big, liberal, ethnic city; and on the
subject of New York it is paranoid.[22] It is on the point of permissive morality
that the 'new right' becomes especially eloquent. Business and media are
perceived to be bound up with social degeneration. The 'new right' coalesces
around a whole series of issues. There are the 'right to work' issues, the
'pro-family' lobby, the education and foreign policy groups, and the powerful
anti-abortion groupings in a category of their own, the law and order groups,
the pro-gun movements. Then, related to all these groups, is the 'religious
right'. Many of these myriad institutions are to a greater or lesser extent
marketing agencies; some are more ostensibly academic than others and they
have of course different target markets, with appeals perhaps to decision-
makers, or to the evangelised, or to the ideologically committed.

Their movement has especially been towards the television medium: this then is marketing for the propagation of particular values and a world view and the common denominator is a full internalisation of the marketing approach; the consequence is legislative dividends which demonstrate how the usage of marketing has contributed to change in the ideological focus of US politics. This is what distinguishes the 'new right' from previous populism, when media was in its infancy and the right carried no organisational expertise. The Draft Goldwater movement gave a base: the mailing lists then generated provided subsequent revivalists with a ready target of appeal and source of funds. According to Howard Phillips, 'Organize discontent. That is our strategy'. This they have done effectively.

The sums of money raised by the 'new right' are remarkable; during the nineteen seventies Viguerie-assisted 'Political Action Committees' (PACs) were raising more money than the Republican National Committee and the Republican House and Senate campaign committees. These groups can even individually bring pressure to bear on Congress. Hence in January and February 1978 the National Right to Work Committee sent out eight million letters, and six million letters exhorted the senate to disavow the common situs picketing bill.[23]

4 Television

> 'When he has been drawn out of his own sphere, therefore, he
> always expects that some amazing object will be offered to his
> attention; and it is on these terms alone that he consents to tear
> himself for a moment from the petty, complicated cares which form
> the charm and the excitement of his life.'
>
> Alexis de Tocqueville, *Democracy in America*

Political marketing employs a constellation of mediums: but television remains the supreme gift to politicians, with their presence
assured in every home, and political marketing is largely a television
activity. It is even employed in minor campaigns. According to David
Garth, television 'can take someone who's relatively unknown and
make him a visible factor'.

Television is inescapable for politicians. Tele-marketing is also
costly, both on its own account and because its successful usage
demands the leasing of professional expertise: it is a medium thirsty
for cash, to obtain which the politician has to trade his central asset,
his influence as a legislator, thus giving external groups significant
political power. The fact that air time can be purchased in large
quantities enables new men to buy entry into the political process:
wealth or rich supporters become a necessary qualification for access.
It is actually possible – we have ex-Congressman John Le Boutellier
to prove it – for a rich young candidate who has scarcely worked to
purchase advertising time, and win.

There are of course two kinds of political television, advertising
and news, the paid and unpaid media, and while the news is the most
important element, advertising is also influential. With television as
the primary political marketing source we see the obituary of popular
political activism, for television is a domestic medium whose audience is immobile in an easy chair, and it has created a politics that
does not incorporate people but is produced for them – they cease to
solicit each other, but are solicited in the collective by the electronic
face. In comparison with the more traditional mediums of propaganda, television is less heroic, more domestic and more abundant: it
engulfs us, part of the anti-heroism of the age, and appeases our
appetite for debunking.

The unpaid media lends itself particularly well to the concept of the

46

perpetual campaign, for the politician–product appears constantly before the public: groomed for the news, purveying stories, avoiding an adversarial relationship with journalists. Television electoral marketing dictates extravagance, with half a minute on prime-time television, retailing at $30 000. It was estimated that in 1984 Reagan and Mondale spent fifty million dollars on television advertising. According to Diamond and Bates, the parties spent about the same amount of money on the national campaign between 1912 and 1952. Television changed all that; the sum per vote had tripled by 1968. Ninety per cent of a politician's advertising budget can go on television. 'Image' and 'issue' commercials are created in superabundance. Nor is such intoxication misguided: one study suggested the previous exposure or specifically media exposure successfully predicted eighty-three per cent of primary winners. Fortunes have been made in media consultancy. Television political advertising also has the function of inspiring the candidate's existing supporters and of providing riposte to a competitor's charges. There is of course the risk of saturation; candidates can be overexposed on television and their public become weary, and this is particularly so in a presidential campaign with candidate exhaustion and staleness as major factors.

THE RISE OF TELEVISION ADVERTISING

Eisenhower in 1952 was the first tele-marketed Presidential candidate with his 'Eisenhower Answers America' series, gaining thirty-nine of the forty states advertised in, and since that year America's politicians have slithered into America's sitting-rooms in increasing numbers. Political advertising began on the political right; as it was not the natural majority party, it was more inclined to innovate in political communication because it had the money and, most important, a commercial ethos and no ideological bias against it.

Rosser Reeves orchestrated the Eisenhower campaign. He recognised and proved to his own satisfaction the comparative ineffectiveness of the traditional mode of persuasion, the set-piece political speech. He tested the audience awareness of a televised speech by General MacArthur and found that nobody remembered what he had said (though it would be fallacious to rest a strategy on this recall measure, since image and impression are also important); subsequently he claimed that only five per cent of the total media audience at the very best would listen to a political speech.[1]

Reeves was the pioneer of television political mass merchandising and in this 'Eisenhower Answers' series he had representative American types, hauled from Radio City queues, put brief topical questions to the presidential candidate. This follows the 'man in the street' idea of commercial advertisers. Here, the target audience influenced the political product. Marketing with its focus on 'consumer' response assists a movement from elitist to more participatory democracy.

The medium was by 1952 ready for political use, since there were now about nineteen million television sets in America with a penetration of 62 per cent of homes in large urban areas. George Gallup established a dozen issues of importance (especially: Korea, corruption, taxation and living costs), and twenty-eight spots of twenty seconds' duration, and three of one minute, were produced: for example, in reply to a question asserting the decency of Democrat intentions, he replied that if a schoolbus is driven into a ditch you do not say the driver's intentions were good, you change the driver. The spots were shown in forty of the forty-eight American states with saturation (four or five spots heard by voters each day) in eleven, and Eisenhower won in thirty-nine. The Democrats superciliously dismissed this barrage as 'political soap suds and tasteless bubblegum'. Subsequent accounts have claimed that the television campaign had scant impact. However, there appears to have been no contemporary measurement of the impact of the spot campaign, while no party had an interest in claiming that it was decisive. Thus assertions that it was ineffectual are conjecture.

Reeves was an eminent advertising theoretician who worked for the Ted Bates agency, a professional applying commercial marketing logic to a tradition, and tradition had been found wanting; he had the marketing operative's concern for effectiveness and measurement. His methods, much copied since, had been inspired by consumer advertising which so often seeks out 'typical' personality types to articulate the product's merits on film.

Presidents and politicians varied in their ability to accommodate television. Lyndon Johnson was an awkward television performer although a massive personality outside the studio, for communication methods that work in more traditional politics may fail when translated to television: for instance, the medium had a nullifying effect on the oratory of Adlai Stevenson.

Eisenhower's team may have established the use of television as a political marketing medium, yet their employment of it remained rather innocent, and it was left to others to develop the techniques, especially the Nixon campaign team. Marshall McLuhan's writings influenced them. McLuhan[2] emphasised an intimate and urbane presentation style as being critical to success, quoting Perry Como as the ideal 'low-pressure king of a high-pressure realm'. The impressionistic and even illogical nature of television campaigning was well noted by Nixon's strategists and, observing that voters were lazy, one of them, William Gavin, added: 'Reason pushes the viewer back, it assaults him, it demands that he agree or disagree; impression can envelop him, invite him in, without making an intellectual demand . . .'[3] This connects very clearly with the 'thematic' emphasis given by later campaign managers and singled out by Etzioni. One of those who made them described the Nixon commercials thus: 'Their message was intended for people who had triteness oozing out of every pore . . . The commercials are successful because people are able to relate them to their own delightful misconceptions of themselves and their country'. Targets for these advertisements were selected with equal cynicism; thus the South 'will like the great nation self-help, fields of waving wheat stuff and the general thrust of Protestant ethic imagery'.[4] The creation of image, especially the use of advertising to counteract the negatives in public perceptions of a candidate, was thus emphasised in Nixon's campaign. The same banal mechanic is then used to promote areas of very different significance. Ivory Snow on the one hand, the government of the nation on the other.

Once discovered, media political marketing was to become a permanent feature of political campaigning and the effect of this was to put up the price of office considerably, for it made the ability to sell on film, hitherto of limited relevance, the most important political skill, and it demonstrated greater power than orthodox methods of campaigning since it could stress the same message repeatedly to large audiences, as commercial marketing does, and be effective for the same reasons. Nixon's 1968 campaign was the most significant event in the incorporation of a marketing ethos into the American political process. By 1968 there was a more general recognition of the marketing concept: for many years it had been an article of faith in large firms like Procter and Gamble and an academic discipline in business schools and had now filtered into public consciousness. The campaign now conceived of the candidate as a product that could be modified in relation to a market, seeking with a conscious marketing awareness to control all factors in the environment and eluding truthfulness to create a plastic man.

Nixon developed and continued the marketed approach during his time in office. To bypass a lukewarm and even hostile media he acquired the arts of symbolic communication, in 1970 actually vetoing a bill in front of the television cameras, and claimed in his memoirs, 'Modern presidents must try to master the art of manipulating the media not only to win in politics but in order to further the programs and causes they believe in . . . In the modern presidency, concern for image must rank with concern for substance'. Communication obsessed him: 'Nixon has been a very hard worker, but with very few exceptions this has been hard work in preparing and delivering speeches'.[5] Seymour-Ure asserts that most of Nixon's 'crises' comprised winning or losing an argument.[6] In 1960 Nixon had failed in the television debates because he used a parliamentary debating style and not one suited to media persuasion, and both the significance and the triviality of the medium left an abiding impression on him.[7] Recognition came blindingly: that an intellectual argumentative style was now anachronistic. He became an adept manipulator of television; he could and did go directly to the television audience, and this as Seymour-Ure points out became a method of legitimising his government.[8] He became a harbinger of the perpetual campaign. His career represented a transit from the old to the new political style, his awakening representing in large a conversion to marketing that so many politicians underwent. Looking back on the Nixon and Carter Presidencies, it is easy to forget – overshadowed as we are by their later debacle – how well a marketing approach originally built and sustained them.

Their failure showed the deficiencies in their overall political marketing strategy, and also perhaps the practical and conceptual limitations of the marketing approach to politics. Both used television well until events began to defeat them. Moreover Nixon could attempt to intimidate the independent commentators, with Agnew rallying the mass – on which the media depends – in derision of the media, as a way of gaining leverage.[9]

By the time of the Carter–Ford contest everything appeared constructed for television marketing and there were now abundant proofs of its effectiveness. The Carter team discovered that people were telling investigators the things they had in fact heard in advertisements.[10] Rafshoon made advertising of Carter in informal domestic settings and also 'executive' postures, in a value-laden campaign with stress on the themes of 'hard work', 'family', 'home', 'land' and 'love'.[11] A five-minute biography was made of Carter and he appeared in blue-collar settings.[12] Ford countered with his 'man in the street' spots.[13] Both sides adopted this symbolic approach, and there was an absence of real debate.

From all this televised political marketing process one man emerges as its expression – and perhaps its vindication. For the Great Communicator himself was past master. He could face a crisis, appear and in five minutes talk away his blunders, his sunny rapport with the American people reasserted. For public expectations from television were determined by the quality of its actors, who set a standard, and from its politicians the public began to expect no less, and wooden performers like Senator Glenn failed. Hubert Humphrey claimed to regret not having mastered television, a sentiment later to be echoed by Mondale after his defeat, and hence an apprenticeship served in Hollywood should not be regarded as aberrant, rather is it a fit background for media politics/ Reagan's television abilities were the explanation for his success, and the measure of how far American politics had become immersed in marketing. For the first time in history an actor had risen to the highest political office. First advised when he entered politics to emulate Efrem Zimbalist Jnr of the 'FBI' series ('Warm, intelligent, never intellectual'), Reagan is undoubtedly a media artefact and without the media he would have enjoyed a sunlit Pacific coast retirement.

In so far as he was the agent and political articulation of the 'new right' he made possible a minor revolution. Under Reagan the image control approach reached its apogee, for while Nixon had at least faced up to the issues, they can be divisive. Reagan's electoral vehicle, Tuesday Team, was filled with advertising men and consultants and represented the fruition of the brand management approach to politics, for by this stage no one was under any illusions and they recognised this as political marketing. The concept had become popular orthodoxy, a demand-led and research-defined view of political communication that is thereby distinguished from earlier and more intuitive notions of politics.

So the consequences of media manipulation are profound. But are they bad? To be effective a president must have a wide and non-sectarian appeal, and it follows that if he can attract mass support by his mastery of modern communication he is also good at neutralising the disaffected. Arguably then he has achieved ʼʼ central task of all statecraft, by using electronically commʼʼ symbolic strategies to reconcile competing factions accept it would give an ethical as well as ultilitarian legʼ

methods of political marketing. Market politics involve the anaesthetising of hostility, and the adoption of the marketing concept as a political ideology means that this therefore becomes a political goal.

In a viewing of many political advertisements several stand in sharp relief: Harriet Wood's 'crying farmer' spot; Senator Tower explaining why he refuses to shake the hand of his opponent; Chuck Percy's *mea culpa*, admitting that the electorate are right in wanting their taxes cut; an actor playing a derisive Castro thanking the American taxpayer; Senator Abdnor acknowledging his lack of oratorical prowess and turning it into a virtue; Sheriffs, rifles at hands, fiercely endorsing a candidate; Reagan's 'Morning in America' soft-focus jingle; a modest-living old man damning Democrat tax policies and vowing to vote Republican; copulating rhinoceri (that was never shown); the anti-Abzug 'Bella we know you' campaign; the 'In 1929 they said the same' refrain on Republican tax cuts; models of ships being pushed over to represent the McGovern defence plan; an Arctic research station based in Los Angeles; Hart addressing 'our generation' on its 'idealism' and ability to 'dream dreams'; champagne spilling over cut-glass cups to illustrate the 'trickle down' effect beloved of Republican economists.

KINDS OF TELEVISION ADVERTISING

After so many years of political advertising it is now possible to make categories and to generalise about it. Sometimes indeed this advertising may be done self-consciously, but even here the intention may be serious – to jolt the voter out of apathy, to create a luminous image for a dull incumbent or to establish identity for an unknown candidate. There are inane political advertisements, just as there are consumer advertisements. The following examples closely parallel consumer advertising since their objectives are the same, to establish the humanity of the person or product with wit, and to relieve tension.

Television advertising can be unrestrained: one advertisement wittily caricatured the corpulent Tip O'Neil, Speaker of the House, attempting to drive a stalling car, with the caption 'the Democrats are running out of gas'. Another, never shown, revealed Mr Mondale facing in three directions: by ingenious cinematographic effect his flesh appeared to wobble and creep.[14] All of the above at least had a

purported meaning even if the format was sometimes gross. Sometimes however promoters choose gimmickry with no aspiration to
higher status: it is one way of getting audience attention and ensuring
that the candidate will at least be remembered if nothing else, so that
Malcolm Wallop, running in Wyoming for the Senate (1975),
appeared mounted in stetson and business suit for his television
advertising complete with posse: 'Wallop is now leading a horde of
cowboys on horseback, resembling a cavalry scene. They parade
through town, as crowds cheer and Wallop waves'. The slogan was
'Ride with us, Wyoming!'[15] And in Georgia a candidate for the
governorship employed a mist-enshrouded, turbaned hypnotist to
chant 'You will vote for Nick Belluso' at viewers.[16] Senator Hayaka-
wa used a mud-daubed windscreen to epitomise his opponent's
record.[17] Perhaps the nadir was reached with Pierre Salinger's
tasteless campaign refrain, 'In the tradition of our martyred
President'.[18]

Political advertising is possibly more bizarre than consumer advertising, because the function of political advertising is often like a new
product launch; the purpose is to attract recognition in the case of the
new candidate, or to strive for memorability. However, there are also
identifiable forms and much is created in sterile emulation of past,
successful formulae. Thus the 'man in the street' interview, or the
'talking head' format, are not arousing but good for trustworthiness
(some studies credit them with high recall).[19] Consumer marketing
uses similar devices to strive for credibility. Another possibility is the
'news' method, with documentary or press-conference style, when
the candidate is able to appear as a restless enquirer after the truth
with all the reliability of the newsman (television anchormen have
high approval ratings).[20] There is a predictability about the content of
much political television: the limited sums involved and the penalties
of failure make people reluctant to experiment. The candidate is
filmed talking to 'ordinary' people (such as actors and party members), and there is a (synthetically manufactured?) rally with national
emblems: patriotism, last refuge of the scoundrel, is the first of
symbols for politicians. A number of totems of Americana are
invariably courted and paraded by candidates for high office – Texas,
mid-western farmers, a Cardinal, the Mayor of New York – all join
the campaign whirligig. And media events abound: the wearing of
funny hats, Red Indian head-dress and the like is mandatory. A
variety of time-hallowed television poses is advisable, depending on
the status of the candidate; when fighting an incumbent he might

adopt the 'clean uncorrupt broom' approach, or appear 'statesman-like'. Henry Jackson won his seat with strategically placed billboards depicting him in severe pose with 'Jackson for US Senator' – contrasting sharply with the blustering incumbent. The aim of political advertising must also be to win attention on the non-paid media.

Over the years television political advertising has developed an orthodox stock-in-trade of recurrent symbols: the shrinking dollar, with the opponent's face inscribed; the weather vane, with opponent's head; the torn social security card (used first in 1964 and powerful with older voters, who exhibit high turn-out levels); the red telephone.[21] Content is then predictable, and often there is a more or less established sequence which begins with advertisements that concentrate on gaining 'name identification' for the candidate; subsequent advertising carves out the issue positions of the candidate in emotive and simplistic terms, and further down in the sequence is the deployment of 'attack' and even negative advertisements: Mondale, for example, displayed a bright red telephone to easily illustrate the 'inexperience' of Gary Hart. In the final bout of the contest more elevated advertisements appear, and on the eve of polling day a quiet, long, and mildly visionary offer is presented. The documentary has sometimes been employed. Thus in Alaska a candidate's half-hour documentary (it was called 'Man from Alaska') boosted his campaign: before it was shown, Mike Gravel was losing 2:1; afterwards he was ahead by 55 per cent to 45 per cent. Effective political documentary is helped by the repetition of symbols that encapsulate basic themes, such as Nixon's use of film of a USAF transport.[22] Symbolism, as with Lindsay wandering around ghettos in his advertising, will always be central. A symbolic appeal is so effective because it imposes no intellectual tax, is imprecise and hence immune from exposure, can be interpreted by many in a light favourable to them, and unites complex positions in the one all-embracing image.

Political marketing is promoting the images of ordinary men and not, in the main, actors; the creative challenge is therefore considerable. The candidate himself may not even appear, especially if the packagers cannot disguise unappealing features, voice and so on. He becomes more essence than physical substance. Hence television political advertising seeks to utilise a candidate's best points: if he is plain it will sell his voice, if he is photogenic his smiling countenance will appear, if he is a fine public speaker action clips will be shown. Henry Cabot Lodge's effective 1960 campaign film was composed entirely of stills, since the candidate was a cumbersome television performer.[23] Only the aggression of the newsmen and the willingness of television to stage debates will expose candidates.

Often television advertising is used to change those areas where the candidate is perceived negatively, to deal with key criticisms directly; thus John F. Kennedy in the West Virginia primary: 'there is no article of my faith that would in any way inhibit – I think it encourages – the meeting of my oath of office'.[24] Here he was attempting to dispel doubts concerning his Roman Catholicism.

Advertising tries to carefully sidestep the vulnerability of the candidate. Thus, in 1966 the unpopular Nelson Rockefeller seemed sentenced to defeat, so puppets of fish did the talking:

Reporter puppet: 'Already one hundred and thirty new sewage-treatment plants are getting under way'.
Fish puppet: 'Yeah, well it was pretty smelly down here'.[25]

Only in later advertisements did Rockefeller himself appear, and he won with a broad margin. One Mondale advertisement did not feature the candidate himself with his lugubrious television manner; instead it showed a roller-coaster, which acted as mobile metaphor for Reagan's handling of the economy,[26] and much of Senator Jesse Helms' advertising showed the Senator only briefly in his opening half-hour advertisement: he himself appeared just for a few seconds. According to Tom Wicker, 'the ordinary voter in North Carolina will see a Helms commercial at least 10 times a week from May until November. A typical advertisement would feature these words being written on the screen and spoken by an actor: "I voted against the Martin Luther King holiday. Where do you stand, Jim?"' This is perhaps the ultimate art of political marketers, to fight an election without candidates: it demonstrates how advertising can take centre stage and how irrelevant candidate and party can become to a process that is ostensibly all about them. The strategic objective of the Helms campaign was to force the opponent on the defensive and shift attention from his personality and entrenched conservative views; according to his press secretary Helms wanted to focus the campaign on 'this politician [Governor Hunt] who's supported by gays, Commies, Ted Kennedy, Julian Bond and the ultra-liberal media'. In 1952, Richard Nixon answered the allegations of impropriety that threatened his political future with a half-hour paid talk. In this, he referred to the 'bribe' of a lovable cocker spaniel. Almost half of all television viewers watched this 'Checkers' speech: one million called or wrote in support. The event was arranged by advertising agency Batten, Barton, Durstine and Osborn. It heralded Nixon's 1968 campaign and showed how the action of the paid media can become in itself a major political event; the paid media's crucial property is that it can bypass the mediating interpretation of the unpaid media. Here, it saved Richard Nixon's career.

On occasion, advertising has challenged vulnerabilities directly. In 1969 Mayor John Lindsay of New York, at the instigation of David Garth, admitted various mistakes in his 1969 re-election campaign: 'The things that go wrong are what make this the second-toughest job in America. But the things that go right are what make me want it'.[27] Others have emulated this approach since, including Brendan Byrne standing successfully for re-election to the governship of New Jersey in 1977 (his popularity had slumped by two-thirds), while Governor Hugh Carey also used this 'politics of apology' medicine[28] by suggesting that the public's pardon would indicate their political maturity. This is a technique that is cynical and effective, an example of what business, especially at the level of tactical public relations, could learn from politics. Advertising often works by confounding our expectations and stereotypes and here it worked because people are so surprised by honest politicians.

Fortuitous camera shots and film footage are also employed. Nixon used film on his 1972 Russia visit, while Reagan's team made and televised a half-hour sentimental documentary, and in 1980 and 1988 George Bush's admen were able to show film of his rescue after being shot down in the Pacific in 1944. Realism is essential in the political product as a guide to the candidate's competence since this is a key consumer criterion: therefore packaging must be disguised as much as possible.

Since political marketing is inherently vague – we cannot know what the future will hold – it tends to be impressionistic. Here it compares with the marketing of services. But there is, too, a deceit at work. Vagueness is sometimes used to effect. In 1968 advertisements showed footage of Vietnam with Nixon's voice saying, 'Never has so much military, economic and diplomatic power been used as ineffectively as in Vietnam. And if, after all of this time and all of this support, there is still no end in sight, then I say the time has come for the American people to turn to new leadership, not tied to the policies and mistakes of the past. I pledge to you: we will have an honourable end to the war in Vietnam'.[29] This says nothing: it merely gives impressions – that, for example, America under Nixon would leave Vietnam fast. Implication without commitment – that is the artifice, for political advertising is adept at summoning mists and dispelling clarity.

Sarcasm is another technique. In the campaign against Jay Rockefeller for the governorship of West Virginia (1972), New Yorkers were asked what they thought of a West Virginian running for the governorship of New York: close-ups of their laughter were shown (this was a Robert Goodman advertisement). Such a satiric quality would distinguish the political from consumer marketing, which tends to be less vindictive because personalities are not so intimately involved.

In 1988 'toughness' was once again a major theme in the advertising, after the smugness and indulgence of the Reagan years.[30] Moynihan used stark advertising such as 'Killer Cop Bullets'; Gephardt had a telling spot about the price of a Chrysler car in Korea and his advance in Iowa was attributed to such media. Another theme, about as old as American politics itself, was the populist credentials of the candidate, Dole thus becoming a self-styled 'someone from the people, someone who made it the hard way', for whom 'A little bit of Russell goes with him everywhere', while the patrician Pierre du Pont was transformed into the descendant of immigrants. Harvard lawyer Bruce Babbit became the scion of a 'frontier family', and voters were reminded of Dukakis's Greek immigrant parents, though not of his father's Harvard medical degree. 'Credibility' shots were as ever important – Simon as a vigorous young newspaper editor exposing corruption, Bush with Mrs Thatcher and NATO chiefs ·and as a rescued pilot, Pat Robertson as a 'businessman', 'educator', 'Yale Law Graduate' – but not the more proximate truth, his career as an evangelist (his negative rating fell by up to 20 per cent in a test run of this advertisement). Dukakis stressed his managerial competence. Negative advertising was the choice of the more obscure candidates: in bleak New Hampshire, Kemp showed Bush with King Fahd of Saudi Arabia to illustrate his support for oil price increases. 'Compassion' was another theme in 1988: Dukakis showed the homeless living within sight of the White House, with the promise that when he met Mr Gorbachev this would never occur. According to *The Times*:[31]

> Mr Dukakis sounds like an old-style liberal – like a Kennedy or O'Neill, but without the flair. His television ads focus on emotional issues, like Central America and the homeless, alternating between

pictures of limbless war victims and footage of shivering old men asleep on the streets of Washington.'

The extent of television advertising showed no signs of abating in this campaign; in the Iowa primaries for example the average watcher would have seen Gephardt's advertising seven times.

CAMPAIGN STRATEGY

The grand strategy of the campaign is crucial and dictates the advertising. Nimmo recommends[32] that the incumbent emphasises his achievements on behalf of the constituency, reminds opinion leaders of debts owed, and prevents opponents creating the issue agenda or defining the campaign's pace. The candidate acts as a receptacle for 'elements of projection that reside in the viewer rather than in the person viewed'. The consultant must provide a contrasting image, exploiting the weaknesses of the opposition. Effective options are also open to the challenger – he may run as a 'citizen' politician, a tactic to some extent employed by Reagan in his California gubernatorial campaign, the assumption being that the voter is alienated from traditional politicians.[33] Finding the right campaign theme is thus essential: the voters relate more comfortably to general themes than to specific issues, and Eisenhower for example fought his election on the themes of 'crime, communism and Korea' as a 'non-political' candidate.[34] Obscure candidates are well advised to use television advertising: 'as the great entertainer television provides the political neophyte a means for shattering the inattention of his desired audience'.[35] Television is also useful for incumbents whose record is criticised, while those who face a hostile press can bypass it through television; primaries, as Reagan found in 1966, are good for establishing a public identity via the paid media.[36]

Another possible technique is to articulate popular doubts about one's candidacy (established through polling?) and assuage them: the very process of admission that he doubts relieves them, and helps the candidate appear honest, with an endearing streak of humility: 'Maybe you wondered whether I'd treat all people fairly, or whether I'd only listen to the problems of the blacks. Frankly, I couldn't win this election with only one block of voters' (Tom Bradley, first black Mayor of Los Angeles).[37] They base these tactics on what they believe to be the common mood, since polling will have given them some insight, therefore the marketing message in a sense flows from the consumer and thus such examples articulate the conventional wisdom, or purport to do so, and express crisply what the man-in-the-street is thinking; a notion of populist democracy is inherent in the concept of political marketing, and it represents a way of healing social discord by showing rulers who are responsive at the histrionic, if not necessarily at the practical, level.

Clever use of imagery is yet another alternative, with Rockefeller's promotion describing how all the roads he had built would stretch to Hawaii – and back (sound of Hawaiian music).[38] Sometimes cynicism is a powerful tactic: 'after eight years of charisma and four of the clubhouse why not try competence?' (Edward Koch),[39] and sentimentality is another, as with Hubert Humphrey playing with a mentally retarded grandchild and describing how she had taught him about love (tears).[40] A blunt pose as a kind of *vox populi* is a well-chosen method: 'No one could have stopped the snow. But good planning could have prevented the collapse of public transportation' (Jane Byrne).[41] Again these actually say little that is tangible, since their purpose is an emotive and not a rational persuasion.

The advert may also seek connection with prevailing social trends: in the nineteen seventies when many felt the need for more discipline in society, David Garth's candidate used slogans like 'Give yourself a Fighting Chance', 'Fighting for the People of Illinois', 'Tough Young Men for Tough Young Jobs', 'Strong enough to speak his mind', 'Tough enough to get results'.[42] Gary Hart attempted 'high tech' political advertising in 1984, using computer-generated videographics. Like the conventional advertising that it mimicks, the aim is to associate the product, that is, policy and politician, with key social values, the context in which most people think. Fear is yet another emotion to be fermented: one advertisement pictured the names of Agnew and Muskie and the sound of a heart, asking viewers who would be their choice to be a heartbeat away from the Presidency. A focus on anxiety is much stronger in political than in consumer marketing, since politics has a greater legitimacy in arousing fear and because the consequences of major political error are so extensive.

Clearly the placement of the advertising is of critical importance, and the decision is bound up with the strategic focus of the campaign and the question of which particular social group it aims to solicit. Thus Richard Nixon began his successful 1968 campaign with advertising on 'Rowan and Martin's Laugh-In', 'Monday Night at the Movies', 'The Outrider', 'Wild, Wild West' and 'Edge of Night'.

Nixon himself appeared on the 1968 'Laugh-In', proclaiming 'Sock it to ME?'.[43] And in 1984, the Republicans adopted a strictly selective approach with their advertising:

- Sixty Minutes ('prestige')
- Local News; 'Hill Street Blues' (mostly high-income males)
- 'Love Boat' (older women, who have a high participation rate in elections).

Exactly as with consumer advertising, political advertising is placed next to the programmes the target audience will most likely watch: senior citizens, for example, who have a high voter turn-out and tend to be more conservative may have tuned into the 'Laurence Welk Show' before its demise.

Political advertising misleads, often deliberately. One diminutive senator was made to appear bigger by being filmed in a chamber with the small nineteenth-century seats,[44] another was seriously ill but sufficient film was made to paste together a credible shot of his re-election announcement.[45] He died soon afterwards. Alcoholics have been made to appear sober, stupid men have seemed wise, and clowns serious (this is not to deny that such tactics are sometimes used in commercial advertising as well – painting and doctoring food for example). Candidates are recreated for television, with electionists, tailors and cosmetic people in abundance. Senator Jackson, for example, had plastic surgery to create trimmer eyelids, while David Garth forces his candidates to exercise and made Edward Koch lose a stone in weight.[46] There being no legal rules, guile is legitimate unless exposed, and the potential exists for fraudulence.

EFFECTIVENESS OF TELEVISION ADVERTISING

According to one commentator, 'The conventional wisdom among political scientists is that televised political advertisements have had limited impact'.[47] He claims that in general elections, as opposed to primaries, the influence of network paid advertising and news has been 'shown' to be small. Those who are still undecided, according to this thesis, tend to ignore political advertising and it is best at 'stimulating or fortifying' the already decided; the function of targeted media is, therefore, reinforcement. If all this is really true one does have to ask why America's politicians spend so much on an activity which is, according to these lights, marginal. They believe in its power, even if the political scientists who study them do not. Clearly it is difficult for advertising to influence citizens who have a strong precommitment, or enough knowledge to found a firm and unshakeable conviction: but when can a majority of voters be comfortably so described? Practical examples of television's continued power are legion. Wallace Wilkinson for example,[48] an unknown millionaire who spent $4 million on his campaign, defeated the incumbent Governor of Kentucky with television advertisements blandly promising 'a new day of new ideas'. Media assume especial significance in the primaries, for there the citizen's stock of information is low and media therefore gleefully assume the civic burden of replenishing it. There are many candidates, and many of them are entirely new faces. What do they stand for? Who supports them? How are they doing? By what criteria do we judge their current performance and likely chances of success? In all of these the media provide a litany of critical cues, especially as that of partisan allegiance does not exist at this stage. Media in this context does, of course, include especially the paid advertising media.

Political advertising attracts far more attention than does television product advertising, which has 20 per cent viewer recall compared with 79 per cent for the political piece.[49] Television advertising can be not only significant but decisive. In this sense, the political marketers' task is easier since the genre commands an automatic attention, whereas conventional marketing has to penetrate a barrier of indifference. Political advertising campaigns can have a significance which no consumer campaign could ever have. The 'Daisy Spot' helped Lyndon Johnson win in 1964; Saatchis' techniques in 1979 (picture of dole queue, slogan 'Labour isn't working' and so on) contributed to British Conservative success. The apparently greater power of political advertising over consumer advertising is not widely recognised. Television consumer advertising from its very beginnings was regarded as influential since it gave a legitimacy and some status to commercial products, though its effectiveness is difficult to measure accurately. How influential then is television political advertising – can its influence in fact be measured? It is difficult to determine the effects of television political advertising and to isolate one particle of influence from others, just as in consumer marketing the power of advertising *per se* eludes scientific proof; for example, in the 1984 Democratic primaries the tedious John Glenn had the best advertisements, but lost heavily. It would appear that television political advertising has different effects on different categories of voter, just like consumer product marketing. According to Rothschild,[50] the voters who are very interested and involved in an election would not be profoundly affected by advertising while the more apathetic voter might be; examples of the two types would be voters in a presidential election and voters in a state election (this is a controversial claim). Viewing habit as well as involvement is also a factor. Heavy viewers' attitudes, those with lower income and education, were found to be more influenced than those of light viewers. Not surprisingly the heavy viewer who does not feel involved is most susceptible of all. Soley and Reid[51] claim that political advertising's impact on voters is as great as that of party and tenure, and another analysis suggests that voter turn-out is proportional to the amount of advertising in that election.[52] Clearly, then, advertising is a significant influence. An additional useful fact is that voters seem not to distinguish between television advertising and television news,[53] something of an answer to those who decry the effectiveness of television political advertising.

Television advertising is influential since the electorate has so little information and its criteria are vague, especially in a time of party decline. Political advertising really influences the apolitical majority; the numbers innoculated against its influence are so small as to be negligible. The lesson is clear: package the advertising in a news-style format and it will be believed in the sense that retrospectively most people will be unable to remember that it was an advertisement at all.

'Image' advertising seems particularly potent and the voters remember these more than the issue advertisements,[54] though one study (by Sabato) claims the latter induces voters to think more highly of a candidate. But these two findings are not necessarily in conflict. Also, by focussing on a specific political issue, advertisers are able to increase its salience in the eyes of the electorate and in a sense make it their issue. Thus one researcher concludes that 'image' commercials are more effective at getting people to remember the candidate ('name identification') than are issue commercials, and also finds no real difference in the effectiveness of one-minute and five-minute commercials.[55] Colour television produces especially high recall, eliciting the requisite suntans in candidates. Similar debates arise in consumer marketing, with executives discussing whether they should give an image and a personality to a product, or concentrate on technical performance criteria. Arguably in politics the 'product' is animate and therefore much more suited to the image-building approach. Television advertising is less well suited to the projection of issues, since these demand time to explain and explore, but an image is something that can be instantly communicated. The significance of image-building lies in the fact that people can identify with personality far more than with abstractions and ideas, whether a political personality or even a product personality is being sold; yet the candidate who is elected as a result may be a naive parvenu unsuited to the task.

So in certain frequently repeated conditions and with certain large population groups television advertising is effective, possibly more so than consumer advertising, and while individual studies cited can be at fault they constitute in the aggregate impressive evidence – particularly so for state government elections where partisanship is so often low. Many people are thus cajoled through their own apathy, and their lack of interest puts their rulers, who know how to exploit this, into power. All this has a moral message for democracy, for in some circumstances the purchase of good advertising is tantamount to the purchase of votes. Advertising can, however actually be counter-productive. In 1978, Jake Batcher was the victim of his own advertising in Tennessee: supposedly his 'self-made' life story conveyed the hidden message that Tennessee was backward.[56]

Political advertising is distinguished from the commercial in that it is an episodic event for a once-only sale, so that the advertising has a different focus – comparable, indeed, to a new product launch. Political advertising is symbolic, more so than consumer advertising since it attempts to connect with key social values and communicate abstraction, and since there is also less money spent the effect is often either high creativity on a shoe-string, or artless hack-work. The lengthy advertisement mini-documentary is unique to politics, and is little used in consumer marketing, which has never transcended the brief spot format by trying a lengthy piece in which to unfold and explore a product's personality. Television political advertising is divisive in nature: its level of aggression distinguishes it strongly from consumer marketing where negative advertising seldom arises, although comparative advertising does. Name identification is much more important in politics since often a politician's campaigning starts from a point of zero public recognition. People can 'know what they want' with greater certitude in product advertising than with politics. They can inspect the goods and little information is required to make a decision, while in politics information is potentially limitless; consequently reassurance strategies are employed more in political communication because doubts and deliberations arise more extensively in the consumer's mind. The impediments to 'purchase', namely the candidate's views and personality, are much greater, whereas a consumer product as a material entity may arouse us less, though service marketing also faces a similar problem of reaction to individual personalities, as indeed does consumer marketing when it attempts to personify a company. Political advertising reveals the interpenetration of the commercial ethos in everything Americans do: its devices are borrowed from commerce, and consequently there are many areas of similarity. Strategic decision making arises in politics exactly as in consumer marketing, where the function can never be merely opportunistic and responsive. Marketers will seek out the best points: and politics will be doctored for television just like a consumer product. Image advertising, over and above selling on functional performance features, is important in commerce; it is central to political marketing.

NEW DIRECTIONS

A conventional political advertisement is no more than an animated slogan. Consultants, perhaps predictably, claim that they would be happy to provide longer and more substantial film, but that the public does not want that. In recent years however political advertising has taken several new directions, and one innovation that was used first during the Carter presidential campaign was the long advertisement. Gerald Rafshoon deemed the usual brief spots inadequate for an unknown candidate, and used sequences of up to five minutes showing a chat from the candidate and such; President Ford employed similar lengths. But such films are still a rarity.

Another trend has been the growth of advertising commissioned by the party for the party, rather than for an individual candidate, and the Republican National Committee has been particularly prominent in this. In 1984 they frequently showed a sequence with a girl riding through the countryside with her boyfriend. They are wholesome and attractive: apparently this is a health advertisement. But no, she begins talking to us about politics. She is intelligent and college-educated, no pretty clone, and explains to us firmly and persuasively why she is a Republican. Such advertising is symbolic – indeed, how otherwise could 'Republicanism' be expressed? The closeness in style to a consumer product advertisement gives a domesticity to the message and is presumably a deliberate intent, advertising for the party organisation. Some would interpret this as a hopeful sign, since it goes against the trend to disaggregation and shows how bodies can defend their integrity by marketing. Under this view therefore the practice of marketing becomes ethically merely neutral since it is universally available.

Other new styles in political advertising gained popularity in 1986; one in particular was a stress on tangible, material achievements for constituents, much used, for instance, by Senator Alfonse D'Amato in New York who had been selected by the GOP for especially strong support.[57] 'These so-called "pork barrel" ads, stressing compassion for constituents and the ability to bring them new bridges, funding for roads, additional social security benefits, have become a Republican stock-in-trade.'[58] The voter is buying benefits for his state and this has clear affinity to consumer product marketing. Again though this is a policy of disaggregation, making the local issue supreme and shirking the national debate.

Also popular in current political advertising is the use of 'real' people, another method borrowed from consumer marketing. Robert Goodman urged political advertisers to show in their spots how their candidate affected one individual life, adding 'we've done some spots that can make you cry'.[59] William Greenen of the Republican National Committee emphasises the necessity of making a 'connection between the public policy discussion and what's going on in your life', and Democrat candidate for a Lieutenant-Governorship Douglas Wilder made good use of a policeman expressing his fears of the Republicans with regard to law and order.[60] Reagan is past master of this method, 'periodically plucking a person from the heartland and weaning him or her into an ennobling national vision ... The technique is to turn an abstraction into a personalized reality' – for instance, the Philadelphia boy who worked among the homeless.[61] This helps to overcome the distancing effect of politics. It is similar to commercial advertising's use of a 'representative' type to lend credibility to a product endorsement.

Not all methods have been successful in politics – not even those that have proved themselves elsewhere. One fund-raising method attempted in the past was the 'telethon'. The Democrats held one each year between 1972 and 1975; essentially the idea comprises a cocktail of televised entertainment and fund-raising appeals, and celebrities volunteer their talents; the objectives here were several: to raise money, to create a favourable impression, and above all to construct a populist fund-raising base in the belief that a liberal party should not merely solicit the involvement of the elite. But on most of these criteria the telethons were a disappointment, and the amount raised in proportion to the amount spent was not great – two dollars to every one spent, compared with the fifty to one ratio of some of McGovern's direct mail campaigns and a four to one ratio in traditional fund-raising events; moreover, although the donor base was expanded (nearly half of contributors from a sample had not contributed before), it increased within the same liberal activist strata of the middle class and not beyond it. In 1973, for instance, 63 per cent of contributors were college-educated. However the party did enjoy some success with the viewing figures early on; thus 22 per cent of the voting population watched the 1974 telethon. Telethons were a tactic drawn from show business rather than marketing: they are really a celebrity endorsement of a 'product' on a large scale.

NEGATIVE ADVERTISING

A further significant trend has been towards negative advertising, a practice unique to politics, the nearest commercial equivalent being comparative advertising, which is relatively tame. There must be some doubt as to whether negative advertising would actually work in a consumer setting, though a transfer has not really been tried, but consumer marketing may well not possess the same legitimacy since the issues are too trivial. There is debate over the effectiveness of the negative approach. It might work well for parties attacking policies of other parties since these are an abstraction and therefore make no claim on our sympathies, but be less predictable when applied to an individual candidate. However, Congressman John Le Boutellier found negative advertising led to success in the short term (at the age of twenty-eight). Choosing the constituency where the least number of people knew who their congressman was, he brazenly criticised his opponent's voting record, junketing, liberal issue positions and so on. A good fund-raiser, Le Boutellier was able to purchase large amounts of television time to deliver personal attacks (his continued style in Congress earned him powerful enemies: ultimately he lost his seat).

Negative advertising became increasingly popular and in the 1984 Helms–Hunt fight it was an issue in itself and received international publicity. But this time it was a liberal offensive, since no faction has a monopoly of political marketing tactics, and Helms was crudely associated with Roberto D'Aubuisson, the Salvadorian rightist leader, amidst pictures of murdered peasants, and with the new Christian right leaders in America. Shots of moral majority rightist leaders appeared (in black and white they looked sinister), making Helms seem the associate and political mouthpiece of some un-American conspiracy. The negativity is also heir to a very old tradition of mud-slinging which antedates any concept of political marketing. In fact one-third of television political advertising is negative. Nor is its success assured: the slogan, 'While Governor Reagan could not start a war, President Reagan could' helped him by creating a sympathy vote in the 1976 California presidential primary. The 1964 'Daisy Spot' by Tony Schwartz was the most famous negative advertisement of all time. Film of a little girl counting and picking flowers in the spring was followed by a clipped accent counting down and a mushroom cloud, and Lyndon Johnson's voice urgent in warning. It was only shown once just before the election and created a sensation. Johnson's own self was projected through the effective carrying out of presidential duties. But his advertising focussed on Goldwater, especially his civil rights and nuclear record; for example, film of a girl eating ice-cream was followed by an announcement saying that Strontium 90 had been found in milk, and that Goldwater voted against the Test Ban Treaty. Republican protests engendered much publicity, as did their own attempts in 1968 to link Hubert Humphrey to urban strife amid Democratic protests. Another advertisement in support of Senator Muskie's 1968 vice-presidential bid proclaimed 'Spiro Agnew for Vice-President' against a background of giggling and laughter.[62] Richard Nixon's 1968 advertising attempted to blame the Democrats for ghetto riots; one advertisement featured a riot, with a broken dummy on the road.[63] All of these were in themselves important political events. They shed light on the potential power of political advertisers. The underlying conception – that of turning advertising into a political act, a political event – was deliberate: the aim was to provoke political reaction, political debate. Political marketing relies for its success on the provocation of negative emotional sensations; it cannot know whether it can always manage the rage it has summoned or whether the consequences will be for the good, and though malicious politics have a long antiquity television gives them more scope. The negative advertisement also by implication caricatures that opponent's supporters with the effect of discrediting before public opinion the whole system in which you as well as he are participants.

No one could ever pretend that consumer product marketing had the potential to incubate social discord. Political marketing does. Negative advertising can be viewed as harming political consensus by importing ideological rigidities into hitherto pragmatic debates, stimulating faction and reducing standards of political argument by its braggart partisanship. But it could be claimed that such an assault is well-merited, that the pursuit of consensus did damage, and that moral and spiritual values must be fought for tooth and claw in a highly secular age. Evaluations differ, pointing up once again the moral ambivalence that permeates every aspect of political marketing.

In 1986 negative marketing became a political issue with adverse press comment. *The Times* described the 1986 elections thus: 'a campaign which has been remarkable for its cost, triviality, mud-slinging and voter apathy'.[64] It added:

> Altogether this year's campaign has been dominated by television advertising, with very little traditional stamping of the constituencies. Vast sums have been raised to pay for the 30-second commercials, which have been increasingly negative in tone, and focussed on local issues.
>
> There has been little discussion of foreign policy or any national questions.

In the *New York Times*, Charles Guggenheim launched a particularly angry attack:[65] 'In the last 10 years Americans having been forced to endure an epidemic of negative political advertising. Visual and aural manipulation abounds. Every tool of the advertising craft has been exercised to prove opponents lazy, dishonest, unpatriotic, dumb, cruel, unfeeling, unfaithful and even criminal'. He adds: 'Ask any seasoned media advertiser and he will tell you what he can do best given 30 seconds. Create doubt. Build fear. Exploit anxiety. Hit and run. The 30- and 60-second commercials are ready-made for the innuendo and half-truth. Because of their brevity, the audience forgives their failure to qualify, to explain, to defend'. The short spot, then, is of necessity intellectually stunted: it cannot be subtle, there is no room for light and shade. Pointing out how the brief spot had become the norm, Guggenheim complained that 'we have created a system of political campaigning that is eroding the dignity of the election process'. However it is difficult to believe that such errors would be reduced merely by embarking on longer advertisements. Generally the judgement of commentators was that the 1986 campaign was extraordinary in its negative vehemence, and represented a new ethical low in its fondness for the *ad hominem* fallacy and devaluation of democracy.

Also popular in 1986 was the use of anonymous surrogates to deliver negative advertising, thus avoiding problems of accountability. Guggenheim counselled: 'What can be done? Strip away the anonymity of negative political advertising. Put the face and voice of the accuser on the screen and you will move in the direction of decency for the American political process overnight'. This device is a clever one: it avoids compromising the 'niceness' of the favoured candidate, and it makes it appear that there is some grand, accusatory moral force out there in society.

Generally there would appear to be no especial distinction in American television political advertising and marketing. Creativity is exhausting: the magnetism of the medium is towards a honeyed mediocrity; and in this quality of obviousness the genre is cousin to consumer marketing. This sameness should reassure those who are convinced that there is some high level of manipulation, a baleful necromancy, at work. There is no great originality or subtle science operative. Such crassness makes it hard to see the results as particularly harmful, unless a bad man can hide behind a mask, as some would claim Richard Nixon did.

NARROWCASTING

The central problem of television political advertising is one of waste since there is no precise selection of target: the audience is general and its segments are broad. For example, the group watching a programme may be defined simply as middle-aged or middle-class and more precise details are often impossible to retrieve economically. Consequently television advertising is often uncontroversial. It has to be. There are too many people it could offend, and for this reason politicians also project themselves blandly in news bulletins. In a 'market' so diverse, a middling image is necessary. This is a problem for the politician who thirsts to address key target groups in uncompromising language.

Political marketing is really looking above all for two things, cheapness and refinement of segmentation. In cable television it finds them both, for politics is even more budget-conscious than commerce. Moreover cable delivers a defined audience: there are national cable channels for sports, news watchers or pop music listeners, and a superfluity of cheap local channels. Cable can be exploited on a demographic basis, with, for example, programmes for women, and so the politician can advocate whatever prejudices are relevant to whatever particular group and there will be no better practical expression of cynicism. According to E. Dougherty 'subscribers can call up lists of systems to reach particular geographical segments nationwide and demographics', and he cites the case of Barney Frank, who was able to retain his seat via the use of cable. By 1988 cable had become a significant player in the Presidential contest (though it was first employed for John Anderson by Garth in 1980), used by Dole, du Pont, Kemp, Babbit and Simon, while Dukakis produced a one-hour cable call-in on the problems of the elderly.

Cable has many other advantages. It is easier for a candidate to obtain a desirable time. Moreover the local focus of cable is an asset; people identify with it as the 'home' medium, and this could influence the perceived authority of its message.[66] Local workers can be put on cable to motivate them. In New Jersey, cable is used regularly by politicians to show their own programmes.[67] A constant problem in political marketing is: how is a message made relevant? One way to achieve this is to localise it. In politics, as in marketing, the driving aim is for a luminous clarity of audience profile, and local channels often cater for particular groups within the locality – groups whose attitudes and prejudices can be predicted with some confidence, such segmentation being the true object of many of the marketing techniques and technologies examined in this book. The importance of local cable in the local campaign is obvious enough, but it is also highly significant in Presidential campaigns. No longer is the local town dependent on national network coverage, so that during the 1984 Democratic and Republican national nominating conventions 400 local stations sent home live coverage; and frequently now they produce their own special reports amidst the network coverage, with, of course, commentary on the ramifications of some issue in that locale. No longer therefore is television subject to the mediation of elite journalistic cadres.

Politicians were quick to perceive the rewards of narrowcasting. One congressman has described himself thus: 'I am not only a newsmaker, but a newsman – perhaps the most widely read journalist in my district. I have a radio show, a television program, and a news column with a circulation larger than that of most of the weekly newspapers in my district'.[68] Nearly half of all congressmen have had cable programmes, and the rest only appear to have been restrained by the fact that cable does not yet exist in their locality. According to Michael Robinson, 'Today's Senate office is a spaceship of electronic communications systems',[69] and some congressmen have used a species of 'video newsletter'; yet others have transmitted their congressional speeches through cable, and some senators have held their local meetings via cable with constituents in the studio or calling by telephone.[70]

But in America nothing is sacrosanct, no institution becomes a fixture, and channel television itself faces obsolescence, for in cable it has a new and commercially glamorous cousin. Cable penetration in the United States reached 40 per cent several years ago, and candidate advertising on all six national stations costs under half the price of a single network television advertisement.[71] Cable can cost as little as $5 for 30 seconds. A half-minute on network prime time cost up to $104 000 in 1984; on a major cable channel it would have cost between $1800 and $4000, and one thousand dollars can buy fifty advertising spots on local/regional cable as against only 30 media spots.[72] In 1982 the Democrats ran a half-hour cable programme at a cost of $30 000.

The effect of cable is to multiply potential information sources. The system is even capable of holding two hundred channels, as distinct from about twelve on conventional television: by 1984 most cable subscribers had access to at least twenty channels.[73] By 1985 there were 5700 cable systems in the United States, and by 1990 a penetration of 60 per cent of homes is expected.[74]

Cable is undeniably attractive and in 1983 less than half of television viewers watched network television (according to a Nielsen study) where cable was also available. Cable households are richer and are also much more likely to be politically involved,[75] though it is not clear whether this is an effect of the community focus of cable, or that its early acquirers were the more adventurous and critical members of society. The cable networks have many subscribers: for example, 29.7 million householders have EPN (Entertainment and Sports Programming Network) and 23 million subscribe to CNN (Cable News Network). Since advertising is cheap, use and experimentation with lengthy film sequences is possible, with long discussions, short biographies, domestic shots and detailed exposition of a programme.

Electronic newspapers sent via cable are another possibility: indeed in Cincinnati one such is broadcast every day of the week and it is a hundred pages long.[76] Clearly if these, or video magazines such as teletext, became popular they would be important vehicles for political advertising and news. Political coverage of local campaigns by cable will also be critical: for instance, Collais Cablevision in Louisiana sponsors a weekly political forum for local candidates.[77] Groups can use communications to shape the agenda and influence public opinion: the US Chamber of Commerce's 'Biznet News Today' is widely aired; 'Biznet' was originally conceived as a political lobbying arm, but was then given a wider mandate.[78]

In time, cable will refine its narrowcasting capabilities. Then, the politician can target a specialised message at individual neighbourhoods and even, ultimately, individual houses, so that it will combine the potentials of telephone banks and direct mail, and this will be achieved through fibre optics, a technology still in its development but whose capacity will be far greater.[79] Fibre optics carry every sort of electronic signal, including telephone and cable, and interactive video; they will be inexpensive, but it could take up to twenty years for them to be common.[80]

The possible political uses of teletext and videotext are particularly interesting. Potentially videotext can offer an infinity of pages and can show colour illustrations; one suggested system would offer 5000 pages, and the potential for information retrieval is endless.[81] By 1990 it is reckoned that up to a quarter of American homes will have teletext or videotext. Currently prices are about $1000 for videotext and telextext receivers but these will eventually drop to around $250.[82] Ultimately the price of half an hour on videotext will be roughly the same as that of buying a newspaper.

Direct response advertising is also available: at its most primitive this would involve simply encouraging viewers to telephone an advertised number, but some cable systems enable viewers to reply via a small key panel, so allowing home shopping and other services: for instance the QUBE system with its decoder box is for sale in a number of major cities, including Dallas, Cincinnati and Houston.[83] Electorate views on general and specific issues could be investigated by such a device; hence geodemographic techniques can be sharpened when census and other data are merged with the evidence of cable television polling. With the videotext programme viewers can respond to items, making polling a possibility. The politician can deduce the issues on which he is unpopular, how effective is his promotion and with whom; clearly this is also a recipe for a more craven politics as politicians gratify every prejudice and fanciful whim of their electorates, one day to be easily and instantly ascertainable via interactive cable. This interactive potential may therefore be a significant harbinger of the future. In one experiment, an 'electronic town meeting' was held in a Columbus suburb with debates and voting on local planning issues. However it is generally recognised that such direct democracy would have to await the popular employment of fibre optics technology.[84] Experiments in direct democracy, with audiences actually voting on legislative issues, have so far been a failure. They have failed to arouse public imagination, and legislators have refused to take them seriously. They have been disassociated from any prolonged participatory debates and public information campaigns and, thus truncated, have been a mere parody of traditional democratic activity. In focussing on the act of voting itself, they have ignored the preparatory activities that give such an act meaning. Hence critics view with pessimism future dreams of a direct democracy: such a vision would demand a much more educated and motivated civic culture than now exists, and the experiments convince some that this is merely another brand of naive utopianism. The experimental evidence is inconclusive, since all the experiments – perhaps because of the sheer novelty of the idea – were at best crudely executed. But, almost without exception, employment of technology by politicians is geared towards better communications rather than better understanding of the issues. Higher specific information for specific groups, lower general information for people generally – this is elitism, a result of the adoption of the marketing ethos with its stress on immediate consumer satisfaction, as well as of the evolution of technology.

Nevertheless the marketing credentials of direct democracy would be undeniable, for marketing takes the consumer's needs and wants as its starting-point, and therefore represents a potentially radical way of interpreting the political 'consumer'. It does however make for a politics of opportunism, not strategy. It could be claimed that this is democracy in a purified form, that the intermediary power of the politician could be reduced once the exact views of his electors on every issue were regularly transmitted. For with the political 'product' it may be important to create a sense of involvement and control of its creation by consumers in order to succeed: this rather distinguishes it from commercial products. On the other hand, cable could perform a missionary function, bringing new groups into politics, and it enables poorer candidates and groups to advertise, counteracting the trend towards elitism and expense. Cable is within the price of low-budget parochial campaigns, thus putting these too on the air and into the hands of the media merchandisers. The aggregate effect could be truly to democratise political marketing by giving it a just entry cost.

Cable, and the political consequences of cable, are also spreading internationally – in the United Kingdom for example. As far as the United Kingdom is concerned, when cable appears local candidates with their legally restricted budgets may not be able to afford much advertising, but it may still have implications for the individual seat, for the more ambitious members of Parliament may use cable local news as a medium for frequently addressing their electorates on national and parochial issues. During elections, opponents will be able to articulate their views and sharpen local contests. One possible consequence could be that the personality of the MP becomes important as for the first time most members of the electorate will see who he is and what he says. Their subsequent judgement could conceivably affect the result in many a safe seat and open new territories for genuine political contest, and the days when a candidate was a mere cipher for his party could be numbered.

Videos are another form of narrowcasting. The making of a video, even if it is not widely seen, can generate high publicity value. The anti-abortion lobby demonstrated this with 'The Silent Scream', though its effectiveness was somewhat undercut by scientific critics.[85] Possibly then videos have more potential in political than in consumer marketing. Video-conferencing is another technique which has already seen some political use.[86]

What of the implications of all of this for the particular kind of democracy America will get? Some authors find it difficult to gauge whether this will lead to a heightened political provincialism, or greater intra-national political debate; cable, clearly, is localising in its focus, whereas satellite is pan-national.[87] Yet targetting contains the danger that, in focussing on particular groups, others will be ignored completely in the political dialogue, for much political material, though actually consumed inadvertently, has the effect of contributing to the citizens' political awareness, and the smaller the inadvertent audience, the more ignorant, possibly, becomes the citizenry.[88] Demonstrably there is a need for some sort of common political culture for democracy to work, yet the constant thrust of marketing is towards fine-tuning, so that a marketing-driven politics is fragmentary and suited to a politics of group-issue interest.[89] Cable and other forms of televisual segmentation will have similar effects to direct mail, perhaps even magnified, speaking to people directly and without mediation. Political scientists also fear disaggregation arising from political usage of the new media; behind this thesis is the notion that some commonality of political culture is essential for democracy to work: 'But if the nation is to be a community in any sense . . . then democratic pluralism requires that there be some identity which unites us as Americans, as well as divides us into hypothetical subgroups'.[90] National network television helped to do this.

Of some concern also is the fear that the instantaneous nature of new communications will corrode the element of deliberation held by some to be crucial in politics: 'what some regard as time for careful deliberation, negotiation and reflection, others see as time spent dissembling, stalling and wriggling away from issues'.[91] They may also increase the pressure the congressman faces, making the legislator less an independent representative than a conduit for transient local passions, reflecting not the wisest in prevailing sentiment but the strongest,[92] and thus Wertheimer of Common Cause speaks of 'a qualitative change in the amount of pressure being brought to bear on Congress'.[93]

TELEVISION NEWS

In many elections unpaid television has played the central role, as with, for instance, the Nixon–Kennedy and Carter–Reagan debates: in each, the candidate with the mature media style triumphed. Four million voters claimed that their 1960 election choice was determined by the Nixon–Kennedy debates; and three million of those cast the vote for Kennedy (whose winning margin of 112 000 votes was the thinnest ever majority).[94] One hundred and twenty million people watched the Carter–Ford debate.

The power of political television is explained by the universality of television viewing in the United States – it is less a recreation than a way of life. Ninety-seven per cent of American homes have one or more television sets, which are on daily for about six hours in the typical home.[95] Between 1952 and 1956 the number of voters claiming that television was their most important political information source rose from 36 per cent to 56 per cent and by the nineteen sixties two-thirds of electors depended largely on television for such information.[96] Those who continued to rely on newspapers seem to be much less malleable; they had more knowledge and their opinions were firmer.[97]

The nature of television coverage and its effects have been perceptively discussed by Austin Ranney.[98] Television viewing is a national habit: the average American watches television for three hours a day. However, Ranney portrays it as a semi-concentration medium, a context in which other events happen, a kind of electronic wallpaper: its moving tableaux are not subject to intense scrutiny and only occasionally will an item excite real attention; for the rest, people converse, eat, read and relax with their television sets. Television is their balm, their Lethe of forgetfulness, an aperture into other worlds and other lives, a space of brightly-coloured movement.

Purchased advertising seeks to exorcise pre-existing disbelief. Even in 1960 more than 80 per cent of those surveyed claimed that the mass media influenced their political choice more than other people did.[99] Americans believe their television: the younger, the less educated and the women would appear to believe it most, and Americans generally think that it is fuller and more objective than newspapers, while there is a correlation between reading and education level.[100] This is an interesting fact, since values and behaviour are more normally determined by peer group pressure, and suggests the high believability of mass media in relation to political choice.

Against this must be set the fact that the television journalist is formally independent of pressure from the politician, though other kinds of influence may intrude, and sometimes indeed he will perceive himself as the adversary of the politician, or as an embodied public conscience. Conventional consumer marketing does not have to manage such an omnipotent and frivolous entity.

The fact that people are so credulous of news is important – the notion that it represents some kind of disinterested objectivity has been successfully sold to them, even though by the very nature of its selectivity it cannot be this. The paid media have inherent bias but the authenticity of news reportage and value of positive exposure makes the rewards of successful news media strategy much greater, so the logic is that 'packaging' must consume much political time – grooming, rehearsing questions and so on; commercial products in comparison do not have the potential to generate this degree of press interest and therefore do not devote time similarly to public relations. Hence the opportunist candidate will devote his greatest resources to the news as an alternative advertising medium, and journalists may be taken in through their urgent need for a story and 'visuals'. But political marketing must also seek to influence the unpaid media if a coherent and credible candidacy is to be established. Stock methods available include gimmicks, media events, speeches, walkabouts, press conferences and strategically chosen themes: all can force entry into television news. All this takes time, and the consequence is that all manner of secondary actors will assume power on the political scene, real power disappears elsewhere in the unlovely pursuit of the opportunities and pressures of the news medium, and scope for administrative attention is correspondingly reduced. The arts of news management raise the price of campaigning, given the costs of speechwriters, planning, hire of sites, the props, bunting and the rest, the publicity stunts, the ubiquitous consultants.

US television is often criticised for a lack of good documentary programming and political discussion, so that the news must carry much of the extant political confrontation. The special demands of the news tend to create a need for specialist advice, again fortifying the power of the consultants in US political life, for they are its brand managers: television advertising and packaging for television news are their specialities. Many such consultants, like Roger Ailes, are from television backgrounds themselves. They coach the candidate remorselessly on how to handle journalists; the consultant conceives and writes the script and the candidate may in fact – as in the case of Jesse Helms – not appear at all. But consultants take existing public opinion as their starting-point and the candidate is fitted to that rather than the other way round, and this makes consultants marketing men by any criteria, for here, as elsewhere, the phenomenon of political marketing is perceived to be cost-driven and expertise-directed.

But how much news is actually absorbed? More perhaps by the emerging political elite than by anybody else, so that items may be tailored to them as the most significant element in the viewing audience. But tight orchestration of the news is beyond the artifice of any political consultant since its independence is jealously guarded.

Politicians must be able to influence the news media, and those who cannot, fail; Ford's ratings, for 'works', for example, would only increase when he was inactive, while Edward Kennedy was finished by a hostile interview (the CBS documentary, 'Teddy': November 1979).[101] Arguably through television 'the process whereby Presidents are recruited may have changed in ways which preselect inappropriate Presidential candidates'.[102] Some politicians have even managed their own programmes: Reagan produced five-minute 'Reports to People' as Governor of California, and both Connally and Goldwater presided over morning television shows.

Television is seen by some as a deceitful and self-deceived medium, with a narrow focus on the promise of instant satisfaction in all things. Television also gives a somewhat misleading impression of politics as a sequence of sudden and disconnected crises, making people feel both anxious and helpless as problems seem to explode around them apparently without warning. Ranney discusses how news creates an impatience with the slow process of influence and negotiation that is an integral part of politics, for problems are described, but their intricacies are not explained, and it also generates unease and cynicism: since problems are intractable, what is the good of political programmes or party loyalty? There is the superficiality of television news, its fitness for conveying image rather than issue, and the short time period of the average news item. This aspect is hardly the fault of political leadership, and its assiduous use of a medium so universally popular is opportunistic but scarcely of itself immoral.

Television affects the interpretation of events. For events exist less as tangible entities in themselves than as the media react to them. Thus when President Ford referred to Poland as free, polling carried out immediately after the debate did not suggest that people regarded it as a major mistake. However the media pundits did and a few days later so did the people, heavily influenced by the media interpretation. Again television gives a disproportionate weight to early primary results, and often interprets them not according to absolute margins of success but rather the extent to which the candidate has failed or succeeded in matching expectations. The media's judgement could thus be a summary and entirely subjective dismissal. As a result of news coverage politicians, especially the President, have to spend much of their time on public relations activities, and influencing the media's interpretation becomes a key activity, since television news coverage is rated much more highly than that of newspapers by viewers.

A CRITIQUE OF POLITICAL TELEVISION

Expense and Consequences

Television constitutes the greatest expense in any political campaign. Expenditure on television advertising by candidates continues to rise and quite often up to 90 per cent of a candidate's advertising budget goes on television; nor are the heavy spenders just the big politicians since the new entrant might have to spend in order to persuade possible contributors of the gravity of his intent. The high cost of television advertising (competing of course with commercial products) is the principal reason for the dynamic fund-raising activities described earlier, with their ramifications throughout the American political system. Television manipulates the electorates who watch it and compromises the politicians who have to buy it. Television advertising consumed twenty million dollars in the final two weeks of the 1984 Presidential campaign and, consequently, it is another factor in diminishing the real independence of politicians since they need the support of managed interests and groups who may in no way represent the general voter.

The advent of telemarketing must influence in some degree the personality of the legislature, so that politics becomes more democratic in that people are exposed to their politicians more often, and less in that by the same token the entry fee is raised; almost by definition the rich men entering politics are not average, and it may be questioned how far they sympathise with the aspirations of more ordinary people.

For Crotty and Jacobson, 'The partyless campaign is a slick and expensive affair'.[103] The centrality of private wealth in this process particularly impresses them: 'By definition, the professionalized candidate organizations are bought by one man's money and committed to only one man's success'. They later claim, 'Television allows those candidates who can command the necessary financial resources to mount impressive challenges to incumbents at all levels' and further add, 'A prospective candidate with sufficient personal wealth or PAC resources can run for office whenever he decides. He need have no previous political experience, no ties to the party whose nomination he seeks and no particular roots in the community or bonds to the people he seeks to represent'.

Triviality of the Medium and the Message

One argument against television is that it often focusses not on essentials but on the periphery. Thus Nixon on his 1960 defeat:[104] 'I paid too much attention to what I was going to say and too little to how I would look. . . . One bad camera angle on television can have far more effect on the election outcome than a major mistake in writing a speech'. A further criticism made against it, which its denizens predictably deny, is that television relays the world in pictographic terms; its information content is minimal and its capacity for analysis and abstraction limited. Ranney further alleges that television news does by its nature distort. The amount of commentary in any newscast would constitute just a few paragraphs in a newspaper, and much of our criticism of political television must lie in the nature of the medium itself; an entire evening's viewing would constitute just a few typewritten pages.

Television is commercial in the United States (apart from public television) so that most programmes must be of the popular film show/soap opera type and the objective is not primarily to inform the listener but to retain his attention. Moreover, although nightly newscasts in America are quite long, much of the material is of purely local interest. Television treats politics much as it does sporting events, with which indeed politics has to compete for attention; 60 per cent of television news reports would come under this 'horse race' category, so that television news trivialises political campaigning since it has to compete with other television programmes for entertainment (conceivably it is in the leisure rather than the knowledge market), so as to attract advertising revenue. If television actually demanded something more of politicians, and was sarcastic about the razzmatazz, it might get it. Television news is particularly prone to the confection of images – building up Carter for instance, perhaps because it was bored. In many ways the moral case against television news is stronger than against advertising since it is more influential, for the advertisement is simply the paid servant, the hireling of the politician. News at least has the freedom to do more: it does not have to accept the triteness it expects, receives and communicates. The long and frequent television news programmes are saturated with irrelevancy and what then remains is a caricature, for American political television is strangely like one of those distorting mirrors in the fairground – this feature exaggerated, that, lost in obscurity.

Television leads to a kind of cloning among political candidates. It seems curious to question whether America is really a culture of individualists, but, since it is a society where organic community bonds are not strong, there is a constant search for synthetic ways of creating them, and conformity to recurrent national personality types may be seen as a principal way of attaining this. The influence of the Kennedy style is particularly strong as candidates try to counterfeit vigour, youth and so on.

To those who take their politics seriously, advertising is predicated upon the assumption of an imbecile viewing public and reduces political debate to a monosyllabic harangue, but while one can feel some sympathy for this position it is not necessarily a fair one, and television advertising has to be clear and repetitive if the message is to penetrate the inattention of the relaxed and disinterested audience.

Creation of an Image – Centric Politics

Of more weight is the charge that the advertising does not reflect the candidate at all, but rather the expertise he can afford to hire, he himself becoming a programmed autodidact. Even if we believe that the images we see projected do constitute some kind of reality, this could merely mean the commonplace that the candidate is a good actor, and the image he succeeds in creating may have no basis in a reality of knowledge and competence. Richard Nixon in 1960 and British Labour's Michael Foot in 1983 were not helped by their reluctance to wear make-up for the cameras, the former emerged looking sinister, the latter cadaverous. Thus commented Miss Phyllis George: 'What matters is whether a candidate is handsome and articulate and has a good smile'[105] (she is an ex-Miss America, married to J. Y. Brown, proprietor of Kentucky Fried Chicken and former Governor of the state). And the whole process is highly impersonal; we do not see the politician as he really is but as his stage managers create him; he is a magic lantern statesman, bland, overgroomed and bloodless.

Political telemarketing is changing the personnel of the US political system, as traditional skills are superseded by those of visual appeal and polished delivery. Under this image (centric politics) television, the great persuader, is barely capable of discussing issues; it is best at putting over images so that those become the criterion of choice, and the issue is relevant only in so far as the particular manner of its exploitation builds up the image. Television advertising seeks to avoid the mediating influence of television news and gives an idealised image of party, programme and candidate.

Once – it is possible to exaggerate – people had no alternative but to read an argument; this is a new vision of a politics of lurid, disconnected images. Are the best put off, leaving things to men clever enough to play the game and stupid enough to think it important; could, indeed a gifted man survive the public dissection of those idiosyncracies which are on occasion the concomitant of intelligence? A Washington ridiculed for his sanctimony and outsize jaw, a Hamilton castigated for arrogance, a Jefferson for being a high-brow? Would the founding fathers have vacated today's climate? And, given the 1987 demise of Hart and Biden, Americans began to ask if anyone could withstand media scrutiny intact.

Manipulation of the Electorate

Those who are ideologically uneasy about all advertising would also be critical of television political advertising on the grounds that it is, similarly, dishonest. Certainly the politician can evade some issues entirely, stress other issues favourable to him; in other words he can set the agenda, observing no larger duty to educate and to inform.

Television news is even more believable since it issues from an ostensibly non-partisan source, and it commands more attention than does printed news; therefore the American candidate must especially learn to manage television news: this is less simple than in advertising since the ultimate source of control is external. Orchestrating the news can become the central political task.

Events and statements – even overseas occurrences – can be manufactured only with the needs of the US news media in mind: 'Reporters covering the civil war in Lebanon between Christians and Moslems reported that both sides in Beirut would wait for the TV crews to arrive and the cameras to be in place before shelling the enemy'.[106] Crotty and Jacobson give another good example – how Hubert Humphrey once had to persuade cameras to enter before he could get senators to come to a committee. Television, they assert, is an ignorant medium, with reporters recruited for visual appeal rather than journalistic ability, and since this is an entertainment medium controversial issues are presented blandly. They cite what they call television's poor record in the exposure of Watergate, and imply that network executives wish not to offend the FCC and Congress.

Undermining the Parties

Television has helped to erode the automatic loyalties of traditional political constituencies; seeing that the other side also has an articulate, defensible viewpoint makes for a fickle and facile electorate whose commitment is seldom internalised. In Congress itself politicians now have a powerful external constituency, and this has led to increased fragmentation, since it is harder to gain the cohesion necessary to advocate a party programme and vote a common party line. In their television studios congressmen can instantly tape a message to nourish their constituents, and many candidates cultivate an image somewhat independent-leaning. But no trend is immutable; the Republican party has in recent years advertised its party label extensively at a national level. Between 1952 and 1968 the percentage of voters marking a straight party ticket diminished from 66 per cent to 43 per cent; in one recent state election only 32.5 per cent voted the party line, and much advertising, with its focus on personalities and issues, perpetuates split-ticket voting. It is not good at conveying abstraction, as a party must be.[107]

Reagan himself continually appealed over the heads of congress to the jury of public opinion to get his programme passed. A real problem of coherent public policy making arises, though it is possible to exaggerate its dimensions. Moreover we can perceive advantages in a less defined party system. Parties could offer endless opportunity for malpractice; and within their incestuous ranks dogged mediocrities were able to rise to a prominence impossible in the world outside.

Certainly the stress is usually on building up an individual; his party, the higher social unit, is correspondingly neglected, and political advertising is thus a highly individualistic and almost anarchistic genre. Parties, their cohesion and their force, are hampered as a result, maybe less able to offer a distinct social vision, for now the aspiring politician can go direct to the voter through paid advertising, and the parties that once took his loyalty for granted are now his suppliants: the essence of political relationships has experienced fundamental redefinition.

CONCLUSION

In television, we meet then a number of recurrent themes. The cost of the advertising exerts fund-raising pressures and the consequent mortgaging to vested interests. The art of politics becomes an exercise in the judicious manipulation of symbols, to which task the pseudo-science of marketing lends its nefarious lore. Arguably elections always have been swathed in the bunting of triteness, though there may be a necessary dignity we are abandoning, a politics without the veneer of sacrosanctity.

Yet promotion is essential to all modern American parliamentary elections. For Irving Kristol, 'It is a world of media, a world where habit and custom are weak before the forces of communication'.[108] To succeed in such a world one must be first an effective communicator: 'It is, therefore, a world where ideas and their articulation are indispensable to effective conservative government, because it is only such ideas that can provide definition and coherence to the conservative constituency'.

Television more than any other factor is responsible for the trend towards sedentary activism we observe elsewhere; the ranks of volunteer labour, canvassers and such diminish: all the emotions of the campaign are available through electronic transmission. Electronic politics certainly contribute to a feeling of lack of involvement and responsibility: there is a distancing effect, and the same expectations are created as with a running melodrama, with which indeed it has to compete. The long-term implications of the lack of significant popular direct participation in politics have yet to be evaluated: electorates could demand of politics a degree of sensation which it is not its proper function to purvey.

There is a sterility to the democracy created by television. Democracy ceases to be an interactive process in the sense that the town meeting of American folklore was. Attempts to resurrect such town meetings via interactive television have been a failure. Television is a commercial medium and concerned with ratings for revenue. This does not necessarily preclude serious analysis, but it does place a premium on entertainment, with the consequence that journalists invariably seek a dramatic story line with interesting visual material. The politician has to fit himself into this context, possibly – as Irangate so memorably revealed – to the exclusion of a proper superintendence of political and constitutional proprieties.

Packaged politics undermines debate. Even set-piece debates have been heavily 'managed' by either side, with candidates trained in the glib response, so that there is no real interchange where rival points are taken and rebuffed; instead extant positions are declaimed. More generally electoral trial by television is not a test of skill or intellect but of physical stamina and the rather negative capacity for avoiding blunders. The processes of democracy cease to be a civic education for political literacy; they license a general cynicism in society.

The influence of political television is demonstrably strong. It would be naive to claim that purchased influence was decisive: non-controllable events in the economy and foreign policy often play the crucial role. But it was not part of the intention of earlier architects of democracy that finance should be so central. Television, in common with the other factors we discuss, has engendered a short-term expediency in political decision making rather than the growth of a long-term strategy. Everything has to be depicted in pictographic form and as pressure groups ventilate their opinions the politician experiences constant emotive pressure. Crotty and Jacobson summarise the contemporary situation:[109] 'The role of the political party in campaigns has given way to the technology of television-centred campaigns built on polls and run by media and public relations experts. The evolving politics is a candidate-centred, technocratic exercise in impersonal manipulation. It is also a politics of extraordinary expense'.

In political advertising simply one view is being advocated as the truth; there is no argument and no rebuttal in the immediate, and none at all if the opponent is significantly under-financed. Moreover politics inhabit a world of abstract claims: there can be no proof where so much is predicated upon future promise. In this reduction to vacuity it is a happy accident if the candidate happens to possess any insight into the complexities of macroeconomics or international affairs. Robert Moses commented dismissively of John Lindsay's campaigning: 'If you elect a matinee idol mayor, you're going to get a musical comedy administration'.[110] Other criticisms abound. There is the argument that advertising politics creates excessively high expectations which will invariably be disappointed.

Yet it may be legitimate to argue that mediability is a justly valued asset in politicians in a television age, for the medium cannot be disinvented and its domination is assured: effective performance deserves therefore to be called a political skill. Banning or seriously curtailing political advertising on television would be an obvious answer, but an unsatisfactory one, for this may not induce television stations to donate more time to political analysis and discussion, since advertising perhaps stifled such a potential at birth; there is some content to political advertising, however saccharine; arguably it does make a contribution towards heightening voter awareness of the issues. Diamond and Bates have some kind words to say in defence of television political advertising: non-paid television may be viewed as more facile still with its preoccupation with 'horseracing', while the candidate's choice of issue-spots illuminates his priorities and agenda.

Moreover as a persuasion device it is open to both sides. The public have been traditionally sceptical about the blather of politicians. Perhaps, too, political advertising helps counteract the negative commentaries, leading to a kind of rough justice, and sometimes good political advertising may actually arouse interest in politics and stop apathy. It can be informative. One may legitimately take a more upbeat attitude: what we witness is merely traditional publicising in modern garb, and moreover the barriers of public cynicism are robust, immunising people from attempts to manipulate them. Common sense says this: does the evidence?

5 The Peevish Penmen: Direct Mail and US Elections

'It must be acknowledged that equality, which brings great benefits into the world, nevertheless suggests to men (as will be shown hereafter) some very dangerous propensities. It tends to isolate them from each other, to concentrate every man's attention upon himself; and it lays open the soul to an inordinate love of material gratification.'

Alexis de Tocqueville, *Democracy in America*

Political direct mail is the best example of the transliteration of commercial ideas to political election salesmanship; it is a necessary adjunct and no campaign is complete without it, for mailings generate an independent, privatised source of campaign finance and instant if superficial loyalties. And they provide the precision targetting so crucial in modern America campaigns. Large-scale political employment of political direct mail began with Goldwater; McGovern exploited it well and since then political groupings of every tincture have assiduously sought to use it. Outside the United States British Conservatives have now made mail technology an article of their political faith. It illustrates how political merchandising techniques, once incubated in America, spread internationally.

We perceive in direct mail, as with the adoption of other marketing techniques in politics elsewhere, the trend towards mechanisation and the impersonal: the illusion of personality is cast over an automated process. Direct mail is the coming mode of political involvement. We wish to explain its widespread popularity and its reputation, why it is the most powerful of devices – an explanatory task that has been neglected, for direct mail is the major fund-raising device and force for cohesion among pressure groups. At a less abstract level we look at the planning of a direct mail campaign and suggest some deficiencies in the conduct of current direct mail strategies.

Direct mail is a junior branch of marketing and was originally developed to sell encyclopaedias and the like. Politics has magnified its importance; indeed so intensive has been its political employment that the medium is probably best understood by political consultants who use it and who would have much to teach commercial marketers – Viguerie with his thirty million names for example. The mail illustrates a business method employed in politics that has found in its political usage more imaginative treatment than in commerce. The medium is especially well fitted to the requisites of a political process. The administration of a direct mail campaign proceeds very much as in consumer marketing and political campaigning is becoming busi-ness-like in the size of its multi-media communication, and the skills this calls for – those of the businessman.

This chapter seeks to analyse the political employment of direct mail, in order to illuminate its qualities and limitations and to diagnose the conditions under which mailings excel other mediums in creating and sustaining target group loyalty.

ASSETS OF DIRECT MAIL

Direct mail is as noteworthy for its versatility in politics as in commerce: the political mailings frequently constitute a cornucopia of invective, illustrations, novelties, trinkets and other assorted items.[1] Moreover its results can be accurately predicted on the basis of pre-testing and this is important in political campaigns with their stress on economy. Direct mail enables full coverage of a political market by reaching forth to remote or isolated electorates, while the contextual 'noise' that affects other marketing mediums (for exam-ple, in the form of alternative television channels) is silenced. Direct mail can boast many successes. Through its agency the US Republi-can party created a populist donor base, rising from 34 000 in the early nineteen seventies to 2.7 million in 1982. Contributions, eight million dollars in 1975, were expected to reach $92 million by the end of 1982 and eighty per cent of this sum came from direct mail solicitations.[2] The Democratic mailing list expanded from 32 000 in 1981 to 170 000 in 1982, but since 80 per cent of its contributions still exceed $500 (mainly through political dinners) we can infer a continued over-reliance on rich individuals.[3]

Mailings can orchestrate intense pressure on legislatures. Technol-ogy enables congressmen to be bombarded with pressure-group letters, almost instantaneously; pro-lifers can have 1000 letters off to Congress with only twenty-four hours' notice. Communications

Management Inc. sent 2000 mailgrammes to Senator Percy in one week on natural gas price decontrol; they had traced sympathetic citizens with a polling census and asked permission to send in their names. Craver Mathews illustrate the point about volume of transmission well, for they can send one million pieces of mail in twelve hours; and in 1982 the California gubernatorial candidate could send out one million absentee ballot applications. One firm, Voter Contact Services, retains a file of fifty-six million voters nationally with all areas matched for telephones, probable ethnic origins, with target analysis, demographic reports and the like.[4] Direct mail thus possesses specific competences as a fund-raising, lobbying and communications tool. Moreover, political communicators do not choose exclusively from a broad array of possible media and technologies: they use them all.[5]

Such a strategy yields various benefits. Direct mail can magnify the message and feel of an original television or magazine display, which would invariably be somewhat bland as the recipients will be more general than a specially selected direct mail audience, so that targets of a political message who are already evangelised receive renewal without the alienation of possible subscribers who might need a less abrasive approach. Direct mail supplies information which in other more expensive media would be an extravagance and an intrusion; specific arguments can be underlined, while the candidate can be presented, free from the cynical mediation of the press, with an idealised image – a property that direct mail shares in common with other marketing mediums. Thus the politician consolidates his loyalists and in the process kneads them into a new and powerful lobby. Moreover a set of direct mailings can build up an argument and give to readers a superficial sense that they have witnessed a rational process,[6] while if different political marketing approaches are used an impression is given of creativity and gathering momentum; and extra television advertising might have limited impact when mailshots would reignite a campaign.

Thus mailings are often joined to other methods of political marketing and can be used to compensate for their limitations – telephone solicitations for instance may antagonise people when initially called, but they can effectively follow a mailing or be used to approach former donors.[7] 'Americans for Reagan' in conjunction with a mailing raised seven million dollars by telephone in 1980. Richard Viguerie, the right-wing direct mail entrepreneur, has advocated a total political marketing strategy with direct mail tied to other media initiatives.[8] Mass mailings portended the public speeches of Senator Orin Hatch and Senator William Armstrong, while Bruce Eberle (a major direct mail fund raiser) has claimed that replies to a television message can by themselves build a foundation mailing list; and direct response technology should fortify this trend. Direct mail, since it aims at the emotionally committed, services politicians as a fund-raising device whereas other marketing methods are employed for the more urbane end of general political communication. Mailings have the special merit of introducing a concept of membership: people are made to feel part of a group, the essence of which is core common values and an unrestrained vocabulary to express them, and with direct mail the candidate's private voice and character can be brought alive at a level of intimacy only television can also achieve: it is almost a case of contrasting private and public media. One effect of television is to make the audience imagine that they are personally intimate with the person appearing, so that there is a pre-existing relationship and direct mail is a synthetic extension of this association: the real relationships of everyday life are supplemented by the electronic connection between the citizen and the visual image, and for many 'participants' in these 'relationships' they seem momentarily satisfying.

Direct mail has advantages as a political marketing medium, a context defined by mobility, fund-searching and segmentation. Since direct mail has been pre-eminent in the work-force of candidates and pressure groups we can isolate reasons for its popularity connected with the specific demands of the political process. It can be produced fast. The mobility of taste and opinion in US politics can be exploited by versatile direct mail which can ignore the contracts, deadlines and the forward planning demanded by other media; nor is it in competition with other purchasers of space. Direct mail, in comparison with other more sedate and bureaucratic marketing mediums, is especially well matched with the high voltage of the political process, with its shudders of mood that may necessitate a change in campaign pace or some deft 'image surgery'. It represents a method of expressing the candidate to different groups in different ways, of modifying his image; and direct mail is an intelligence resource, sending signals to the campaign manager and fuller information than can be provided by a television advertisement. Given the cost of television in some cities like Los Angeles it has considerable financial advantages.[9] Only with the widespread use of cable in the 1988 campaign could television begin to rival direct mail in its key strengths. Direct mail has the further merit that it creates strong loyalties, since it is intimate, and because it implies recognition of the needs of particular groups its recipients appear to be specially chosen; and where people make the effort of reply such public commitment reinforces loyalty to the cause and they are reluctant to re-think a stance publicly avowed. Also congressmen are concerned about cultivating their districts and constituency service is relevant for re-election, so that direct mail has a central task in marketing them locally.[10]

Direct mail supplies that familiarity of tone necessary to marketing's ability to persuade. Through its agency pressure groups approach the individual constituency; loyal politicians owe a debt, opponents are intimidated. The danger is that it could make for political timidity if politicians anticipate the weight of nationally-based resources targetted against them. Politicians can flatter electors that their support is of significance; the mail is a way of recreating national issues as local ones; it can be used to call volunteers and is a lobbying instrument.[11] For example Alaskan legislators were influenced over balanced budgets by constituents encouraged by a direct mail campaign.[12] Often mail is used simply for political advertising.

SEGMENTATION

Yet the above are marginal assets compared to the central competence of direct mail, its talent to harvest political market segments to the full.[13] And here it is superior to television and to everything else apart from the individual call. The central task with all political communications technology is to identify sub-groups and fashion appeals to them as is the practice in business. While segmentation is a key element also in commercial marketing, in politics it remains absolutely crucial, given the social differences among people.

Of course, most kinds of marketing to electorates involve segmentation. Mail offers an intensification of this property; with other marketing channels such as television the appeal must necessarily be more bland, whereas mailing can be sharpened as much as information on lists permits, and the widespread availability of data today permit a good deal. Contradictions in a political platform can be cosmetically hidden: an innocuous public stance can appeal to general values while mail shots can be hard-hitting and specific. The future will take this process of selective segmentation further as politicians find ways of knowing more about people, so that their likely resentments and hopes can be predicted with greater accuracy. The manipulative ability and intent of this medium becomes apparent. It is polarising, as finely segmented mediums are bound to be, more so as targetting technologies improve: and while marketing also makes distinctive individual appeals in the commercial product world, the effect in politics is not so innocent.

Direct mail consultants adopt many of the same processes as other marketing executives, for they must seek out the exact group of consumers most predisposed to their product. Political direct mail facilitates the selective communication of different messages among different constituent groups, such as import issues in industrial states and environmental matters among 'yuppies'. In 1972 Senator Griffin, a Republican who represented Michigan, used mailing to target white car-owners on bussing; blue-collar families on pensions; affluent areas on the need to reduce property taxes, farmers on agricultural issues;[14] while a remarkable 1975 congressional result in Michigan[15] was assisted by mailings to ten different market segments – youth, senior citizens, blacks, and so on – even though the candidate could not afford to employ television, which illustrates the potential power of cheap and non-televisual mediums if imaginatively used. Pat Robertson solicited evangelical Christians in 1987–8.

LIMITATIONS OF THE MEDIUM

Direct mail has various disadvantages. It yields dividends over the long term; persuasive campaigns are structured over at least a year, and the candidate suddenly faced with an election will find scant use for direct mail. But politicians who forge their candidacy into a perpetual marketing organisation (like Senator Jesse Helms who has his own PAC, the Congressional Club) will be well rewarded by direct mail, as list building is a long business and not all politicians can manage a six-year course of mailings as Helms has done. These technical demands of direct mail make consultants necessary since they understand the conditions for its effective deployment.

A further problem with direct mail as a marketing medium is the popularly noted danger of over-solicitation, the image of saturation junk mail, since the average American household receives fifteen items of such mail weekly. Many groups feed from the same lists. Some believe that direct mail has an effectiveness point after which it declines – this might be true if every mailing was comparable, but ingenuity of composition can put off such a saturation point, assuming that it actually exists. Regular mailings to the right target may strengthen their adhesion since, when a person has given once, they may give again, as past actions can be decision precedents. Once a gift has been made, the size of contribution requests is often increased. The consultant Morris Dees believes that during an election most loyal donors can be solicited every three weeks; nearer the close of campaigns weekly letters are practicable.

A major criticism of direct mail as a political marketing medium is its potentially high cost, for while nationally eminent and controversial candidates and major parties are its beneficiaries (Richard Viguerie has said that people will donate more easily to a cause than to a candidate), obscure candidates pursuing a national market will fail; Representative Fortney N. Stark invested $26 000 on a nationwide mailing for a $14 000 return.[16] However direct mail can be influential within individual territories, as Representative Les Aspin found with a valuable 8000-name local list.[17]

OTHER STRENGTHS

The marketing strengths of direct mail remain significant and they are not merely the mechanical ones of precision of reach and versatility, for direct mail satisfies unarticulated needs that explain its continued success and its ability to excite.

Direct mail gives participation without depth involvement, the pleasure of partisanship and the privileged information which political association gives, without the usual cost to the individual; this feature has re-defined the political 'product'. Active support is time-consuming, whereas direct mail, a fund-raising medium, well suits the contemporary dislike of collective activities.

In making people feel special the mailings fulfil a venerable advertising cliché: thus Reagan in seeking annual membership of the Republican Presidential task force ($120), claimed, 'I'm not asking anyone to join this club – only proud, flag-waving Americans like you.'[18] This may be seen as creating a new type of political cadre defined by distance involvement, a passive action political elite. Many would say this is a consequence of democracy rather than a perversion of it. In the field of product marketing, people are made large in their own esteem by personalisation – the target appears to have been chosen by external authority and a sense of exclusivity is always satisfying – whereas with other marketing mediums everyone is exposed to the same message. America is increasingly a society of groups as national cohesion diminishes, of rival tribalisms, and membership of such groups supplies a coherent identity less easily found in any national and now much diluted concept of Americanism.

Direct mail has other merits as a marketing approach: people do not really believe that substantial effort has been invested in reaching them, but the delightful illusion persists, for technology has become fraudulently adept at lending a personal gloss to a mechanical and remote process.

Moreover with direct mail a guilt-driven imperative may operate, as recipients feel that they cannot reject the call of a cause they strongly identify with. Direct mail represents a way of mobilising mass allegiance by soliciting it in a personal way: flatteringly the party or lobby shows its vulnerability and reliance on ordinary people. In addition, given the size of the United States, parties and pressure groups may seem remote and involvement awkward; direct mail by contrast gives ease of entry to the political process, since participation asks only the return of a reply card. Unlike other forms of political organisation the membership is powerless: direct mail is an authoritarian form of political involvement since the donor is unquestioning, and the object of his charity is, within the puny world of cause and constituency, omnipotent.

THE PROCESS OF DIRECT MAILING

Thus far we have discussed direct mail's target marketing properties which in some conditions create a central and unique advantage. The mechanical process of a campaign is, however, also crucial. The primary phase of a direct mail campaign establishes the nature of the relevant segments – the groupings to be cultivated and those to be discarded. Identification of the market segmentation is obviously a pre-requisite of a direct mail campaign: this depends on intuitive comprehension of the political market, as it does with any other market, since the data need to be interpreted. Trial and error is one way of finding the relevant segments; and more quantitative methods exist, such as multi-statistical techniques, attitude and perception research (for example, perceptual mapping), though many of these are confined to consumer marketing and political direct mailers still largely operate on impressionistic insight as much as by technical expertise. The more advanced methods will assuredly appear, but time pressure will always limit somewhat their applicability for the individual politician's campaign, though the real length of campaigns is growing. The aim is for a glaring clarity of audience profile.

But discovering names is the foundation of a direct mail marketing campaign, and a reliable 'house list' to which all future solicitations are targetted is constructed from two sources – names that the candidate or lobby has already, and names obtained by writing to ('prospecting') lists supplied by research and commercial purchase from the list brokers.[19] The quality of these lists is vital. A shoddy list containing names of members apathetic or absent could waste resources, and so the definitive elements of any political mail marketing strategy are: finding sources for accurate lists; updating lists; including as much relevant information as possible so as to divide the list into sub-segments. There is a need for a richness of understanding which only consultants can supply, for it cannot be simply taken from text books.

THE ARTICULATE RIGHT

Yet much of what has been said does not explain the degree of success direct mail has enjoyed among the political right. For direct mail has come to represent a conservative response to the radical direct action. Whereas before conservative activists could claim substantial but inarticulate and therefore impotent and even unde-monstrable support, direct mail gives that support voice and its call to the more authoritarian disposition is clear – one that commends itself to the remote, the elderly and the surburban. It does not ask for any of the embarrassing or tedious public rituals the radical is asked to perform. It offers a low entry price for a hitherto costly product. Previously even the radical right could rarely match the vigour of the left.

The genius of the new pressure groups of the right and their direct mail consultants has been in discovering and developing a marketing medium for achieving money, publicity and a cadre of supporters without making exacting demands. Interestingly, the right has mimicked the style used by the left in their direct mail campaigns, the single-mindedness and the crude slogans, while turning it from propaganda into marketing. For a long time such methods worked; the rightist PACs helped to defeat twelve liberal senators between 1976 and 1980. Using direct mail the National Right to Work Committee increased membership from 20 000 to one million, and the National Tax Limitation Committee from 2000 to 600 000.[20]

Direct mail was thus the major instrument in creating the 'new right' as a political force. Essentially the attitudes of the American right developed in opposition to what was perceived as a sentimental and sententious liberal status quo, and they regard the social change of the 1960s and 1970s as having been negative. Single issues are thus highlighted in rightist political marketing as symbolic so that the subscriber can be persuaded to try to stem one small aspect of this universal erosion. There is a desire for that trenchant affirmation of values, which direct mail is in a position to provide, for direct mail does not create its market constituency, it pre-exists, and the mail simply stimulates an underlying emotion. The marketing style of direct mail is often demagogic in utterance, striking a vein of nostalgia, 'rugged individualism' and a sense of insecurity. But it is also the echo of a tradition of right-wing gut reaction (Huey Long, Father Coughlin, Senator McCarthy, George Wallace, etc.) and in its ability to articulate a clear line on an emotional issue it circumvents the constraints of ordinary party politics and ordinary marketing mediums.

As to the style of new right letters, the late Terry Dolan said that the shriller the tone the easier it is to raise funds. The letters share resemblances of style and technique: donors are informed as to exactly what their money will do (highly effective). The fate intended for you personally is described; rhetorical questions employed; blame attributed to a rather ill-focussed 'enemy' and some sort of solution offered.

Thus vociferous minorities are seen to accumulate an influence out of proportion to their numbers. The mail increases the seeming redundancy of parties by giving politicians an independent cash source, one which only the richer of their number once possessed: high expense is a result of the political marketing imperative and direct mail helps to defray it. Mail is also important in image-building – a task centred on the anti-party and pro-personality kind of politics that America sustains today. And mail is, like television, a way of communicating with electorates directly and outside the control of party, helping the entry of new men. Direct mail, more so even than other marketing mediums, bypasses the press, therefore jettisoning its mediating influence to consolidate key constituencies with an unadulterated propaganda, one never before possible. But it mortgages a politician to his more extreme supporters since it is the emotive propaganda that works.

The political and historical significance of mail is that it has helped to shift the ground in American politics, giving sway to groups that did not hitherto possess it, making respectable and giving weight to opinion hitherto discounted, calling forth regional forces, extending the franchise of actual political participation. But then, there is something clinical about the democracy so created, and a problem of such involvement being at a superficial level – a politics of restlessness that is a mirror of its host culture. Such forms of political activity may contribute to public cynicism: a dangerous contribution given the need to have government's legitimacy respected so that laws are broadly obeyed and social strife averted, to convey a sense of the obligations as well as rights of citizenship, to respect the aspirations of others in the same nation state.

But is the mail simply a new marketing way of giving expression to an old phenomenon? The real commitment of small numbers has always been a key to political movement: political change has always been precipitated by dedicated minorities and possibly those who are most politically aware merit their disproportionate influence. Direct mail is an integral part of this interest group pressure, and as such contributes to the instability and the familiar vices of US politics; the mail helps give lobbies potential leverage and makes Congress more beholden to them.

As one observer has remarked, direct mail reflects two political trends, from mass media to tailored and targeted media, and from direct action to the armchair approach.[21] Americans have witnessed a curious evolution from soapbox to letterbox. In spite of this the medium arguably remains imperfectly comprehended and therefore not fully harnessed, for promoters must integrate it with the other tools of marketing and the conditions for its success have not been defined and prescribed by political lore. Rather, direct mail is sometimes added to a campaign haphazardly. It is infrequently trusted with a pivotal function and this junior role may make it a relatively unfruitful use of resources.

6 The Monopoly of Midas Congress and Political Action Committees

'No sooner do you set foot upon American ground, than you are stunned by a kind of tumult; a confused clamor is heard on every side; and a thousand simultaneous voices demand the satisfaction of their social wants.'

Alexis de Tocqueville, *Democracy in America*

Political marketing is a consequence of the gradual recognition that a consumer society, where individual personality becomes almost an aggregate of consumption experience, would accept a politics clothed with the identity of such consumption experience.

Marketing is expensive. Ninety per cent of campaign spending is consumed by television advertising. American campaigns thus luxuriate in large quantities of money, and most Senate campaigns have a price tag of at least three million dollars. A total of $900 million funded the 1981–2 elections. A grand sum of $20 million was spent on the election for governor of New York, while the contest for each New York and Californian Senate seat absorbed the same sum. By no means untypical was the Missouri race in 1986. Each candidate planned to spend about four million dollars on their campaigns, with 60 per cent of this for television. In their final month the candidates were spending $250 000 per week on television. And in 1984 Jay Rockefeller, West Virginian Democrat, led all candidates in outlays per vote cast, spending some $12 million and receiving 368 483 votes for the Senate seat he won – a per capita cost of about $32.56.

The costs of campaigning are high as a result of the need to advertise on the media, a cost that can be readily met by the pressure groups, so that politicians can be put in their debt: attempts to control all this have a record of failure. Therefore the politician must find something to exchange. And, clearly, politicians do have something substantial for the exchange relationship. The rise in marketing costs reflects both inflation in media prices and also the broadening of the conception of a marketed politician.

Nevertheless post-Watergate America sought to diminish the role of wealth in American politics. Individual contributions were limited to $1000 per candidate or $5000 to a multi-candidate PAC. No sooner was the new law minted than it was devalued, and it proved to have been a mistake to legislate in a vacuum with no reference to the contextual factor underlying those high costs, namely the pressure and opportunities for political marketing, especially via television.

Now that rich donors had to play a less active role, small donors were solicited instead; business professions and conservative groups formed 'Political Action Committees' (PACs), since these were less inhibited by donation rules. Management and employees may be approached and asked to donate to the PAC sponsored by that business. Similarly, political action committees are also attached to professional associations, while America's trade unions have underwritten their own PACs longer than anyone. The major preference of such committees is for incumbents as the safe bet (two-thirds of PAC money in the 1980 campaigns went to incumbents) and in uncertain contests the money appeared when the winner began to emerge. Business and professional PACs tended heavily to favour Republican candidates and in 1982 Conservative PACs spent four times the outlay of their liberal counterparts, while PACs paid nearly thirty-three per cent of house candidates' campaign expenses. Often they will have a string of candidates, and conversely the candidate will have a shoal of PACs supporting him. Nearly half of the 'Fortune Five Hundred' companies have political action committees.

There are many explanations for the existence of political action committees. The extent of laws and regulations affecting US businesses, the elaborate superstructure of support, special protections and concealed subsidies, make organisations want a clear way through. Moreover donating large sums to political causes – as well as to charitable causes – is a time-honoured tradition in the United States, and there is a high level of group participation in the country, of which political action committees are simply one manifestation, for 62 per cent of people are members of some voluntary organisation.[1]

These developments are thus a malign consequence of good intentions, for the objective of the post-Watergate legislation was to cleanse the process of monetary contagions, a catharsis. The opposite occurred, for in the act of broadening the contributor foundation the potential sources of funding were also multiplied. There is however a distinction between monetary political support and corrupt purchase of actual favours. The post-Watergate era increased not so much the need for honesty as the need for concealment and cosmetics, and what elsewhere would be simple bribery is elevated into something ostensibly better by wholesome-sounding PACs. Yet their existence is not hypocrisy but a rational answer to a need. For where corruption is integral to a culture – or a political culture – exorcism is impossible and the need is to contain it; and this is achieved by legitimating some acceptable measure of corruption. PACs have proved the ideal vehicle for rendering laws a nullity, and since all parties derive benefit from them there is no move to expunge that by which all are enriched, and we may imagine the trading when PAC and politician meet, furtive, with a vaguely decadent aura, as support is bargained for support. PACs are allowed to give up to $10 000 per candidate, half to the primary, half to the general election campaign, and they can also give up to $15 000 per year to the political committees of national parties. Individuals can contribute up to $20 000 each year, some tax-deductible, to national parties.[2]

The PACs also have great relevance to the phenomenon of the perpetual campaign. For a PAC will not be active simply at election time. It will closely monitor the performance of its sponsored candidate: it becomes critical to his re-election and is therefore a constituency he must continuously solicit throughout his period in office. PACs also foster a tactical as opposed to a strategic approach to politics. This is because the PAC will have its own legislative programme, and the legislator's support for these items will be taken as a token of his continued commitment: the politician is bound by the time-scales of the PACs. At the presidential level, however, the PACs are less relevant, since candidates receive state subsidies; 18 per cent of private financing comes from individuals, and dinner at $500 a plate, celebrity parties and the rest are used extensively.[3]

RECEIPTS

After the 1984 elections the *New York Times* claimed: 'overall, the winners received an average of $595 908 from political action committees. That amounted to 20 per cent of their total receipts'.[4] This was a slight decrease from 1982 and 1980. Some Senators however had particular reason to be grateful to political action committees,[5] especially:

Senator James J. Exon, 59% (Nebraska)$_D$
Senator Max Baucus, 57% (Montana)$_D$
Senator Ted Stevens, 49% (Alaska)$_R$

Senator Thad Cochran, 36% (Mississippi)$_R$
Senator William Armstrong, 27% (Colorado)$_R$
Senator David Pryor, 39% (Arkansas)$_D$

Senator Vermont raised 74 per cent of his money from PACs and Representative James Jones led the House with $694 212.[6] Of course, the 'independence' of such pressure groups from the candidate they in practice assist can become somewhat academic.

But after the 1984 election the dimensions of PAC involvement and contributions grew (see Exhibits A and C below). According to Bolling and Bernstein 'the immense influence of PACs pollutes the democratic political process'. They pointed out that chief among the favoured were members of congressional tax committees. Republican Leon E. Panetta, Democrat, of California, claimed: 'Congress is literally being bought and sold by PAC contributions'.[7] And Congressman Barney Frank of Massachusetts (D) said, 'we are the only human beings in the world who are expected to take thousands of dollars from perfect strangers and not be affected by it'.[8] In the eighteen-month period before September 1986 Political Action Committees had raised $254 million; two years earlier the figure had been $195 million. One survey sampling 114 Congressmen found that one-fifth of them admitted that political donations influenced the way they voted.[9] Moreover fund-raising is a time-consuming activity, with 65 per cent of Senators claiming that fund-raising pressures restricted the time they could spend on legislative tasks. A total of 43 per cent of Congressmen saw PACs as a negative influence on politics.[10]

EXPENSES

It has been justly observed that 'one may look at American politics from the beginning of the Republic as a contest played and replayed, in different keys and with variations, between the people who command the votes and the people who command the money'.[11] In the nineteen eighties campaign costs went even higher (see Exhibit B). In 1980, 205 members of the House of Representatives received over $200 000 each in donations (in 1968 most House candidates spent under $25 000); most campaigns spent half the total sum raised on fund-raising.[12] Costs, adjusted for inflation, rose by 117 per cent in the years 1976 to 1982.[13] With fund-raising totals adjusted, the overall cost of winning a Senate seat increased by 30 per cent from 1982, a much smaller increase than the rise of 54 per cent from 1980

EXHIBIT A Price of Victory: PAC's and Politics

Winners of 1986 House races who received at least 75 per cent of
campaign contributions from political action committees.

	Total Receipts	From PAC's	Percent
Augustus F. Hawkins, D-Calif.	$ 87,403	$ 80,688	92%
William J. Coyne, D-Pa.	110,445	101,100	91
Melvin Price, D-Ill.	127,045	113,475	89
Harley O. Staggers Jr., D-W. Va.	157,285	133,695	85
Dale E. Kildee, D-Mich.	96,113	80,510	83
Clarence E. Miller, R-Ohio	85,901	69,349	80
E.(Kika) de la Garza, D-Tex.	169,004	134,500	79
Howard C. Nielson, R-Utah	118,151	94,200	79
Joe Kolter, D-Pa.	280,064	218,642	78
Joseph M. Gaydos, D-Pa.	159,192	123,425	77
James H. Quillen, R-Tenn.	472,265	363,300	76
Cardiss Collins, D-Ill.	304,744	230,571	75
John D. Dingell, D-Mich.	495,665	375,177	75
William L. Clay, D-Mo.	197,938	149,817	75
Frank Horton, R-N.Y.	134,988	102,100	75
John J. Duncan, R-Tenn.	531,190	402,302	75

Source: Common Cause, based on Federal Election Commission reports

to 1982.[14] In 1968 most candidates for the House of Representatives
spent under $25 000.[15]

In 1986 the trends continued unabated. $425 million was spent on
House and Senate elections, compared with $130 million in 1976,[16]
and PACs contributed one-third of this sum, while by mid-October
spending was 25 per cent more than in the 1984 elections. In 1976 a
Senate seat cost $600 000: now it was $3.1 million.[17] By 1986 also
nearly half the members of the House of Representatives, 194
candidates, received half or more of their campaign money from
PACs, and one-quarter of the Senate got at least $1 million from such
groups;[18] Ampac alone gave $4 million to candidates. In 1982, the
House figure was 94; in 1980, 85; in 1978 it was 63.[19] Certain
individuals continued to benefit substantially. Claimed Barry Goldwater, 'It is no longer we the people, but PACs and the special

EXHIBIT B Campaign Spending

Election	Total amount spent (millions of dollars)
President*	
1980	
Ronald Reagan	$49.3
Jimmy Carter	48.0
1984	
Ronald Reagan	66.6
Walter Mondale	67.4
U.S. Senate* (all candidates)	
1980	103.0
1986	211.1
Californian Legislature* (all candidates)	
1980	34.3
1986	60.0
British General Election (all candidates)	
1979	6.0**
1983	10.3**

*Totals include primary and general elections.
**At May 20, 1987 exchange rate.
Source: Federal Election Commission: California Fair Political Practices Commission: British Information Services

interests they represent, who set the country's political agenda'.[20] Political Action Committees favoured incumbents over challengers by a factor of six to one.[21]

Individual expenditure in the 1986 election was high, Kemp spending $2.5 million, Joe Kennedy $1.6 million, and Bainum, Bentley and Townsend all spending over the million mark in House races (in 1976 a House seat had cost $177 000) and much of this spending was a consequence of television advertising, on which candidates spent $200 million (a half-minute television spot cost $100 000 in the Dallas–Fort Worth area).[22] Republicans spent most, twice as much as the Democrats in the Senate.[23] The Republicans' National Committee was especially generous, giving $1 170 000 to d'Amato and $1 112 000 to Zschau.[24]

The inflation in campaign costs was also considerable:[25] the cost of a thirty-second advertisement increased by over 63 per cent between 1984 and 1988, computerised lists of a party's state voters by 100 per cent and even campaign buttons by over 66 per cent. In 1988 the government was to give $46.1 million to each party's major campaigns. Such costs have to be paid by some means, so that the advertising imperative may be viewed as compromising the entire political system; since PACs are often the chosen means, they have become the primary medium for the articulation of vested interests in US politics. Could political advertising be restricted, an impossible task in our view, such special interest groups would disappear as financial agencies. PACs are therefore both a cause and a consequence of political marketing. The avenue of strict limits on spending, permissive access to the media and media motivated by commercial considerations to the exclusion of any higher concept of public duty, create urgent monetary pressures on politicians which PACs help to satisfy.

WHO BROUGHT WHO?

Of course, business does not give to politicians out of public spiritedness or a disinterested concern to promote a political philosophy. These are commercial judgements; what must be remarkable is the low cost of political investments compared to the other things corporations spend money on, and we may even speculate that their market price is low and will rise as businesses compete with each other to buy shares in political influence. Some tangible return is expected and there are many testimonials to success; as Justin Dart (Chairman of Dart Industries) has said, dialogue with politicians 'is a fine thing, but with a little money they hear you better'. The effect of the adoption of the political marketing conceptions has therefore been that politicians 'sell' the only commodities they have to offer – helpful legislation.

Thus representatives voting for a hospital cost containment bill got one-quarter the amount its opponents received from the American Medical Assocation. PACs have been able to lather the political process.[26] American citizens in the end help pay the price of political marketing by having to buttress inefficient established interests that can purchase shares in political goodwill, and thus in 1978 businesses attempting to avoid regulations from the Federal Trade Commission gave $4.4 million to congressional campaigns. As many as 83 per cent of representatives voting for an amendment backed by the National Association of Realtors (that emasculated a bill containing measures against dishonest developers) had been given campaign finance by the Association's PAC in 1976 and 1978. Top contributors in 1984 were:[27]

National Association of Retailers	$2.2 million
American Medical Association	$1.9 million
National Association of Home Builders	$1.7 million
United Auto Workers	$1.62 million

The *New York Times* gave a list of other examples:[28]

- The United Automobile Workers gave $2 million (1982), with domestic-content legislation on the agenda.
- Dairy PACs donated one million dollars to congressmen voting against removing price supports.
- Industry gave $200 000 to twelve members of a House sub-committee who voted to weaken the Clean Air Act.

USA-Today claimed: 'five of the top six recipients of big money from the banking PACs serve on the House Banking Committee', and 'four of the top five House candidates getting big money from defence contractors are on the subcommittee that approves the Pentagon's budget'.[29] The American Medical Association (AMA) is the most generous donor of all, and over the years its PAC has bestowed $10 million in political campaign contributions. Nor does such largesse go unnoticed. When a bill to exempt doctors and dentists from Federal regulatory jurisdiction came before Congress these professions donated more than three million dollars to congressmen.

All this would be regarded as corruption in any language, but since it is done openly it is not somehow so regarded; 'corruption' therefore would appear to be a contingency of secrecy, and when performed publicly apparently loses its negative aura. The ease with which politicians have fallen for these practices and their inertia in seeking to discipline them, reflect the intensity of marketing press-ures and the unavoidability of their costs.

Certain individuals were outstanding beneficiaries (see Exhibit A). Kip Fernand St Germain as Chairman of the House of Representa-tives Banking Committee received handsome sums from banking

PACs, while transport groups were uninhibited in their money support for the Chairman of the Transport Committee.[30] A *USA-Today* survey also revealed that nine out of ten candidates enjoying fat funds from the farm lobby were on the House Agriculture Committee, and its Chairman, Senator Helms, was particularly well looked after: his customary antagonism to state hand-outs was miraculously stilled when it came to the interests of farmers.[31] Republican Dan Rostenkowski, a Democrat, must have been pleased with the receipt of $168 000 from PACs in 1983, and the PACs must have been pleased with enlisting this Chairman of the Ways and Means (tax) Committee,[32] while in 1981 twelve oil companies donated $1000 or more to one Senator's campaign treasury: two weeks later he introduced a bill mitigating the windfall profits tax.

These sums do not go to jollify the private life of the politicians concerned: they go to pay the high marketing costs. In a sense, the most corrupt – defined as the one most likely to exchange the credit of legislation for the currency of money – is the one most likely to win.

THE RIGHT-WING PACs

The right recognised, perhaps earlier than anyone, the salience of aggressive marketing in the political process. They saw that it represented a way of short-circuiting the media, and mobilising and directing the provincial support of whose existence they were certain. The 'new right' has assumed the paraphernalia of modern marketing.

Their activities were given a major boost by a judicial decision enabling them to spend unlimited amounts. In a critical decision of the United States Supreme Court (*Buckley* v. *Valeo*), political action committees can spend whatever they please against whom they please. But they must hold no communication with the opposition candidate. The consequences of this decision were interesting to observe. The ideological right-wing PAC pressure groups became prominent, and their titles are self-explanatory: Gun Owners of America, Stop the Baby Killers, Moral Majority (Liberty Lobby), Americans Against Union Control, Citizens for the Republic, Americans for Life, Fund for a Conservative Majority. They were able to spend unlimited amounts on limitless independent marketing, and their demagogic utterance sometimes embarrassed orthodox Republicans and sometimes backfired. Between 1976 and 1980 they helped

EXHIBIT C
Growth in PAC Collecting and Spending

These figures show the political action committees that contributed the most money to Federal candidates over the 18 months from Jan. 1, 1985, to June 30, and the top money-raisers in the same period among the so-called nonconnected political action committees, which are generally noncorporated and nontrade groups working in the interests of a certain candidate or cause.

The Big Contributors

1. Realtors Political Action Committee	$1,387,429
2. National Education Association PAC	1,034,220
3. Build PAC of the National Association of Home Builders	949,772
4. American Medical Association PAC	869,098
5. Committee on Letter Carriers Political Education	839,255
6. Association of Trial Lawyers PAC	803,600
7. Seafarers Political Activity Donation	768,956
8. National Association of Life Underwriters PAC	737,317
9. U.A.W.-V.C.A.P. (United Auto Workers)	711,470
10. Democratic Republican Independent Voter Education Committee (Teamsters)	709,426
11. Machinists Nonpartisan Political League	637,500
12. Active Ballot Club (United Food and Commercial Workers International Union)	622,510
13. Airline Pilots Association PAC	594,500
14. National Association of Retired Federal Employees PAC	580,755
15. Transportation Political Education League (United Transportation Union)	554,109

The Big Money-Raisers

1. Fund for America's Future (Vice President Bush)	$8,249,387
2. National Congressional Club (Jesse Helms's associates)	8,099,908
3. National Conservative Political Action Committee	7,738,709
4. Auto Dealers for Free Trade PAC	2,742,554
5. Campaign for Prosperity (Jack Kemp)	2,260,577
6. Fund for a Conservative Majority (conservatives)	2,176,332
7. Citizens for the Republic (President Reagan)	2,019,098
8. Voter Guide (bipartisan California group)	1,947,267
9. Fund for a Democratic Majority (Edward M. Kennedy)	1,942,751
10. Campaign America (Bob Dole)	1,874,449
11. National Committee for an Effective Congress (liberal Democrats)	1,604,050
12. National PAC (Israeli interests)	1,453,446
13. Republican Majority Fund (Howard H. Baker Jr.)	1,241,517
14. National Committee to Preserve Social Security PAC	1,118,757
15. Council for a Livable World (antinuclear, environmental)	990,094

Source: Federal Election Commission

defeat twelve liberal senators. In 1984 right-wing conservative groups provided eight million dollars, either given to Republicans or spent against Democrats.

Perhaps they have greater political legitimacy than the other PACs since their motives are politically ideological rather than commercial. The increased political influence of the 'new right' was certainly an unintended consequence of liberal legislation, and it looked to a different and less pluralistic kind of America: its role in shifting the ground of political debate in the United States was a major one, so that by the end of the decade democratic candidates were saying things that had once been the exclusive preserve of the radical right.

Implicit in the decision of *Buckley* v. *Valeo* was the old belief that the money of true believers should be allowed to speak. Note again the moral entanglements of the politics/marketing mixture, for a respectable defence can be made of this position – those who feel committed and are prepared to devote their resources to fight a cause are entitled to more influence than the uninterested. The question arises, however, as to how much influence they should be permitted to accumulate before the term 'democracy' becomes redundant and some may argue that the most 'committed' can be actuated by base motives, their commitment really being prejudice.

Issues of urgent concern to such groups include bussing, prayer in schools, abortion, sex education and so on. Thus they are often single-issue groups, formed with particular legislative objectives in mind and aiming to lard the campaign coffers of friends and intimidate opponents. They have adopted an issue-oriented approach, one less concerned with image, and this gives their marketing promotions a different flavour from that of many main-stream politicians. Their favoured vehicles have been television advertising and direct mail, while television evangelists lent influential support. Certain consultants have been able to accumulate great power as a result of the ideological PACs: they are the *éminence grise* of the movement, manœuvring in the shadows.

The groups create a precision of focus which is highly valuable in marketing terms and is derived from their single-issue preoccupation. However the nature of their propaganda, and of their attacks on opponents, became legendary. A rightist pressure group distributed comic-style biographies in which Senator Kennedy was depicted as an obese black sheep, twisting and cheating through life.[33] It was entitled 'Every family has one'. Elsewhere leaflets showed a black man pointing a pistol at a judge's head, while anti-Salt II mailings gave you two stamps to stick on the return mail: a white flag of surrender, or the Stars and Stripes. Christians for Reagan urged clergy to support opposition candidates in nearly fifty legislative districts and compiled a rating list of incumbents based on their voting records. Often such promotion is crude: the aim is to jolt the 'consumer' out of apathy. We should not see such methods as merely the outcome of prejudice but also as a calculated marketing ploy, succeeding more when everyone else was bland, than when such merchandised aggression began to become universal.

The most pre-eminent of rightist political action committees was the National Conservative Political Action Committee.[34] It nullified its attacks by their continuity, and they became issues in themselves. In Idaho there was the Anyone but Church Project; in South Dakota, People Against McGovern, while $700 000 was spent in a vain effort to unseat Senator Paul Sarbanes. In 1981 NCPAC spent almost half a million dollars trying to oust Senator Kennedy. NCPAC successfully helped to unseat Senator George McGovern in 1980, and also campaigned against Senators Church, Cranston, Culver and Bayh, and in one case NCPAC's television advertising depicted a basketball player dribbling a ball and the words 'Globetrotter is a great name for a basketball team, but is a terrible name for a senator'. This PAC spent $800 000 on advertising in 1980, and liberal senators found above $100 000 was spent against each of them by the 'new right'; typically their advertisements were 'tough, strident, and accusatory, portraying the senators as big-spending, high-living Washington bureaucrats who have lost touch with the conservative beliefs – and real needs – of their constituents back home'. Another advertisement pictured a piece of baloney with the price tag of $46 billion stuck on it and the words: 'That's how much deficit spending Bayh voted for last year alone. So, to stop inflation, you'll have to stop Bayh first'. Many commentators believe that such negative advertising is initially successful but ultimately counterproductive, hence in Iowa NCPAC were much more influential because they concentrated their attack in the last few weeks of the campaign: elsewhere the longevity alienated voters. In 1980 NCPAC opposed six candidates: four were defeated. Their expenditure on political marketing was not small and forced opponents to spend more, so that their intervention further propagandised the American political process.

PACs have given a new prominence to the role of the emotional appeal in politics, and the rightists groups played on it ceaselessly in merchandising their sentiments for ordinary folk. It is possible that the political left began this current coinage of abrasive political language in the United States and that the simplistic diatribe has a reverend historical pedigree; the right's behaviour was a reaction to the arrogance of American liberalism and its apparent success in getting its way.

Some liberal congressmen may have been more reluctant to vote controversially, knowing that they were subject to such scrutiny. Not them, but a parody, would be placed before the electorate, a pantomime caricature. The marketing appeal of the rightist groups is that of simplicity in a complex world, and the strength of this appeal (with all its consequent distortion) should not be underestimated; in particular they promoted that single-mindedness which is such an effective political resource. For a time they made the political atmosphere much more ideological: liberals say they poisoned it. They testify to the power of the focussed one-issue marketing appeal rather than the general one; there is much more coherence in the 'consumer's' mind, and therefore political marketing has had some influence on the unfolding of modern American history via the right's enthusiastic sponsorship of the genre.

But the legionnaires of the 'new right' who populate some of the political action committees are not elderly reactionaries. Many, including Richard Viguerie, are graduates of Young Americans for Freedom: an organisation that was influential on America's campuses in the nineteen sixties and, though less visible than its liberal contemporaries, its commitment was as deep. In a curious way the rightist groups are a product of the same cultural trends as the liberals they deride, and in their fondness for the platitude instead of intellectual labour they display the impatience of the instant-gratification society. Marketing draws its creative resources from the contemporary culture, whose occasional shallowness it reflects.

Political influence was therefore purchased by marketing, though it is difficult to calculate the total effect of the anti-incumbent rightist PACs. They had a subtle influence on the political climate. Yet there is some residual notion of decorum in politics and people do not like to consciously have their intelligence manipulated – perhaps it was not the aggression but the unsubtlety that put off voters. Moreover the intensity antagonised: people become bored with constant nega-tivity, with a repetitive world picture forever dour and glowering. Marketing cannot contradict perceived reality for ever.

In the eighties the negative advertising of the right began to backfire as voters became uneasy at the ideological rigidity of their promotion, and above all at the long periods through which it was sustained; it never graduated from propaganda into a more mature form of marketing, failing to draw from the target consumer since it claimed to already know what he wanted, and any marketing tactic will backfire when over-exploited. Ultimately the right was limited by having a clear but unsophisticated understanding of persuasion.

Thus attacks became issues in themselves.[35] Senator Eagleton's lead at one point dropped from 50 per cent to −10 per cent under the NCPAC barrage, but in the end he still retained his seat. In Iowa, however, 25 per cent of voters claimed they were less likely to vote for the incumbent, Senator John Culver, because of well-timed NCPAC advertisements.[36] Generally NCPAC learnt nothing and forgot nothing: its policies became increasingly resented and in 1982 nineteen out of twenty senators it selected as targets won again. NCPAC tactics typically comprised advertising that focussed on the voting records of the intended target and, moreover, whether deliberately or not NCPAC were often wrong:[37] for instance legislators Melcher and DeConcini were charged with voting for abortion whereas they had in fact opposed it, and the nervous media began to reject their advertisements.

Thus the rightist PACs are less a threat than when they first appeared because their world of moral absolutes is too alienating for continued success. One strategy adopted by some politicians has been to disavow such groups, while benefiting from their exposure of the incumbent's voting record. Liberals have their own political action committees with the specific aim of opposing the conservative PACs and imitating their tactics; liberals too now have target lists of those they would extinguish.

These examples are lurid. Perhaps they are overly selective. Nevertheless, on this evidence alone, in the aggregate it amounts to an indictment: congressmen are bought and sold. No amount of integrity on the part of an individual politician can diminish this, for he needs money and has to turn to the interests to get it. Only the collective will of Congress could change things: and that would be like asking a drug addict to renounce his narcotic.

PERSECUTION BY PAC

The PAC movement derives its strength in part from the pre-existing vagueness of the party system in the United States; one consequence of this is that the personality and views of the individual candidate loom much larger, and it is therefore easier to isolate those whom a group finds objectionable: it is more difficult for the targets to take refuge behind the party programme.

The gun lobby provides the best example of the power of PACs. Annually 20 000 Americans are killed by hand-guns. Since 1938, according to Gallup, majorities of Americans have consistently wanted control, yet they did not convince Congress, which voted more permissive laws in 1986 – rifles could now be sold across state lines; interstate transport of weapons was allowed.[38] Nor was the gun lobby's appetite sated here: legislation against plastic guns was in jeopardy after the Attorney General withdrew support when he met National Rifle Association officials.[39] Well might he have feared the NRA's clout, given its annual legislative budget of $5 million, its three million members, the seventy million Americans who own guns, the billion dollar per annum gun industry,[40] and consequently not one member of Congress, despite their vaunted liberalism on other subjects, voted to strengthen the laws passed in 1968. The police in contrast could muster only $15 000 to oppose the 1986 legislation. States, notably Florida, moved to make gun-owning easier.[41]

The *New York Times* was vitriolic in its denunciation on the issue of armour-piercing bullets:[42]

> The N.R.A. seems cornered, but Senate supporters of the bill remain concerned about Steve Symms, Republican of Idaho. Running to re-election next year, he seems determined to impress gun enthusiasts with a last-ditch effort to stop the bill. He defies the Senate's leadership with irrelevant and dilatory amendments . . . The vote in the House was a lopsided 400 to 21 – for who does oppose a bill that protects police officers? Yet the ban on harder alloy bullets capable of penetrating police vests came to a vote only after a bitter six-year struggle against the gun lobby.

Another instance of persecution by PAC was the race in South Dakota. Senator Abdnor, who was of Lebanese descent, had always voted both against aid to Israel and against all foreign aid. Fund-raising, much of it from outside the state, raised $90 000 to fight Abdnor:[43] 'Inquisition, pogrom, anti-semitism', accused one letter from a congressman, appealing for funds to support Mr Darch. It denounced the radical right's 'requisition' in South Dakota, 'bigotry and hate' in the state, and attacked Senator Abdnor's refusal to authorise aid to Israel.[44] This, like so many direct mail letters, was crude: but in under-populated South Dakota television advertising is crucial and, therefore, so is raising the funds to pay or it. Even though there were only 605 Jewish people in his state Abdnor flew to Israel to assure them he was no anti-Semite. He still lost. Pro-Israel groups had also helped defeat Senator Charles Percy (Chairman of the Foreign Relations Committee; he had $86 000 spent against him) and Congressman Paul Finlay earlier.[45]

UNIONS AND DEMOCRATS

America's corporations have become generous donors; even in 1978, of the $35 million given to Congressional candidates by PACs, 35 per cent was from the political action committees of corporations. But PACs are not a formal arm of businesses, who are forbidden to participate directly in politics; rather they are associations of individuals, including shareholders, within the companies; however, corporations can pay for the administrative expenses of a political action committee and donate 'in kind' services.[46] Most corporate employees do not join, however: between 20 and 35 per cent of a company's employees who are asked to join a political action committee will actually do so.[47] They are unlikely however to meet other campaign members, at least according to US law which forbids meetings between campaign and PAC contributors.

PACs are a way of involving business more intimately in politics than anything yet devised. By the 1984 elections it would appear that business was being almost as generous to Democrats as to Republicans, for the smart political investor recognised that the Democrat exclusion from government was not permanent: he did not wish to alienate future leaseholders of power. Democrats had received $20.7 million, and Republicans $23.6 million, and in the 1984 campaign business and conservative groups accounted for more than two-thirds of PAC money spent.[48] Representative Tony Coelho, a Democrat, told businessmen: 'The Republicans got you into a lot of races where you made enemies' of the eventual Democrat winners.[49]

The chief House of Representatives beneficiary of business largesse was in fact a Democrat (James R. Jones, chairman of the Budget Committee), and Democrats with prize committee positions found a new popularity with business.[50] In the Senate however the Republican Charles Percy was the largest recipient of corporate funds with $661 336, yet he still failed to gain re-election.[51] Like many of the phenomena we depict, the business PACs were a reaction to and imitation of the political left with its public interest groups, but applied more efficiently.[52]

Predictably the adoption of a marketing orientation, whether conscious or not, by the political right in America so consumed Democrat votes that Democrats then turned to it as well. After the defeat of 1980 a luxuriant growth of Democrat political action committees appeared, and they include:[53] Democrats for the 80s; Independent Action (which raised $700 000 in 1981 and ran negative advertising against Senator Helms) which specialised in direct mail; the Committee for the Future of America and the Fund for a Democratic Majority (they help Democrat politicians); the Center for National Policy and the National Policy Exchange which are concerned with policy analysis. The Parker-Coltrane Political Action Committee assists southern blacks and black candidates, while the Progressive Political Action Committee orchestrates aggressive advertising against Conservative Republicans in mimicry of the 'new right', and the Committee for American Principles aims to spotlight rightist illegalities.[54] 'Fair Play Committees' have been formed against the conservatives. To a significant extent the style of all these groups emulates the right: they testify to the hostility of a party not only defeated but made so, in its own eyes, by illegitimate means. Therefore there existed a determination both to imitate and to expose; the aggregate seems a lowering of ethical standards, a vulgarisation of tone in American political dialogue, and even if the ideological right had limited subsequent effect they provoked opponents into similar tactics and collectively they debased the coinage of political debate.

Is marketing to blame? In itself it is morally neutral. So, perhaps, is a gun. It provides a method and technology for hostility to express itself more forcibly. Union political action committees were the first such organisations, and they are still potent. Perhaps they need to be since there is only 22 per cent unionisation in the United States. They can endorse and promote a candidate to their members; they produce literature and raise money for him, canvas and operate telephone banks.[55] Usually the Democrats would be the beneficiaries of this large manpower resource; COPE for instance can supply a list of 12.5 million union members to candidates, with data on each member.[56]

PAC GIVING

	Cash spent	Given to Democrats	Given to Republicans	Independent Spending
Business	$126.8	$20.7	$23.6	$0.1
Labour	52.1	14.7	1.0	0.1
Conservative	49.6	0.4	2.4	8.0
Liberal	31.5	2.7	0.3	0.1
Other	9.2	1.6	0.5	0.0
Total[57]	$269.2	$40.1	$27.8	$8.3

Many kinds of PAC proliferate – from the National Rifle Association to the National Association for the Advancement of Coloured People – dealing with issues for which other countries would use political parties as the conduit. There are also PACs for countries with a special interest in Washington's decisions, including Korean, Arab, Israeli and Taiwanese lobbies.

A miscellaneous group of PACs account for 3 per cent of giving and are dominated by pro-Israel committees. Financing totalled $9.2 millions, from which Representative Paul Simon (Illinois) at $150 600 prospered most.[58] They gave Representative Clarence D. Long $93 700 as chairman of the strategically valuable Appropriations Subcommittee on foreign operations.[59] Administrations of both parties have claimed that the Israel lobby distorts American policy in the Middle East. The American Israel Committee has 51 000 members, eighty staffers and five million dollars a year to spend, dwarfing the diminutive National Association of Arab Americans; thus most of the Senate publicly disavowed the sale of AWACs to Saudi Arabia. A further issue has been the PAC-directed influence of foreign companies. In 1986 they spent $2.3 million on Congressional campaigns, so that Senator Bentsen proposed legislation against this. Arguably the commercial and professional PACs have less legitimacy than the issue ones, since the universe of their work is entirely self-service; their numeracy, their growth, testify to their success; they are a consequence of the size of the state, for there is no particle of modern American life in which the state is not involved and therefore the desire to influence that state is natural if moderately corrupting: some would argue that people cannot be blamed for attempting to govern their governors.

ETHICS

The supremacy of marketing and with it the need for money has serious implications for the kind of men to be found in American politics. The candidate is probably rich in his own right. He will almost certainly have to be adept at the soft technology of fund-raising, and possession of such money-gathering qualities, while laudable in itself, is not synonymous with being an informed and effective legislator, importing no especial political benison, such as knowledge of international affairs or maturity of judgement. Congress, like the Ritz hotel, is open to everyone, but large categories of people are effectively excluded by economic status from participation in the American electoral process at its highest levels, for it still helps to be rich in this business. Senator John D. Rockefeller of West Virginia made loans and contributions to himself of $9 850 722.[60]

The effects of big money on the American political process were described with lofty condescension by John Grigg in *The Times*:[61] 'But we can more reasonably ask why the Americans, whose democratic instincts are in many ways stranger than ours, continue to tolerate the subversion of their democratic system by the unbridled use of cash'. And of the Americans he wrote:

> To the extent that they tend to regard money as the most reliable index of merit and virtue, they cannot grasp the urgency – for their democracy's sake – of modifying that attitude to take account of other indices, no less valid, and also to take account of the corruption, prejudice and injustice that may flow from making wealth paramount.

For Representative R. R. Cheney, 'A person who has no assets simply cannot afford to participate; to spend $50 000 on his primary', for the 1976 Federal Election Campaign Act permitted the candidate to spend any amount of his own money, while, according to McKay, PACs are not as significant as the candidates' private wealth.[62]

Individual politicians demonstrated other types of initiative: thus Lloyd Bentsen, chairman of the Senate Finance Committee and later Democrat Vice Presidential Candidate, invited people to join his 'Council' for a monthly breakfast at $10 000 a time; Quentin Burdict, chairman of the Senate Public Works Committee, offered pins in the price range $1000 to $5000 to joiners of his club.

When the House of Representatives attempted to reduce contributions from PACs the bill was stopped by their principal beneficiaries, the United States Senate. A survey of attitudes to state financing of campaigns showed 51 per cent of Democrat Congressmen strongly in favour and 49 per cent of Republicans negative.[63] The Boren Bird Bill sought to control PAC giving via a part public financing and spending limit in Senate elections.[64] Three other Senate bills dealt with the same theme. Only a few Republican senators endorsed the bill. Forty-four senators signed it altogether, and eight bills on the subject were presented in the House. Detractors of the bill argued that advertising costs and not PACs were responsible for such sums, representing surely a confusion of cause and effect. Certainly in Presidential campaigns public funding was a success (Reagan netted $90 million from this source).[65] 'In eight years, the cost of a typical Senate race has gone from $609 000 to $2.9 million', Boren commented, 'the mushrooming influence of political action committees is beginning to threaten grass-roots democracy'. His bill would have created ceilings of $2000 for individual donors, $100 000 for House candidates and between $175 000 and $750 000 for the Senate, according to size of population.

LOBBYISTS

Great personal wealth is one way of paying the bills created by politicians' adoption of the marketing notion. Another is the PACs. A further alternative is via the favour of the lobbyists. In 1986 20 400 lobbyists were officially registered,[66] that is to say thirty for every member of Congress, and their expenditures were reckoned to be $1.5 billion.[67] Over half of all political action committees support lobbyists in Washington.

Lobbyists are part and parcel of the political market/marketing approach to politics that has evolved in the United States and is evolving elsewhere. Many of their methods, such as phone banks, are drawn straight from commercial marketing. But the 'product' offered by the lobbyist is targetted pressure, so that he frequently has to call on an external constituency to create this, and such constituencies are built by marketing methods, so that doubt might attach to their genuineness: 'these middlemen can quickly manufacture and channel public support that otherwise would not exist'.[68]

The services offered by this golden horde are extensive: they raise campaign funds, give strategic advice, lobby (on behalf of corporations mainly), help freshmen Congressmen onto committees and their seniors onto subcommittee chairmanships.[69] They influence the content of bills, especially in the direction of retained or increased subsidies, special tax brackets and the like. *Time* described lobbyists 'laboring to spare their favorite federal subsidies from the exigencies of deficit reduction'. It described how 'By day, Boggs lobbies Congressmen, often the same ones of whom he has raised money the night before', and it called one firm, Black, Manefort and Stone, the 'ultimate supermarket in influence peddling'. There exist several firms whose task is simply to service lobbyists, providing them with texts of bills, committee calendars, voting records, data-bases or political contributions and so on.[70]

The influence of lobbyists is all-powerful, and the anecdotal evidence is particularly striking.[71] Black, Manefort and Stone were able to create a strong Washington constituency for Joseph Savimbi. Senator Dole ceased to oppose tax rights for commodity traders when they increased contributions to his PAC. Even the conduct of international relations can be influenced. Thus Senator Boschwitz was given a question on Israel to ask King Hussein by Jordan's lobbyist, who also assisted the king with his reply.[72]

Major controversy has been generated by the lobby participation of former politicians and administration officials. Fourteen top Reagan administration officials had become lobbyists by 1988, including of course Michael Deaver, Richard Allen and Lyn Nofziger.[73] Such officials have overseas governments as their clients. Black, Manefort and Stone all worked for Reagan's campaigns.[74] The attractions of lobbying are not difficult to fathom: thus the former White House political director Ed Pollins earned ten times his former income as a lobbyist.[75] *Time* commented that 'For many, public service has become a mere internship for a lucrative career as a hired gun for special interests'. Such men of course have especial esteem as lobbyists, a trade which depends on such intangible and ephemeral qualities as 'access' and 'influence', and an illustration of their potential is provided by Richard Schweiker's campaign on behalf of the insurance industry, where five million dollars were spent on a television blitz, seven million pre-printed cards to Congress and so on, so that the campaign achieved its objective of restoring special privileges. Mr Schweiker is a former Secretary of Health.

Lobbyists pay up to $21 000 to get a congressman to dine with their clients (presumably the dinner is free). Such 'honorariums' are also paid for other forms of 'service', visits to factories and the like.[76] Collectively such sources paid $4.5 million in 1982.[77] The *New York Times* commented:

> as for the so-called honorariums, Representative Bill Chappell, Democrat, of Appropriations Subcommittee, received $4,000 for one day's appearance at plans of AVCO, which makes engines for

the M-I tank, as well as $2,000 from Lockheed and $2,000 for two appearances in Pratt and Witney.[78] Representative Trent Lott . . . accepted $2,000 from Brown and Williamson, a tobacco company, to attend a seminar on tobacco. The junket included an all expenses-paid trip with his wife to the Kentucky Derby.[79]

The paper added: 'It is not at all clear that we should distinguish between those who work for a candidate by handing out leaflets and those who give money to hire people for this purpose'.[80] It is, however, important to distinguish between those who give money to a candidate whose views they support and those who give money with the understanding that the candidate will adopt their views.[81] The *New York Times* claimed that the need is to 'devise a compromise that will allow us to live more easily with the ambiguities of the reciprocity relation',[82] and, while arguing that special interest groups have a legitimate place in a democracy, it suggested that costs should be controlled by law and argued that free television time for candidates is the best means of achieving this.[83]

EFFECTS OF PACs (I)   PAC AND PARTY

PACs are undermining the party system by enabling faction to come alive and finance its political representation. They give the individual an alternative source of funds and publicity, and his appeal must be adjusted not to the general interest of the party but to the sectarian constraints of the PAC. Single issues exact a greater emotional appeal than aggregate politics: they throw into relief the great ideological fissures in society. They are therefore much more effective ways of attracting money. Moreover people seem to be more satisfied by partnership in a single-cause group than by party politics; since it can give measurable progress to a tangible result, it becomes 'my' cause – and to a hedonistic society this is the more fulfilling alternative. Tip O'Neil claimed that people running for Congress since the Vietnam War and Watergate 'had no loyalty to the party whatsoever. They looked down on it'. They said 'the party didn't elect me, and I'm not beholden to the party'.[84]

Elsewhere we discuss the consequences that flow from this weakening of the party, a weakness partly attributable to the centrality of the marketing approach to politics in America today. With so many diversified sources of funding, and the necessity of tapping them, legislators are bound to adopt a much narrower conception of their own self-interest and cease to identify it so strongly with that of their party. Parties cannot therefore rely on their votes; the programmes its leaders conceive must perforce be modified out of existence, in order to please the legislator and by extension the funders on whom he is dependent for this political life. This new format of American democracy would not be endorsed by a view of democracy that concentrated more on outcome than on process, on the ability to produce workable government rather than on representativeness.

Party activity has to some extent been replaced by the operation of strategic coalitions, but these are a much less robust vessel, where issue groups with some loose relationship with each other collude and their sponsored legislators support one another.

Single-issue PACs may be more nefarious than business PACs. Business wants favourable legislation, things too minor to be called a policy or even affect society very greatly. Single issues are different. Such groups have been able to turn into issues areas where previously there had been accord: they represent a much more extreme intrusion than the commercial PACs, demanding not only the vote but the soul of the politician: is this a good or a bad thing; are they awakening the conscience of society, or propagating needless discord?

In a country as disparate as the United States, the parties were and are a major force for cohesion. Dean John Pittenger has argued persuasively that contemporary evolutions in the United States have weakened federalism, the power of the states, and strengthened the hand of central government. He points out that many congressmen today have had previous careers in state legislatures: 'Nowadays, the tendency is to convert fame earned in some other walk of life – as an astronaut, for example – into a seat in Congress. One outcome of this tendency is a Congress markedly less sympathetic to the claims of a federal system'.[85] He adds that the political supports of federalism are being eroded as the result of the debilitation of the political parties: 'the parties were important in two ways: they provided both career ladders and cash', and as a result members of Congress were inclined to think twice about offending governors, especially of their own party, and other major state and local actors. No similar delicacy restrains most members of Congress today. The parties have become largely irrelevant, their place taken by political action committees that operate most effectively at the national level and for whom national legislation is the badge of success. The best way parties could have helped their survival is by limiting the opportunities for political marketing.

Crucial to the success of PACs is that consciously or not they apply the market segmentation approach: marketing will always advise a division of any total market into more refined subgroups, to which distinctive appeals can be fashioned as long as the groups are economically viable, and the creators of the PACs recognized instinctively the power of a specific and targeted appeal over the bland, platitudinous stance of a political party. But segmentation implies disaggregation: the power of the specific is magnified but the power of the general grows smaller.

The Economist commented acidly on the Congressional anarchy created by powerful PACs and lobbies: we quote it at length, since both the substance and the rhetoric are memorable.[86]

Just 14 of the 182 Republican members of the House of Representatives were at first prepared to let the tax-reform bill even come forward for consideration by the Full-House . . . The national interest? Fair taxation? Economic efficiency? Both the initial and amended proposal for tax reform held some advantages for all of these, but such concepts seem remote from the minds of congressmen these days. They are swayed, above all, by the army of lobbyists that infest Capitol Hill, proffering the financial support of their innumerable political action committees and arguing for particular rather than general interests . . . In the case of tax reform, traditional opponents coalesce to fight for these single common interests.

Thus employers and unions join forces to lobby for special treatment for investment in industry, particularly theirs, while building unions, construction companies and property developers all combine to secure tax breaks for thrice-mortgaged holiday-home owners. Congressmen, faced with ever bigger bills for their constant and interminable campaigns, are too craven to resist the blandishments of the lobbyists, let alone to risk their wrath and be 'targetted' as undesirables.

Indeed, congressmen now find it hard to say no to anybody. As a result, they have so burdened the federal budget that the tide of budgetary red ink is lapping at the steps of the Capitol. This tide, unlike that which immersed poor old King Canute, obeys the laws of man, not of nature, and could be reversed with taxes or spending cuts. Yet in the last days before they went off for Christmas, congressmen were voting to spend money on everything from crop-price supports to chemical weapons. Their prodigality was particularly incongruous because, only a few days before, they had passed the Gramm-Rudman Act, a device designed to bring financial discipline to their deliberations on pain of having it done for them automatically, indiscriminately and with much suffering. President Reagan has now signed this extraordinary legislation, which will, if it is not ruled unconstitutional, deny both Congress and president discretion over a range of future spending.

The Gramm-Rudman legislation is one of the most desperate Acts ever to have come out of Washington. It is like a girl who can't say no, so she puts on a chastity belt and throws away the key. Congress is now composed of 535 one-man parties which combine in small groups and shifting alliances among numberless subcommittees, each led by a chairman jealous of his narrow fief and limited power – which is the power not to promote but to obstruct. The most notable victim is the budget, which emerges from an incoherent and interminable process punctuated by deadlines that are not met, debt ceilings that are lifted at one-minute-to-midnight several times a month, and catch-all continuing resolutions that make a mockery of any claim Congress still has to be a serious deliberative body. Against this background congressmen can without any embarrassment declare themselves determined to attack the budget deficit while voting to spend more and more on their favoured projects. . . .

His tax cuts have indeed brought economic growth, but, given his adamant desire to spend so much on defence and to leave untouched such sacred fountains as social security, the growth in the budget deficit means that the national debt, which was below $1 trillion in 1981, is passing $2 trillion now. . . .

If the constitution is not to look its age in 1987, may the spirit of the Founding Fathers by then inspire more leadership from America's President, and a greater willingness to be led from its shambolic Congress.

EFFECTS OF PACs (II)   INERTIA

PACs, and the issue-oriented politics they sponsor, create stronger adherence to a narrower cause. They do not create loyalties to any of the broader social and political entities in society, so that a political structure of mass loyalty to larger bodies is replaced by a system of casual loyalties to smaller groups, signified by donations rather than activism. This can hardly be said to enhance the perceived legitimacy of law-giving bodies: and it is interesting to speculate on the consequences of the great deeps of apathy and non-involvement beneath the surface activism of US politics, for while the action is orchestrated in Congress and in the media by the officers of the PACs, their donors and contributors simply agree, and often rather passively, to the requisite donations being made from salaries. PACs though would not exist if congressmen did not have to advertise themselves so heavily, and so often: the advertising imperative is both a cause and a consequence of the prevailing political culture in the United States. Weak parties create a vacuum which marketing fills, necessitating fund-raising and therefore PACs which in themselves further loosen the ties and loyalties to party without replacing them with any strong political adhesive.

Elsewhere we have described loyalty thus created as rented allegiance; this suggests a lack of rootedness and the ability to be simply 'brought' by somebody else. Politics themselves become defined by the market ethos, issues peddled, sold and discarded as new ones come into fashion. The treatment of issues as products is not a perversion but logically consistent. The PACs themselves behave as single or multi-product firms, with strategies to expand and update their offer, collude, add new 'products', that is, to conceive the issue or cause as they would a commercial product.

We have also stated that such a political culture makes for a moribund democracy, because it would not appear to invoke those levels of physical activism usual in a democracy and once traditional in America, which are an earnest of real popular interest and involvement. Elections are battles between rival candidates and the companies each has hired. Such a process however is created by a cessation of political activism in the traditional sense – it is a politics of introversion rather than the old extroversion, predicated on popular lack of interest in attending speeches, hustings, rallies, walking the streets.

But we would not cease to call the new process democratic, merely perhaps that it is a less 'full' democracy than its predecessor, if we accept as one measure of the value of democracy the degree of popular activism it arouses. But the logic of such a view is open to question. Mass activity may be symptomatic of deep social discord, for instance, and indicate not the health of a democracy but its failure. This was the case for example in Spain in 1936, with society certainly politically active, but polarised between the left Popular Front and the nationalists. Telemarketed democracy though superficially polarising may by its very existence signify a deeper calm and therefore represent a sign of health.

PACs: AN EVALUATION

A conundrum exists in that the public demand high ethics of a system wherein only the less-than-ethical can afford to participate: they ask for the morality of the cloister fortified by the lucre of the casino. Since wealth is sometimes created in the grey ground between legality and illegality, this leads inexorably to the kind of embarrassments demonstrated by the Ferraro affair.

There is no way of insulating American campaigns from serious money. Interest groups will always discover some Byzantine entry: they need politicians, and politicians need marketing, and marketing needs cash. Political mass marketing has therefore come at the price of some diminution in political integrity and many politicians are in bondage to the PACs. 'America has the best politicians money can buy' would be an exaggeration but, obsessed with the next election, a Mephistophelian whisper from a rich group might illuminate congressional minds on many an issue hitherto unclear. So long as marketing remains central – and how could the position be reversed? – there will be no way of protecting American campaigns from high finance.

Political marketing, then, while it frees a politician from party bondage, diminishes his status as an independent agent even if his voters imagine him still to be independent, for he must give satisfaction to his paymasters. One form of servitude is exchanged for another. This tension is historic, between the dedicative aspect of a politician's role – his loyalty to the movement that put him in power – and other forms of obligation to constituents, to conscience and to personal vanity.

The universal use of expensive marketing techniques in American politics has created a massive financial imperative, since politicians' need for money gives power to its possessors, and this equation is the heart of the dilemma. Indeed, if the primary focus of electioneering was television documentary and debate, if only limited marketing was purchased, a different political system would emerge with governments different in kind. A process of competition now operates, with politicians outbidding each other in the usage of marketing techniques: the marketing concept has been internalised by the current generation of politicians, and yet the costs of sustaining such an appetite continue to soar since they must compete with commercial buying of advertising time.

Such politics make it hard for truly independent to succeed. While it is perhaps difficult to say whether lobbies have now become more powerful despite all the laws to put them down, it is clear that few can now afford to do without them. For a long time the whole PAC movement favoured the ideological politician. In the past the middle-of-the-road pragmatist may have beguiled the dollars from a few rich men: but it became harder to get PAC money because he could not persuade its donors individually and so the finance went to the man with the clear profile, the reputation, the firm issue positions. The politician must market himself to potential funders and financiers. In the late 'eighties however incumbency rather than ideology became the chief attraction to political backers.

Political action committees are both a cause and an effect of political marketing. But can they be avoided? Given the reality of commercial media, and the wealth of those interests that seek the benison of government, it is perhaps best for reformist legislators to channel these energies rather than seek their extinction. Special interests have historically been privileged operators on the American political scene: as McKay says, 'Indeed the growth of the Republic can almost be described in terms of successive moves of populist revolt against the undue influence of organised groups'. So what is new? Woodrow Wilson noted, 'The government of the United States is the foster-child of special interests'; arguably their power is greater now.

PACs are the primary medium for the articulation of vested interests in modern political society: nevertheless they have their defenders. Since every major sector in society appears to have its own PAC a kind of rough justice is established, though it would be naive to equate aggregated sectional interests with the national interest. But this must surely alienate those with less access. Indeed in one survey three-fifths believed government was managed by large, egocentric interests, and two-fifths felt they had 'no say' in government action. As McKay suggests, such interest groups hardly have neutral distributional consequences.

Yet it is possible to be overly critical, and the PACs have made one positive contribution to US politics: they have broadened political involvement. For a PAC must be based not just in the boardroom or among the heads of a profession: to work it has to be rooted in some kind of popular support. Such a trend to breadth of involvement is apparent also in many other developments we have discussed, part of what might be described as a movement towards a political nation, an informed and involved and middle class-dominated elite, distinguished from an apathetic mass by its possession of intimate information. One effect will be to buttress the status of members of such a group as opinion leaders in office, factory and so on: in politics as in all forms of marketing 'word of mouth' is an important persuader. The marketing process discovers and involves the most committed. Such elites are not particularly distinguished by social status or talent, merely by political commitment, and this process is democratic in the sense that anyone can enter, and there is no significant economic price to be paid. Their numbers may be limited, but their dollars spent on marketing influence others. The PACs possibly involve in democracy's processes more people than parties did, and more ordinary people at that; yet the broad mass, characterised by inertia, are still not involved. Not their interests, but those of the most politically forceful, are taken into account: however in various ways this has always been true of democratic politics.

So the PAC system is not without defenders. In common with other elements in political marketing it permits new talent to enter the process, at least in theory, without needing the support of party; critics would say that this is merely exchanging one form of bondage for another. However the PACs are diverse entities in a way that a party never was, and therefore permit a broader range of people. Critics would reply that the graduates of such a system do have an important point in common, for they are all similarly indebted to their paymaster.

Yet there remains the issue of how far democracy can license the disproportionate accretion of power by small groups who represent nobody but themselves, and some might ask rehetorically how far democracy has matured since the days of property-qualified suffrage. Organised interests must help determine the kind of candidate who emerges in US politics, since they are such a major source of funding, and partially determine then the personality of the legislature. The consequences are manifold. Perhaps political establishments are brought into disrepute with electors and better men and women discouraged from participation, and certainly it gives more political power to corporations – a good or bad thing, depending on one's political orientation.

Also, donating to corporate or union PACs and to favoured lobbies calls forth no effort, re-evaluation or deep-seated commitment. This must surely have implications for political loyalties since to work for a candidate or party represents direct investment while, arguably, giving a trivial sum is much less binding. So technological society will get automated politics, with everything experienced impersonally in the antiseptic late twentieth century.

It would be easy to exaggerate the democratic credentials of the new PAC participation: even if the rich are not as influential as before, their influence is still great. Each individual can give $5000 to a PAC; but he can end up giving a great deal of money to a string of PACs. However the need now is to solicit myriad numbers of the semi-rich and the effect is to transfer a portion of political influence not from the rich to the average but to the organised group, the self-identified class, the professional associations. This is a mildly democratic move. We may envisage the new political maestro, not as a fat man with a huge cigar, but rather a row of fattish men with smaller cigars.

7 High Priesthood, Low Priestcraft: The Role of Political Consultants

'All the domestic controversies of the Americans at first appear to a stranger to be incomprehensible or puerile, and he is at a loss whether to pity a people who take such arrant trifles in good earnest, or to envy that happiness which enables a community to discuss them.'

Alexis de Tocqueville, *Democracy in America*

Political consultants may be described as the product managers of the political world, and they made their first recognisable appearance in California in the early nineteen thirties. The success of these pioneers became legendary; their growth was rapid and by the fifties they were firmly established on the political scene. California, with no ancient political loyalties and only light party organisations, provided fertile ground for political marketing, a genre that is inherently anti-party and whose growth is intimately bound up with the demise of parties and which depends for its effectiveness on the absence of strong loyalties.[1] A total of 5000 consultants and their assistants now work on campaigns, with an extra 30 000 drafted in at peak periods.

THE RANGE OF POLITICAL CONSULTANTS

Consultants come into their own in the United States where one-third of the electorate is not pre-committed to any political party (indeed such a statistic is a prerequisite of their existence). They really are marketing packagers.

Political marketing has important consequences for the local political battle. Consultants operate extensively at the state level: thus in California Butcher-Forde helped to orchestrate the passing of Proposition 13 and arranged a contract with Howard Jarvis. Consultants work with a broad range of elections, referenda and initiative campaigns; judicial elections, for example, use them frequently, with bizarre packages of advice such as 'Campaigning with Dignity:

Maintaining the Judicial Image'.[2] One advertisement offers the services of 'One to One', a pro-Democrat communication organisation, and these include: fund-raising; getting out the vote; field training; political polling; voters' ID; voter persuasion; phone banks; co-ordination; script writing.

The ramifications of these marketing techniques are not confined to America: by osmosis the rest of the world will absorb them, with American consultants as missionaries, and even non-democratic regimes may seek to copy them and 'sell' their autocracy like soap powder. The consultants will expand internationally, for some of them have already handled numerous overseas campaigns: this would of course cause controversy, since their political power would be much more direct than that of other multinationals and they could be used to maintain pocket tyrants in power, and manipulate naive electorates. Herera of Venezuela was elected with a Garth campaign aimed at poorer groups and costing $28 million (the ruling party spent $110 million): the campaign focussed on the size of Venezuela's debt.[3] Joseph Napolitan conducted a classical American political marketing campaign for Giscard d'Estaing in France.[4] Robert Squier operated in Spain and the Philippines.

The very complexity of the new political marketing technology makes consultants necessary; for example, it is they who are behind the explosion of direct mail. The consultants offer a broad range of marketing services: polling, advertising, direct mailing and so on, and often they maintain a self-seeking allegiance to some political party. However each firm tends to have one particular marketing specialisation: other services are performed less well and are often subcontracted. Consultants are not interested in the substance of policy; they are tacticians and not innovators: they tend not to supply any long-term policy creativity.

Many of the largest political consulting firms are in fact primarily polling firms. Pollsters have in many ways enjoyed more power than any other member of the consultant species. They constitute market research agencies, and campaigners cannot do without the polling component. For Sabato the pollster is 'an analytic interpreter, a grand-strategist, and to some, a Delphic oracle'.[5]

Elections are not the only or even the main business of political consulting firms: many of them prefer work for political parties or political action committees, where circumstances are more predictable and free from the pressures and smouldering tempers of elections, and where they can have permanent contracts and perhaps charge more. Most firms have between one-third and two-thirds of their business as political.

THE FEES OF POLITICAL CONSULTANTS

Consultants demand and receive large fees, helping to inflate the price of office in the United States. The compulsion to market entails high-cost professional advice and organisation of the type supplied by consultants, making politicians dependent on external interests for financial backing, as has been seen. Money remains an important motive with consultants and by its dividends they gauge their success. And the money-making issues are the emotional and therefore polarising ones. They behave exactly like brand managers and their allegiance is rented. For example, of the $2.5 million raised for Republican Philip Crane, $1 200 000 went to Richard Viguerie's enterprises which sometimes take as much as three-quarters of the sums raised.[6] The liberal consultant David Garth's monthly fees range between $10 000 and $15 000 with 15 per cent for broadcast billings.[7] To pay the consultant for the marketing services he offers the politician must issue dividends to the pressure groups, fattening their disproportionate share of the power in the US political system, or pay the marketing bills out of his own wealth, in which case the system may preselect among the very rich, and a politics of rich men is inherently a conservative politics. Twenty per cent of the average campaign budget is probably spent on consultation fees, expenses and commissions.[8]

Yet the money to be made out of political consulting is not so great by American standards: consultants could earn much more from commercial marketing engagements, though the plush creative fees and the commissions have made consultants rich men, so that those who participate in consultancy are actuated by other motives too. Some are ideologues trying to achieve their particular world vision. Others are great egotists and seek a sensation of power. Certainly the consultants are in the game as businessmen. But not only as businessmen: they are there because they are fascinated by their product, politics, and many of them emerged from political-type backgrounds. They are high-tech zealots, and perhaps this makes them more sinister than if they were just cash-motivated. Consultants are not idealistic about the political process and their condescension often comes across; they enjoy many of the benefits of political power and few of its costs, and this kind of career is attractive to a certain type of intelligent operator; they exhibit the confidence and brashness of men who are too powerful in the state. (Towards candidates in particular their attitude can often be patronising.)

Richard Viguerie was one of the first to recognise the right's problem as a marketing one, and he became the most dynamic, and the most ideological, of consultants. Like any entrepreneur he began by perceiving a gap in the market-place: he recognised that rightist ideas needed to be packaged and sold, that the right needed 'someone who could take ideas, the writings and the books and market them to the people', and a ready source of inspiration was available in the techniques of the left: 'We've taken close to 100 per cent of the left's tactics'. He argued that the old right 'expected and needed defeat because defeat certified its opinions'; mass direct mail campaigns[9] were his method of changing all this, which demonstrates the circularity of the process of political marketing with a cross-pollination among the various political factions.

Viguerie's remarks reveal a clear perception of himself as a marketer and packager, choosing a somewhat neglected marketing technique and developing it into the most potent piece of campaign artillery ever invented, having defined the essential weakness of the right as one of communication and not ideology: he recognised that with the adoption of marketing techniques it could be resurrected. The fact that zealots adopted these marketing practices and made them their own demonstrates that commercial motives are not exclusive in political consultancy; but they are important – certainly to Viguerie – and it is always possible that other consultants assume a mask of ideology when their true motives are financial. But against the permeation of consulting by ostensible ideologues must be set the liberal influence of the orthodox media.

CONSULTANTS AS MARKETERS

Consultants are the natural outcome of the political marketing culture we have described, and from the very start they were closely associated with the visual marketing medium. Consultants are experts in media. While media can never really be dictated to in a free country, much can be done to influence it, although consultants themselves deny charges of manipulation. Consultants are the consequence of a media-centric political process. They throw into sharp relief how the media is vulnerable to professional manipulation; media calls consultants into existence because it is a phenomenon that requires specialist knowledge, something the candidate and the old-time party boss were unable to provide. Thus, in the end, the explanation for the power of consultants in American politics is reducible to the power of television in American life. TV is an American's retreat and his cares are charmed away in the mesmerised contemplation of the illuminated trials and tribulations of others. Consultants can create media events and stories, train the candidate into media mannerisms and catechise him to deal fluently with hostile questions. The candidate's political act becomes about as spontaneous as the 'have a nice day' of restaurants and diners. However some would argue that all the above merely counterbalanced the traditional adversarial of journalists.

In the commercial world management consultants are pre-eminent operatives, specialists hired to advise on specific problems. The notion intruded naturally into the world of politics, for the campaign is a specific problem, but the politician is a general practitioner just like the general manager: and like him, he brings in the expert to resolve the special dilemma. Consultants bring to the conduct of political campaigns business acumen and strategy exactly as if they were the marketing executives of corporations, and may accumulate a large and tradeable bank of experience.

Consultants think in terms of the perpetual campaign – in part because of the business nature of their vocation, they want not a temporary but a lasting contract so that their initial efforts in winning and fulfilling the arrangements continue to pay dividends. Therefore they help the candidate throughout his time in office, in the preparation of strategic plans and generally close involvement: here perhaps, commercial and political wisdom coincide.

Its defenders can legitimately describe the process operated by consultants as 'marketing' because the direction in the end does emanate from the elector, since consultants interpret what the political 'consumer' is looking for, and while they are certainly manipulators it is not the case that people have policies and personalities foisted upon them with which they disagree. Joe White for example pointed out how, in 1986, drugs became an issue not because consultants unilaterally decided this, but because young parents who had themselves known drugs at school had become by that stage seriously alarmed.[10] Thus our attitudes to the ethical value of consulting is coloured by our attitudes to consumer marketing in general – whether we see it as being primarily a responsive or a manipulative function. Sensing the public mood, what it will buy, what it is looking for, via research and the interpretation of that research and the asking of the right questions, constitutes a consumer orientation which certainly justifies the term 'marketing' even though consultants may not have originally thought in such terms or appended such a description to themselves. Consultants can put new issues on the agenda: issues which perhaps deserve articulation but which conventional politicians with their lack of a real marketing orientation would be slow to recognise.

CRITICISM OF CONSULTANTS

The power and practice of America's political consultants have not gone unmolested. Their critics are legion. Certainly they make the process more soulless: as Perry said, 'Political technocracy . . . is sexless; it has no soul and a computer for a heart'. He quotes an early critic of Whitaker and Baxter:

> The sad fact is that their manufacture of slogans and wielding of labels has led to a grievous debasement of political debate . . . Whitaker and Baxter's peculiar contribution, however, has been to make a precise art of oversimplification, to systematise emotional appeals, to merchandise the images they create through a relentless exploration of every means of of mass communication.

Consultants can be ideologically motivated as Whitaker and Baxter certainly were – early primitive conservatives, supportive of the Republicans and vehemently against any monolithic welfare state. They undertook a five million dollar campaign against compulsory health insurance. And they anticipated the future power political consultants would accumulate in acting in an autocratic way towards their candidates. Consultants may also have a vested interest in polarising politics, for as businessmen it is natural that they should seek to expand the scope of their enterprise. Consultants are not simply hired by just anyone, they actually choose to whom they will lend their expertise, that is, to those most exploitable by the media, on such criteria as an attractive wife. They will also choose the richest. The implications of having business firms influence the personnel of the legislature must be significant indeed.

Gillian Peele[11] has pointed out that the consultant, and not the electors, selects the issues, with opponent vulnerability rather than national significance being the criteria of choice: thus political marketing issues are sometimes phoney, dictated by technology and consultant as much as by candidate. Hence the more marketing becomes central to the political process, the more actual political power will consultants obtain, since the nature of the product cannot be divorced from its communication, and where communication is central those who advise on it will necessarily help create the product. This, if true, would be a substantial addition to our point about marketing manipulation. It is one thing for people to be influenced in a particular direction over issues about which they are already concerned. It is quite another to create and market artificial 'issues' and then engage people. The claim could be made that such an approach is naive, that politicians have always created issues and the press has always provoked popular sentiment: this is true, but seldom did they do it with the calculating coolness of the consultant, and such developments are inevitable and implicit in the adoption of the marketing concept. Materially irrelevant but perceptually impressive features are stressed in product advertising, and politics similarly looks for 'saleability', no matter how peripheral.

The notion of commercial organisations arranging the political agenda therefore certainly has profound implications – some might accuse them of perverting this agenda by selecting emotive issues, knowing that they will 'sell'. The individual issue may be chosen as symbolic, one around which to hang an entire campaign, or for its exploitability by the media; consultants, being in business, conduct their operations according to the business ethos and they seek market expansion and new applications.

THE POWER AND THE GLORY

Consultants are unelected, subject to no professional rules of conduct, but number among the most powerful politicians in the United States and are indispensable to the needs of the modern campaign. Increasingly the candidate is scarcely controlling his own campaign, so that his role becomes more symbolic.

Naturally enough the real power of consultants is growing. In the nineteen fifties consultants were not involved in strategic decisions. Now they are, and in much else – sometimes they are hired to reorganise state and local parties,[12] and sometimes they even recruit candidates; Nixon for instance gained his first progress in politics by replying to a political consultant's advertisement and being selected.[13] Deardourff admits that his firm actively searches for the right candidates.[14] Business marketing is a similarly holistic concept, for in the marketing-oriented firm no aspect of the business will be ignored by the marketing department.

As Blumenthal points out,[15] consultants can provide access to political leaders for aspiring candidates and they enjoy influence with past clients. They can constitute an independent political power in their own right: hence Deardourff can claim of his firm, 'We are one of the centers of moderate Republicanism' (his firm superintended the 1976 Ford campaign and the election of 11 out of the 18 Republican governors).

However, consultants have been regarded by some as agents of corruption, the mercenary pimps and whores of the political water-front. Their power is certainly now extensive. They have evolved from technicians to the choosers of issues; as Sabato has said, 'Propagandists are necessarily strategists and strategy in politics involves choice and interpretation of issues as a matter of course'.[16] Other rewards besides continued influence also await the victorious consultant, including work from the state once his patron is in power. Even when their protégés are ensconced in power the consultants may still hold sway, advising on the conduct of policy and returning in swarms for the next election. Carter's pollster, Patrick Cadell, and his media consultant both became significant figures in his White House with Caddell influencing important decisions.[17]

Thus consultants inevitably accumulate substantial political power in their own right, as a consequence of the increasing synonymity of politics with communication in the United States. The consultant has a clear hold over the politician, since he is familiar with his weaknesses and would be invaluable to an opponent. The politician becomes more of a cipher, a phenomenon that is not so much anti-democratic as a re-definition of democracy: consultants after all consult in what the electorate actually wants, or can be persuaded to want. In an article in *Electoral Studies*, Gillian Peele[18] warns of the potential power of consultants: 'Most who have it are well placed to influence candidates not merely on the details of how to package himself to the electoral constituency but also on broad policy issues as well'. And she adds: '. . . the role of political consultants poses serious questions of accountability and control'.

It is possible to speculate on likely future developments in political consultancy. Some of them have shown signs of becoming political figures in their own right: Richard Viguerie took several well-publicised positions of hostility to Reagan, including the Beirut hostage crisis.

In spite of ideological bias consultants remain antagonistic to the parties themselves, their structure and what remains of their power. Whitaker and Baxter were early critics. Party and consultant are in competition and see each other as rivals: to some extent they duplicate each other's functions. Consultants perceive it as an obstacle to their business, one to be short-circuited, and they envisage an even more liberated system. Consultants provide a structure independent of the party. Consultants help make congressional coalitions more fickle, Congress more anarchic by providing an external locus of strategic support. The politician owes less to his party, and the loyalty he returns for its label is of a qualified sort. But these are merely prerequisites of the central function a party performs, which is the provision of a programme, platform and legitimacy. Deprived of these, and in spite of the strong hold parties might have at times exerted in the past, the deliberative processes of the American state will become dangerously volatile. Moreover the consultant is an individual, one of hundreds such, between whom there is no co-ordination and scant affinity, while the party by contrast is a national organisation and thus has to think in terms of broad policy and reconciliatory initiatives.

Consultants do not build great political movements: traditional political activism took a longer-term view, both seeing itself in a historical perspective and looking to the future. Responsibility only to oneself can easily become irresponsibility; consultants promote squarely self-interest and not nationalised adherence; along with the technologies and arts they peddle they help to create a politics of hired loyalty. Party in the US context is a medium for moderacy, since demands have to be assimilated, reconciled and packaged in a programme: its weakening could create a vacuum and give extremists correspondingly more power.

The growth of consultants is clearly related to a decline in public political involvement and an increased voter apathy, thus a higher proportion of the vote is uncommitted and therefore amenable to commercial-type persuasion.

Widespread use of consultants highlights a number of trends we notice elsewhere; they reinforce the movement towards armchair politics and make the volunteer unnecessary, so that again we see politics becoming more impersonal. It is part of the decline of the amateur, and the tendency to use specialists in every aspect of American life. The consultants sever an umbilical relationship with party but in the process diminish the amount of popular political activism that is a result of a strong party sytem. The professionalisation of political campaigns is an inevitable concomitant of their mechanisation, for a local branch of a political party is ill-equipped for this marketing task: marketing is 'at' people and not 'with' them, inducing people to identify less with their political leader. The consultants' milieu is an electronic one; under the commercialisation of the American political process all becomes antiseptic and lacking in human spontaneity, and this contrasts with the politics of the past which was an ineptly charming activity of ordinary men and women. The electronic democracy they sponsor is restless because it does not involve people. Consultants match well a contemporary culture whose essence may sometimes appear to be instant gratification and disposability, the creation of nothing that will endure.

In the past a candidate had to be physically seen by his electorate, to perform at public rallies and perhaps supply a record of public service. This may have produced a limited and parochial kind of politician, but to an extent also it brought forth men who were in touch with their publics and who could offer a record of pedestrian service and local roots; a cadre of professional if uninspiring politicians.

Consultants are hired propagandists: their aim is not to enrich democracy, but to influence its processes so as to win. Consultants promote the trivialisation of politics. They promote image not debate, for debate is a process of intellectual reasoning which is governed by the skills of individual candidates: so that the public meetings that were once the fulcrum of the process could expose candidates in a way that manicured image creation never can.

THE CONSULTANTS CONSULTED

The number of powerful consultants in the United States is small, although the country contains in total legions of practitioners. We interviewed some of the top consultants, and researched others, our criteria for this being the regular handling of Senate, Congressional and gubernatorial campaigns, and sometimes Presidential ones. The numbers who operate in this league are few: these are the moguls of their craft; they are the originators and the trail-blazers.

Richard Viguerie

Richard Viguerie has attained an empire of influence that Whitaker and Baxter could never even have imagined: his business grosses $15 million a year, and George F. Will has referred scathingly to 'quasi political entrepreneurs, who have discovered commercial opportunities in merchandising discontent'. Viguerie aspires to half-hour television programmes comprising a political 'discussion' followed by a fund-raising appeal. Ironically it was the post-Watergate legislation, that great attempt of American liberalism to cleanse the Augean stable, that gave rise to the virulent breed of right-wing political consultants who saw themselves as liberalism's nemesis: an unanticipated consequence of liberal legislation, as the rightists would say.

Viguerie's influence has been extraordinary.[19] He was largely responsible for supplying the 'new right' with its direct mail facility, for example in 1980 his total fund-raising was between thirty-five and forty million dollars and he possessed twenty million names. Direct mail was the technique by which he reached his market, his essential constituency, with the pre-packed right-wing ideas. His firm and his institutions have acted as marketing as much as ideological seminaries for the 'new right': it is no accident that 80 per cent of major direct mail political consultants are on the right wing of the Republican Party, and *apparatchiks* trained by him enter the bureaucracy of the Republicans and the network of rightist organisations.[20] As Blumenthal has commented, 'The New Right is more dangerous because of his pedagogy'.[21] Viguerie superintends various 'new right' institutions. The Committee for the Survival of a Free Congress selects and trains candidates: in 1978 they contributed to the election of five senators and twenty-six congressmen.[22] And his Council for National Policy assesses America's foreign policy.

David Sawyer[23]

A forceful defender of the political marketing concept is David Sawyer. He believes that you can have strong leadership alongside a merchandised politics, and does not agree that it makes for a politics of blandness: Reagan, he says, has firm policy ideas and great self-belief. Moreover he believes that the impact of new communications technology on political marketing has been exaggerated: things are merely done faster and better. Sawyer also argues that negative campaigns have now reached their peak, since they are the issue of heavily ideological conflicts, and now that the Democrats have become much more centrist there is a depolarisation. For Sawyer political marketing is reactive rather than proactive, a vehicle for the communication of ideas; thus polling allows a politician to be responsive, and Johnson suffered through ignoring it over Vietnam. He perceives Reagan's 'permanent campaign', predicated on polling, as simply aimed at control of the agenda; that agenda has been to cut down the size of government and have a strong defence. Reagan made his permanent campaign effective, for example showing flexibility on social security and the Lebanon when polling revealed public hostility to his projected path.

Sawyer perceives the principal changes in US politics as being, amongst others, the longevity of campaigns. Once campaigns were short: but now they begin one and a half to two years before the election. And there has been change in the political agenda: by 1986 no Democrat dared mention 'social programmes'.

Sawyer would like to see campaign reform, but not in the way that Common Cause advocates. He wants laxer rules on contributions, so that individuals are permitted to give more, say from $1000 to $5000. He thinks that the way to prevent abuse lies in having tight disclosure rules. A candidate accepting money from, say, environmentally irresponsible corporations, could then be destroyed – 'I lick my lips'. According to Sawyer, in technology the Democrats have now caught up with the Republicans.

Joseph Napolitan[24]

Joseph Napolitan, one of the doyens of American political consultancy, has a rich fund of memorable anecdotes, but most especially concerning the 1968 Presidential election. He entered the flagging, failing campaign for the last nine weeks and his candidate Hubert Humphrey only ultimately lost by $\frac{7}{10}$th of a point.

Napolitan is a pragmatist, and there is no stereotypical 'Napolitan style'. He was an early exponent of advertising that resembled a television news feature; more generally, he perceives the key role of television political advertising as being to counterweight negative perceptions of a candidate. Thus in Venezuela a candidate of his was running against a popular figure and had rather an aloof image: therefore Napolitan made him talk about his early political experiences, his fight against the dictatorship and four years' imprisonment, a man who had fired machine guns (somewhat removed, this, from the blandness of American campaigning). Such techniques were particularly important given the limited Venezuelan political memory, with 80 per cent of the population aged under fifty.

Napolitan, for all his overseas experience, is somewhat sceptical of the international spread of American political consultancy techniques. Latin America is the most favoured place, with many new democracies and a willingness to take outside help; television and radio can be purchased, making American-style campaigning workable, and both sides to an election hire American consultants. Britain however, with its many restrictions, is a non-starter, and only rarely, with the occasional project, is western Europe suitable, though in Germany there is much training in political communication and internal consultants are widely used. Asia has few democracies, lacking therefore the essential prerequisite, and Africa is twenty years away.

Roger Ailes[25]

Roger Ailes has been consultant to George Bush and many major Republican figures. He views the key Reagan contribution as being to re-define the rhetoric of American politics, so that tax cutting and strong defence become common ground: as a consultant he would actually see the connection between significant political change and a re-definition in communications.

He does not regard negative advertising as being a new and painful intrusion – the public expects their candidates to go through fire and negative advertising has been around since the beginning. However the important thing is the perception of fairness: negative advertising is here to stay but careful use must be made of it and candidates cannot be attacked unfairly. He points out how the Democrats are now using tougher negative advertising; but their key problem remains fund-raising, since a party so pluralistic ('lesbian Navahos') alienates too easily. To Ailes, the unpaid media and debates, not political advertising, are key elements in Presidential contests, but with senate and governorship campaigns the commercials have great effect.

James Severin[26]

Republican consultant James Severin (consultant to George Bush and others) points to the generation gap between the consultants. The older ones he describes as 'plumbers not philosophers', narrow and pragmatic men with the exception of David Garth. The younger ones however are 'TV babies' and this influences their entire outlook. According to Severin, a key to campaigning is conveying the impression that there are many volunteers in a campaign: in practice, there is no real room for unskilled people.

Severin described the successful campaign of his candidate, James Hunt, in Alabama, the first Republican to be elected for 115 years. Hunt benefited from a 'throw the rascals out' sense among the electorate. Electors craved a 'sunbelt' image, where money and jobs would flow down from the north. The Republican candidate's answer was to play an 'above the fray' role. They did not style their contest as one of Republican against Democrat: indeed, they did not mention the word Republican. The stress was on 'problems we all share' and practical solutions that worked: it was a non-partisan message, not ideological. Such an 'anti-political' format for political marketing was both novel and effective.

Video Base International[27]

Sally Hunter of Video Base International is eloquent in defence of the role of political consultants. They save the candidates' money. The brevity and superficiality of their product is the fault of a network television that is parsimonious in its allocation of air time – pressures on television time are 'horrendous', and it is impossible to buy a five-minute spot in a major market. Indeed if consultants had five minutes they could do much good in increasing the information content of the campaigns, developing themes and giving background to candidates and issues. She emphatically denies that America's political consultants are 'merchandisers of discontent': turbulence is natural in politics, and its public airing is merely the American way, and a reflection of the openness of US society.

VBI spots stress the issues: they also do 'enthusiasm' spots which are important in Latin American campaigns with exuberant jingles and the like. Hunter also expressed some caution about 'image' spots, stressing that they make some candidates look merely foolish, and cites those of Richard Nixon walking along the beach wearing formal shoes. In other words, the advertisement merely served to reinforce his stiff and 'buttoned-up' image. Image advertising can only work 'where the person is comfortable'. But she would disclaim any guiding paradigm for their campaigns: rather it is a case of re-thinking for each contest.

This firm is especially noteworthy for the international dimension of its campaigning activities; they have fought campaigns in Venezuela (Presidential), Costa Rica (Presidential, against Joe Napolitan) and the Dominican Republic as well as in Hawaii and Puerto Rico.

David Garth[28]

David Garth, the vendor of Koch, Carey, Anderson, Adlai Stevenson and others, is the pre-emininent name among consultants. His activities have been identified with New York, but he has international experience, fighting campaigns in Venezuela, Colombia, Bermuda, Israel (Menachem Begin) as well as the John Anderson campaign.[29]

The creative marketing styles and methods of consultants differ however. Garth is a past master of the campaign gimmick. It was he who gave the Anderson campaign its essential boost by instituting a ticket-signing pilgrimage. During the Lindsay administration David Garth conducted what amounted to a perpetual marketing campaign for New York's mayor, with his protégé even hosting call-in talk shows. In *The Candidate* the consultant is modelled on Garth, and in one scene Redford, unable to answer a reporter's question, replies 'I don't know'. The response is a hit: 'The cynical consultant hypes it as refreshingly honest, a new brand of politics'.[30]

There is, he admits, a Garth style. People became cynical as a result of Watergate and therefore Garth advertisements project a visual integrity; bills for example are given their numbers and the dates they were passed. He calls these the most 'unproduced' of political spots, and they use real people.

Garth emphasises information. Facts cram the screen just as David Ogilvy, the great exponent of commercial advertising, would fill his adverts with information, illustrating again the parallels between political and commercial promotion. His candidates face the camera directly,[31] and there is sound marketing reasoning behind this approach: such a method confounds our expectations, while he claims that in recall people confuse his advertising with television news. His notion is that people will be stimulated by a high-energy information bombardment, but there is, he claims, 'no mood stuff'. His appeal here is ostensibly to reason: perhaps we are being affected by a pseudo-rational appeal where real impact is emotional not intellectual. Another Garth hallmark is scrawling handwriting travelling across the bottom of the film.[32]

David Garth himself disputes the employment of the term 'marketing'. While advertising can be good it can also trivialise, and according to Garth, 'we chased advertising out of the field, and it came back with Reagan'; the bland 'mom and pop'-type Reagan advertisements work only in the absence of tough opponents. Advertising therefore might create a good campaign – accidentally.

Garth claims that the belief that consultants trivialise the political process shows a lack of historical perspective on how people have traditionally gained political information, for they obtain more knowledge from political spots than from anything else. Although five million claim to read the *New York Times*, they are in fact lying. Today we may enjoy more information about a candidate than ever before; in a single campaign, for example, the Garth organisation make twenty commercials about candidates, each of one minute's duration.

Garth is sparing in his use of negative advertising. People will not perceive an advertisement as negative if it concentrates on the record. But Garth is expert at 'turning' negatives, at making an opponent's charges an asset, and using them to establish a candidate's credibility. Negatives must be taken immediately, head on, and not ignored; people are thrilled with honesty. Garth also favours an aggressive media strategy. He wanted Carter to 'go right for the situation' in the hostage issue, noting the subsequent success of Reagan's 'macho' role. He felt Mondale should have abrasively challenged the President to show how he would balance the budget. Garth thinks the less dramatic spots are more politically effective. But what can you really say in thirty seconds? According to Garth, a great deal.

Garth stresses historical continuity, and is sceptical of the notion of modern American politics being different in kind from those of the past; and there always were political advertisers. Thus, he says, big money is nothing new: the Harrimans gave $4 million to Democrats in New York in 1913. Prestige has been conferred by the vogue communications media; speechwriters were central when the printed word was supreme, and with television new skills become relevant. And image always was a traditional political skill: those of Churchill and de Gaulle held their countries together, and his first candidate Adlai Stevenson was highly aware of image.

Garth accepts that political marketing cannot change what people are: the consultant has to look at a candidate, uncover the best qualities and seek to transmit that. Nor does he feel that political marketing involves dishonesty: politicians do not have to change position – since consultants find ways of making that position saleable.

Tony Schwartz[33]

Another distinguished consultant is Tony Schwartz, who sells Coca Cola, Ford and American Airlines and Democrats. It was he who stepped in to bolster Carter's second presidential campaign, blocking the leakage in his popularity by tailoring sympathy to specific market segments. Some of the most famous political advertisements of all time are the handiwork of Schwartz – the anti-Agnew 'heartbeat away from the Presidency' advertisement, the 'Daisy' advertisement. He has worked for Johnson, Humphrey, McGovern and Carter.

Schwartz does not perceive the modern candidate as an arch-seducer of the popular will but as really being in rather a weak position: the candidate has less control of his campaign than heretofore, with the pressure of discussion shows and the like. The campaign is enacted in the living-room, and people know more about the candidate than in the past.

For Schwartz the key ingredient is effect, not memorability; advertisements must 'represent the feelings of the voters, which is not necessarily the same thing as representing the voters on the issues'.[34] According to Schwartz the consultant is 'selling the voters their preconceived notions; in voting for the politician who can mouth their notions in an evocative manner, the voters reaffirm themselves'. This is classic marketing thinking, the attempt to dramatise people's thoughts and desires. Television is good for 'surfacing feelings the voters already have', while 'The question is which candidates will feel more like you do in relation to an issue'. The notion here, then, is not to assert leadership but to court existing tastes and even prejudices. To Schwartz, people will only identify with personal experience and they check political communication against that. He criticises the 'transportation idea of communication'. What a voter hears politically must 'resonate' with what is stored in his or her mind and commercials must 'evoke connections', a process in which language itself really becomes obsolete. People call such activities 'manipulation' but this means nothing, and Schwartz suggests the word 'participation' – you have to participate in your manipulation, you bring things to it.

Schwartz is known best as a craftsman in sound, and radio is his chosen medium: 'we have a God-given faculty: people are born without earlids'. We hear what interests us. The electronic environment is acoustic and invisible, hearing is an 'inner trip rather than an outer trip', an internal process generating an inner picture. Moreover current sound relates to all else stored in the mind; we recall previous registrations and anticipate future ones: 'I use the voter as workforce'.

Schwartz, as illustrated by his notorious 'Daisy' ad, favours aggressive advertisements – though he would disown the label 'negative' advertising. He took exception to the 1984 Democratic campaign, arguing that Reagan was not attacked because 'everyone liked Reagan' – a self-fulfilling prophecy in Schwartz's view, since of course he was liked because of the failure to expose him. To Schwartz, Reagan should have been shown as a 'liar', the cutter of spending on the aged, hungry and so on. McGovern similarly was not hard-hitting enough, while in 1968 Nixon's case was a mere bubble and his honesty on defence matters should have been impugned. He himself would have brought to the surface the 'confusion people had over Nixon': 'Good communications are what the viewer brings to the viewing'.

Schwartz, like many consultants, eschews an issue-oriented approach to political marketing. Nor does he bother with 'image' advertising, a favourite among consultants; image is merely the sum of attitudes towards a candidate and can only be retouched. But if we substitute the word attitude for image we get a more workable concept, for attitudes can be measured. Schwartz thinks it important that the public feel a candidate is qualified: therefore, he makes biographical commercials.

Schwartz is contemptuous of orthodox commercial advertising:

political marketing has a strong task orientation, reacts quickly to problems and can get a commercial on the air in two days. He demonstrated this for us, making a health-care advertisement there and then in his remarkable windowless studio, via a satellite link with a Californian actor. The advertising community have not understood the essence of competitive advertising: 'Any planned fight is a ballet'. Conventional advertising demands a six- to eight-month period of gestation. The concept of the old advertising campaign is dead. He disclaims any borrowing from commercial advertising, disdains the word 'selling' and adds, 'I wouldn't sell soap the way they sell soap'.

Hal Evry

Hal Evry perceives emotion as the hard core of the persuasion process: people do not wish to vote and therefore they must be seduced or provoked into voting; a negative feeling, an inertia, must be overcome. Evry is unusual in seeing things exclusively as a marketing operation, and he claims an average win of 93 per cent, but he has no doubt about the centrality of money, saying that the candidate who outspends his opponent wins four times out of five and adding: 'I firmly believe that poor people should not be allowed to run for public office'. He is eccentric in his attitude to the electoral process – elections are 'simply a marketing job' and he asserts, almost in self-parody, 'It doesn't make any difference to the system who gets elected'. Like Whitaker and Baxter before him he is dismissive of party and party men: the disdain of the professional for the amateur. He takes to an extreme the notion that the election has little to do with the real candidate and in his first campaign actually sent his candidate to Burma on vacation in a gesture of bravado.[35] He apparently believes candidates perform best when they are invisible!

Evry is clear about the influence of race and religious bias, so that in New York each ticket must have racial balance since ethnics vote for each other (political persuaders use these factors without being overt). His polling assesses the extent of the prejudice, unmasking it without the overt statement that people would never admit to: for example people are asked whether they would like to see a minority group moving into their neighbourhood.[36] Clearly such techniques were important to Evry, since in the 1970 gubernatorial elections he acted as George Wallace's consultant and needed to engage in some image surgery. One particular refinement of polling Evry introduced was the employment of animal images – was a candidate an elephant? A hyena?

Thus he was the first to make political polling humorous, and like all consultants engaged in gimmicks, having candidates throw symbolic coins across stretches of water, teabags into it, and so on. He stresses name recognition – one campaign simply consisted of the slogan, 'Three cheers for Pat Milligan', and that was all; the candidate won. These methods bear some comparison with consumer marketing: among consultants connections with the world of commercial marketing with its greater facts and certitudes, and larger tedium, are never far away.[37]

Joe White[38]

Another generation of consultants is well represented by the Democrat self-described 'campaign fixer' Joe White, a McGovern graduate. Deeply influenced by Schwartz, his advertising carries a powerful moral message such as the 'Republican' lady claiming that the Republicans were cutting her social security; or the war memorial with the message that when old men cover up the truth, young men pay. Commitment does not restrain him from being politically adroit: one of his gubernatorial candidates, a man with a stutter, won thanks to a campaign which turned this disadvantage into an asset with the candidate explaining what a handicapped childhood was like, how one had to work three times as hard at everything, and with the unscripted words of an eighty-five-year-old widow endorsing him.

For White, good negative advertising is not perceived by voters as negative. In 1986 he found it difficult to use negative advertising because of popular criticism and public hypersensitivity to fairness. Today, Democrats do not stress party affiliation in their advertising: but White criticises the 'trend' of conservative and western Democrats who 'out-Republican the Republicans' – this will not work, since voters recognise who the real Republicans are. The positioning strategy of a Democrat political message should be: these people are not unlike you, they understand your lives and don't represent radical change.

White regards the dimensions of monetary involvement in American campaigning as a mixed blessing. However, he asserts that the voters manipulate the politicians more than politicians manipulate voters. He believes that the cost of campaigning should indeed be

regulated, but that the Supreme Court will never permit limitations
that they perceive as reducing free speech. Moreover there is the
argument that able people can raise enough: thus his candidate
Harriet Woods raised three million dollars, all in small donations
averaging $100, and since no one can give more than $1000 the
process is more 'democratic' than when nominating procedures were
controlled.

The consultants present an almost theatrical contrast in personalities:
they have nothing in common. The witty, urbane Severin admires
David Garth but could not be more unlike his old mentor. Then there
is Schwartz, a sage Buddha, sad and delightful in turn; White, his
protégé, youthful, reflective, idealistic without being ideological and
Garth himself, sentimental and irrepressible. The competent and
corporate David Sawyer intimates none of the drama of Roger Ailes,
a strong, certain man, and neither resembles Joseph Napolitan. One
contrast, however, is noteworthy, between the intuitive approach of
the elder generation, the political commitment of the middling and
the clinical technocracy of the youngest (represented by Philips of
Aristotle Industries). The younger consultants specialise in campaigning technology. Thus the 'Campaign Manager' service from
Aristotle Industries offers the following products: candidate scheduling; direct mail fund-raising; campaign budgeting; 'accurate' polling;
media buying; 'precinct targeting'; file cards; treasurer's report;
opposition research; voter list services; constituent service software;
videos.

CONCLUSIONS

Do consultants, like so many of the tools of political marketing,
increase public scepticism? Do they fortify the image of a comprom-
ised public life as they question the integrity of opponents and expand
matters out of proportion? It might be argued by some that they do in
fact sharpen political debate; by others that they create a sort of
comic-strip politics in their grotesque over-simplifications. But possibly a dangerous inexperience can enter the political system at a high
level, one which lacks those apparently intuitive recognitions which

1. 9.2.84. Popeye: Vice-President George Bush, visiting Norfolk Naval Base to commemorate the 40th anniversary of his rescue at sea.

. The Invisible Hand. Bob Teeter, Roger Ailes and Lee Attwater discuss the campaign.

3. August 16, 1988. One for the Gipper. (*The Times*)

4. Head and shoulders. George Bush TV commercial.

(*above*)   Two-Dimensional
Man. (*The Times*, August
15, 1988)

(*right*) Cartoon from *The
New Yorker*, February 8,
1988.

*"Listen, pal! I didn't spend seven million bucks to
get here so I could yield the floor to you."*

7. Hail and Farewell: The Revd Jackson speaks.

8. Cartoon © *The Chicago Tribune*.

9. (*left*) Bland, Blond, Bond. Turning Mr Bond's assets to liabilities.

10. Demonstration in Atlanta, July 21, 1988.

THE UNCOMMERCIAL

There's not one spot our reel that looks like a typical mmercial. And we're proud of it.

Video Base International ializes in spots where the thing you need is mmercial look.

We design the kind olitical spot that the voters eive as credible. The kind of that meets their unconscious ctations about television.

he kind of spot that vs them to *feel* andidate as they learn t the candidate.

We have a lot of respect ne candidates we work for.

We know how to convey that conviction to people who know the candidate only through our spots.

We're award-winning producer-directors who know how to create the "documercial," the uncommercial.

So, if you have 30 seconds (or more) that you want to look like *60 Minutes,* call the experts at Video Base International.

VIDEO BASE INTERNATIONAL
250 West 57th Street
Suite 1110 • NY 10019/NY
212-641-9811

SALLY HUNTER
President

11. (*left*) Political television from 'The Uncommercial' (Video Base International).

12. June 9, 1988, Houston, Texas. 'My Fellow Americans . . .'

13. A wider shade of pale. (*Daily Mail*)

14. Meet me in St Louis, August 6, 1988.

15. Through the Looking Glass, September 4, 1988. (*Sunday Telegraph*)

16. (*left*) Ecce Homo: mural by prison inmates, New Orleans.

17. (*left*) 'Lest Auld Acquaintance...' Cleveland, September 26, 1988, Democratic Candidate Michael Dukakis closes his rally speech in Cleveland's Public Square.

are not intuitive at all, but the consequence of sustained pragmatic experience.

All of American politics now, however, exhibits a professionalism – gone are the eccentrics; but in another sense the conscious marketing of politics has led to an avoidance of the further reaches of extremisms: 'issues' are fomented mischievously, but racial and other kinds of excess will be avoided. Voters are now influenced, however, by specialists in the art of manipulation: the traditional politician and his crony the traditional party boss was never this subtle. Theirs were well-thumbed tricks of the trade and part only of a larger public role, so they never acquired the guile of the modern consultant. But the argument can be made that the consultant is a much more innocent figure than this, an interpreter of public will and temperament, an agent for the delivery of what they want.

It is not so easy to claim a qualitative decline in American political life generally, and a risk-free generalisation would be that there has been merely a revolutionary change which has consequences, some good, some evil. Again we observe the moral ambiguity of the new merchandising of candidates. Consultants give the candidate greater freedom from party constraints. Consultants assist the entry of new talent into politics, obviating the need to perform pedantic service to the party and the conspiracy of mediocrity this can lead to. The morality of political consultancy is by no means clear: however easy consultants are as targets of satire, whatever the temptation to lather them with sarcasm, how we evaluate their merit or otherwise is a function of political philosophy, and a perception of politics as having more to do with the realm of symbolism, exhortation and accommodation, rather than honourable administration, would award consultants a critical if not a righteous role in modern politics. Much depends on the degree to which we accept the legitimacy of political marketing and whether it fits our conception of the democracy. It could be said that they do no harm as they counteract each other and both sides to a fight will probably employ them. While this is true it does not alter the fact that they change the nature of political debate in the United States.

8 Washington's Space Cadets: The Centrality of Polling, Computer and Other Technologies in US Politics Today

'In the absence of great parties, the United States swarm with lesser controversies; and public opinion is divided into a thousand minute shades of difference upon questions of detail.'

Alexis de Tocqueville, *Democracy in America*

COMPUTERS

The advent of the computer enables a greater clarity of segmentation, and illustrates both the transforming power and political consequence of the new technology and the indispensability of professional advice, with real power going to those who purvey it; the right with their business linkages became the first fully to integrate such technologies. Political marketing and its antecedent, propaganda, are really technology-led, and such technology demands the leasing of a specialised expertise which has to be paid for. The progress is towards the elusive ideal of ever-refined segmentation. For segmentation is a key element in marketing since we derive our political identity from major social groupings we belong to.

The techniques used to determine ethnicity, a major element, are often very cunning. The computer can remove very rare names from lists; it is told what names belong to what countries and then goes through the list picking and sorting into groups. It can be used to choose Black names, once Hispanic names are subtracted from lists of their areas (this was done by Los Angeles Mayor Tom Bradley in his 1982 gubernatorial campaign). It is also for example possible to get a list of upwardly mobile Hispanics[1] by combining census data with driver's licence holders and a programme that sorts out Hispanic names. According to Richard Wirthlin, 'information is power. It could restore some of the party's central role'.[2] *Business Week* claimed: 'They know where voters live, what they spend, what they eat, and even the colour of their collars'.[3] Computers enable perpetual campaigns to be conducted through their facility for digesting and categorising quantities of rough-hewn data. A further method is to identify Blacks by combining uniquely Black first names with certain surnames, and this is especially important for areas where Blacks are integrated with whites,[4] while computers have even been used to identify gays[5] by picking out people of the same sex and different names in areas popular with homosexuals. Geography is an important variable.[6] According of Frank L. Tobe to Blow, Tobe and Associates, 'a good number of the 11 000 surnames we identified as being Jewish in Los Angeles can be German in Wisconsin'.

Pollsters gather, and computers process, political market intelligence. Without the computer, many of the other political marketing techniques and technologies we discuss would be redundant, for it can sort out the data and provide a mobile picture of public opinion and the relevant breakdowns: strategy can be fine-tuned. The computer enables and encourages a much more intense focus in the short term, an expediency, since it brings into view such a detailed picture. The computer is vital in the perpetual campaign since it enables masses of research and polling to be assimilated, correlated and interpreted. Without computers polling would be much more difficult to use – the task of disaggregation would be so laborious that its political utility would be much weaker.

Computers are employed to make telephone calls in the all-important drive to voter registration, so that the Republicans were aiming to register two million voters by the election: they telephoned over 20 million potential voters, often via computer and recorded solicitations. The claim is that the computer-operated system is as effective as volunteer labour, much less expensive and more smoothly administered (there is good evidence for this). In one example, nearly 11 000 people were registered out of over 75 000 initial (computer) calls.

Key factors of modern mediums are the volume of information digested and the speed and volume of its transmission. Reagan's people for example possessed 75 000 items on Walter Mondale. They could be relayed instantly to local operations: local party headquarters could give the local media the latest information, and it would also be receivable on board the presidential aircraft.

There is a temptation to cynicism in observing how marketing techniques and technologies magnify all the vices of the traditional politician; for politics all this remains, soliciting every sector and merchandising the appropriate promise, well matched to the characteristics of America with its regions, ethnic groups and so on.

COMPUTERS AND PINS

Reagan's pollster, Richard Wirthlin, and his associates acted exactly like the research agency of a corporation. They developed a computerised election simulation called PINS (Political Information System). Demographic and other data on states, together with the results of constant deep-probing polls (300 interviews, 150 detailed interviews per day) were engorged by the computer system, and those polls were conducted among all relevant segments – housewives, middle-aged blue-collar workers and so on.[7] Census data on age, sex and race, government statistics on unemployment, economic condition and the rest, details of party-registered voters, all were fed into this system, plus analysis by campaign directors and information on voting behaviour in past elections and on the amounts of money spent in the relevant county by Democrats.[8] Periodically samples of about 1000 Americans were taken, with the details of other Republican polls, and polling results are ready in Washington first thing the following morning.[9]

Simulation is more significant in political than in conventional marketing, for the condensed time period of a campaign leaves a politician no time to recover from his mistakes; simulation encourages aggression by pinpointing the opportunities for attack. Computer simulation was first tried at an early stage. In 1960, 48 state contests were simulated using 480 voter categories, and this was predicated on attitude-change theory in psychology, that is, that people attempt to hold consistent attitudes towards related subjects. This exemplified sophisticated political usage of high technology. In addition to these elements, PINS incorporated the collective judgement of political experts so that intellectual input could influence other data; opinions were given a mathematical weight and so there remained a strong qualitative input: for the human and judgemental elements were not being entirely abolished, and such 'experts' also included those with strong specific knowledge about a particular county, and into the PINS system went diagnoses of the strength of the Republican campaign in each state and assessments of voter motivation.[10] The computer enables an especial sensitivity to be accorded to those local and regional factors so important in US politics.[11] By 1980 the ability of PINS to adjust to the impact of certain variables had been greatly improved and it could now gauge how electors would react to specific character perceptions. The simulation was also used to test the ideas of in-house political experts so that the PINS system told what groups to court and instant tactical decisions were possible on its results. For example, after the first of the Mondale–Reagan debates support among the 18–30 group, previously rather Reaganite, dropped and Reagan quickly emphasised visits to young audiences in his schedule.[12] What is especially important about the PINS system is that each state contains a specialised contest with a specific identity and the system is able to reflect this idiosyncrasy. Information is produced in diagrammatic form for the campaign's strategic decision-makers.

By 1980, then, PINS had become a more powerful weapon. The US Census Department had proved obliging, selling conveniently packaged and well-dissected census data. Wirthlin had employed PINS in hundreds of congressional elections; it now had an error rate of one per cent in the prediction of victors. During the preceding years Wirthlin's company, DMI, had been engaged in a deep-seated exploration of underlying public attitudes. The yearning for 'leadership' was central, and Wirthlin was able to spell out exactly what the American public meant by leadership and expected from it. PINS illustrated clearly that the key to a Reagan victory in 1980 would be the steady attrition of Carter's 'nice' image. So Republican strategists had to provoke him: malevolence had to be aroused and made publicly demonstrable, and the other strategic objective was to concentrate on leadership, yet also illuminate Reagan as a man of peace. This latter was not easy. The strategy set forth by PINS dictated the particular tactics employed by Reagan. Central to this was the manufacture of euphemisms, just as consumer product advertising invents labels to change perception: 'peace posture' became the substitute for 'defence posture', 'margin of safety' replaced 'arms race'. Reagan adopted a 'reasonable' tone of voice and logical-sounding arguments. This cool image was enhanced by Carter's rising aggression; by remaining at ease Reagan could appear more credible and 'peaceful', and this is exactly what he did: merchandising defined his dramaturgic role. In campaigning personally Carter induced the 'meanness factor', especially when Reagan by contrast deliberately remained unprovoked.

Hence at the start of the campaigning in 1980 half at least of America's voters feared Reagan's militaristic aggressive posture: his pollsters told him to use the word 'peace' at least five times in every speech. He did. It worked.[13] By Mr Reagan's second Presidential campaign the PINS system had been developed into a major strategic weapon, far more sophisticated than the 1980 prototype (which accurately predicted Reagan's surprise winning margin one week before the election and induced him to divert $5 million from California and Texas, since it showed his strength there; it also revealed Carter's difficulties in the South and West).[14]

But marketing is a live information system. In those final weeks the polls sent alarm signals to the Reagan camp: superficially Carter appeared to be rising and three weeks before the election he rivalled Reagan in the polls. Wirthlin however regarded such developments as illusory; he had planned the television advertising campaign for the last weeks and counted on the histrionic abilities of his candidate and the damaging of Carter's image. In the event he was proved right. He knew that once sufficient credibility had been built up for Reagan direct attacks on Carter could commence, and he repaired a fatal Reagan flaw, the tendency to reveal ignorance under interrogation and blunder in the act of talking spontaneously. Stuart Spencer was appointed special political adviser, a kind of overseer, and Wirthlin himself superintended the speeches. Resources, diverted from the Midwest, could also be concentrated on pivotal Southern states in those final weeks: thus does communications technology now dictate the whole campaign. Reagan began to advance in the South, the Carter heartland, and soon he himself was descending from aeroplanes all over the South, while television revealed him speaking intimately to a camera in a clutter of advertisements. Only later would the more difficult states be attacked, when Reagan's image, and that of Carter, was fully clarified there in the ways the Reagan camp wanted. The Democrats possessed nothing like PINS and again they were seen to be far less mature in campaign technology, the result of former complacency.[15]

Republicans had been using the fruits of their direct mail solicitations[16] for major investment in computers and the strategy had paid dividends, though this is not to claim that the Democrats were themselves computer illiterate and did not make extensive use of them; indeed they possessed the names and addresses of well over one-third of all Americans, but they used computers for less ambitious objectives – voter registration, fund-raising and scheduling campaign appearances.

Is the kind of election that is a consequence of this a truer kind of democracy, one more exactly judged, or a coarse mechanism for manipulation? Certainly the question is at the heart of the ethical debate on political marketing, which may be viewed as encouraging aggressive and cynical strategies but in another sense as democratic since it uses popular wants as the starting-point (but what electorates crave in the short term may not necessarily be an ultimate good).

Does the electoral employment of a computer enable a new form of social control, or rather is it a means for interpreting the national will? Clearly such work draws from people's registered perceptions, yet it is also strategic in that it indicates that such beliefs can be changed to get the candidate elected.

THE LOCAL CAMPAIGN

We observe the universality now of the technology of political marketing, its employment at the bottom of the system and the automation of all campaigns. For computers now influence local contests. Small ones have had an impact at the parochial level,[17] for they can be used to deploy volunteers, manage direct mail campaigns, locate key segments of support for all the 492 000 elective offices in the United States (including 20 000 mayoralties). One senior citizen candidate used computers to target older voters and direct mail at them: the appeal worked and he won his race.[18] Computers have significant democratic potential since they do of course lower campaigning costs, and in that sense they go against many of the trends generated by the adoption of marketing which we have discussed, which are towards elitism and expense: the lowest level race can replicate everything that is done in the highest race.[19] A new generation of microcomputers and programs has appeared since the elections in 1982, and these cost from $2500 upwards, pointing out the cheapness of the technology[20] on which modern political marketing depends to achieve the localisation and segmentation so necessary to it. Specialised political programmes are even available, and computers with their massive amounts of data categorised and dissected, their lists of names and all the rest, potentially give the local campaigners almost as much information as senatorial candidates or the party high command. Programmes for personal computers can schedule the candidate's appearances, co-ordinate volunteers and target critical areas of the constituency: thus, in Harvey Gent's Charlotte mayoralty[21] race, voter turn-out was high compared with past figures since apathetic voters were being specifically singled out; he became the city's first Black mayor.

Certainly the old-time party boss once attempted to do all this. He relied on his gut instinct, a sometimes formidable institution and one he invariably regarded as infallible. Computers therefore have subtracted a pleasant illusion from politics.

Even for the local council men, technology is geared for the permanent campaign. The IBM personal computer can perform tasks that formerly cost $20 000 to $30 000 and computer software programmes have also been developed for smaller campaigns. The first, 'Campaign Manager', appeared in 1983:[22] 'The $750 program runs everything from fundraising to poll analysis in International Business Machines's Corp.'s Personal Computer and Apple Computer Inc.'s Apple II family of personal computers'. There should be a market, since half a million candidates stand for election every two years, while one candidate–businessman is developing a programme to help candidates to stay in office once they get there by emphasising supporter opinion and the way electorates are thinking.[23]

ETHICS

Such technological developments have populist import, for by pandering to public sentiment the political system could be capable of some over-reaction and susceptibility to the calls of demagoguery, and while the idealised statesman of democratic tradition has always detached himself from the immediate emotion and looked to the long-term consequence, the characteristics of the new methods are an impulsion towards the immediate, a reversion to political adolescence. Political marketing and its technological articulation can conceal real intentions, fine-tuning the lie.

But if marketing as a concept is rooted in the search for what people actually want, in a sense people manipulate themselves; the ethical problem here is that however superficially manipulative political marketing appears, it is really their own desires that people have bizarrely reflected back at them – a self-parody.

The tendency of merchandised politics is to promote the personality factor: its provocations could induce entirely the wrong judgemental criteria in electorates, making opponents show the kinds of frailty that are really irrelevant to their effectiveness as elected officials, but not to a system that evaluates solely on image. Carter's vacillations and weaknesses for example were real political flaws; but can the same be said of his 'meanness' which although made a central issue was hardly significant to the realm of presidential policy making? Merchandised elections have therefore changed the conventional political criteria for use in a democracy.

Critics would say that the consequence of the electoral use of technology is the creation of an image-centred politics which is often irrelevant to the conduct of policy, frivolous, and a species of theatre, and also making for an adversarial system so strong that no one can emerge from it whole, a politics whose perpetual focus is on the feet of clay. Marketing has to create contrasts to succeed; the 'product' must shine against a drab background, and political marketing may breed a disenchantment which cannot be good for the future wholeness of democracies.

Computer machinery and software do also contribute to the high marketing costs of political campaigning. The machines must be bought or leased, programmes purchased from specialists, users trained or hired. Yet with computers essential for all campaigns the volunteer and the activist are made less necessary. Traditionally they reported back their canvass returns and supplied personal evaluations based on comments received, but the computer supports this latter function and this is a gain to the parties since party workers were always notoriously optimistic in their assessments and people would often tell what they wanted to hear.

Direct, physical participation is going. Could this affect public attitudes to politics in the long term? The point is speculative. However, with this diminishing human involvement and its synthetic substitute in armchair activism, loyalties become weaker, and Americans might see negative changes in attitudes as citizens cease to feel collective responsibility for the actions of politicians. High-tech electioneering may be conducive to greater public apathy. Yet this is not necessarily the end of the story. Some would measure political worth by the success of a politician and programme in the redistribution of surplus resources. They would neglect the histrionic function of politics which is arguably a more central one. It is also a function which marketing technologies facilitate, but which is suspect to many commentators since it is located in the dreamy world of inspiration, symbolism, rhetoric, leadership and the confection of contemporary myths.

The computer is literally a machine for running political campaigns. Today's party activists are trained not in public speaking and door-to-door technique but in programming computers, and this resembles the graduation of warfare from the age of hand-to-hand combat to that of push-button war. Hence, anaesthetised of the personal sparkle, the volunteer does not direct his enthusiasm straight to another individual but to a keyboard. This is robot electioneering. Little perhaps do electors suspect how they are dissected and scrutinised with all the thoroughness of a military operation.

It is possible though to conceive this process in overly mechanistic terms, for in the end these computer-assisted directives need a person capable of expressing through manner, voice and language what it is that electors are seeking: so personality may remain at the centre of the political stage. Yet the word 'stage' here is apposite. The qualities called for are those of delivery, the qualities of an actor. There is something mildly chilling about the redundancy of the more traditional skills in such a context. The PINS system is tailor-made for Ronald Reagan and under a different candidate such as George Bush would be much less of the mighty asset it has been for him.

None the less, PINS was still rooted in the democratic approach and it is arguably mistaken to perceive it as sinister, since its counsel was a derivative of public opinion; moreover it was open to the Democrats to create a system similar to PINS, and in Caddell they have had an extraordinarily adept pollster. Their failure lay in the inability of their candidates to communicate effectively what their polls had counselled, a failure of histrionics. We could also claim that the PINS approach is a fair one since it incorporates a heterogeneity of public opinion, so that the resulting political messages and legislative agenda are addressed to the political aspirations of many of the key groups in society, and it is inherently anti-elitist.

Computers also demand specialised expertise to organise and run them for political purposes, so that once again the politician is dependent on the consultant, especially in the more sophisticated higher-level campaigns. Thus computers give power to those who really know how to exploit them well, and Richard Wirthlin himself is a good example of this.

POLLING METHODS

Polling provides the nutrition on which the computers feast. It is performed by consultants or by their professional subcontractors. The supremacy of polling in America's campaigns justifies employment of the phrase 'political marketing'. For the essence of marketing is reciprocity: the firm should not manufacture what is convenient, rather, it consults that market and works the confusion of wants into a saleable product. Politics has taken the same route. People themselves set the agenda and define the parameters of policy, they become represented less by the verbalists in Congress than by others exactly like them who are selected for the pollster's interrogation. However the pollster becomes a strategist, not merely a technician,[24] since the data need interpreting and the scope of choice has to be clarified. Polling has become one of the central institutions of the permanent campaign: according to Patrick Caddell, 'Essentially it is my thesis that governing with public approval requires a continuing campaign'.[25] Polling gives a salience to issues that would otherwise be neglected. Provision of a central sophisticated polling service could also help to revive the parties.

Polling also facilitates a segmentation approach to the political market since it is able to give shape to the inchoate mass of public opinion, to divide and sub-divide it, so that the attitudes of each politically significant segment are known, and such knowledge is incorporated into the framing of policy.

Polling is commissioned by American candidates to gauge the dimensions of voter opinion; the polls illuminate new strategic areas for possible assault and they attempt to rate the issues voters regard as important and their opinion of the candidate; they can highlight those areas where he is perceived negatively. They demonstrate how effective his advertising has been. Louis Harris, who acted as adviser to John F. Kennedy, was the first to develop polling in strategic ways. But he was by no means the first political pollster, for in 1932 George Gallup had conducted a poll for his mother-in-law who was running as Iowa Secretary of State,[26] and in 1946 Roper conducted one for Jacob Javits in New York. Amateur polls have sometimes been conducted with considerable humour. The Blevins Pop Corn Poll came within 3.3 per cent of Kennedy's winning margin in 1960: people at theatres would buy popcorn boxes decorated with pictures of either of the Presidential candidates.[27]

PROCESS OF POLLING

Sabato delineates the process of American political polling in some detail.[28] A general survey is conducted well before the election to establish with broad brush-strokes the public perceptions of the candidates, issue salience and so on, until further polls search more deeply into all of these areas. Segments of the electorate whose allegiance is in some way critical to victory are polled and analysed in depth, and during the campaign brief polls are taken in response to the issues that arise; panel surveys may also be introduced. Some of the participants in a previous poll are subsequently reinterrogated to chart the fluctuations of opinion over time. The maximum size of a sample tends to be around 1500.

Polling proceeds in many ways exactly like the consumer market research from which it is derived. Polling must commence with the sampling unit. This defines who is consulted, that is, the population of interest, and selecting the wrong population leads to the wrong results. Sampling procedure determines how the sample of respondents is to be selected, and the basic choice is between probability and non-probability sampling. The various kinds of probability sampling include, first, random sampling, but this presupposes that each member of the population can be located and selected in the same way, and it is expensive. Systematic sampling is an alternative, and consists of choosing every nth unit (for example, every tenth house in a street): the danger is of the selection coinciding with some periodic event that biases the result. Next there is stratified sampling and this involves dividing the population into strata such as demographic categories, and drawing random samples from each stratum. Area (cluster) sampling divides the population into areas; a number are then selected at random and a proportion of the sample is selected from within the areas chosen, but this method demands far more people than the others.[29]

The other kind of sampling is non-probability sampling, and here quota sampling is the major approach; the interviewer is given a description of the types to interview and the number required, and this freedom to select respondents gives rise to unknown biases: thus statistical analysis cannot legitimately be used to estimate the probable error and the gulf between target and sampled populations may be very wide. All proposed studies and reports need to be evaluated against the criteria of: relevance, adequacy, cost in relation to usefulness, timeliness, presentation and user orientation.

Sampling methods include interrogation, and this assumes of course that the audience is accessible and willing. Various kinds of interview are available. In the structured interview, there is a set wording and sequence of questions and thus the freedom of the respondent in replying is limited, while questions are simple, concrete and unambiguous, and answers are frequently to be given in yes/no terms. There are also unstructured interviews, such as free association where respondents just give free rein to their thoughts, or focussed interviews, where there are formalised introductory questions but otherwise respondents are at liberty to answer as they wish. However, unstructured interviews are very expensive and the results are difficult to code and interpret; yet they do bring out the respondents' categories.

The actual design of the questionnaires is very important. This is something of an art, and various factors can bias replies; to check the consistency of replies questions are often repeated in a different form, for example in questions on drinking we do not know the frame of reference being used by the respondent. Answers reflect what the subject thinks is being asked. Nimmo describes the typical questionnaire as comprising: validation data, then filtering of the questions to gauge the respondent's political awareness, information questions, unstructured questions that encourage free comment but elude easy analysis, explanation questions and structured interview questions.[30] One method of survey is to use the mail. This has the merit of cheapness but the disadvantages of a low rate of return; there is a need to sample some of the non-respondents by personal or telephone interview to gauge whether and in what way they might differ from those who responded. Then during the campaign groups of people are rung every night to garner further intelligence.

IMPACT OF POLLING

The results of polling have profoundly affected many a campaign. Thus a Democratic image of corruption, charted in the polls, impelled Milton Shapp to run as a 'man against the machine' candidate in the 1966 Pennsylvania Democratic gubernatorial primary, and in a Texas campaign polls recommended 'warmth' and moderation for George Bush; posters subsequently showed him with a jacket over his shoulder and on film a child ran into his arms. In Texas the polls also told Senator Tower to become more moderate, so his opposition to the Medicare Bill was explained on the grounds that he wanted a better answer, while race was not made an issue since the polls counselled that any stance would antagonise more voters than it would attract.[31] Caddell's polls told McGovern that he would not be able to recover from the Eagleton affair.[32] On the advice of pollsters, Edward Kennedy focussed his first senatorial campaign on a reassurance strategy to show experience and information: no mean achievement for a thirty-year-old.

Polling has proved critical at the highest strategic levels of the most important campaigns. Polling heavily influenced Carter's 1976 election strategy.[33] It told him which groups to court, and in his public utterances he would continually reel off their names. It told him where his support was weak – young mothers, for instance, perceived him as 'fierce' and 'cold' and therefore mistrusted him. In particular, Caddell's polls threw into sharp relief the alienation factor in the South: he needed the Wallace anti-Washington constituency and solicited it with the slogan 'Send them a President'. Carter sought a strategic coalition of southern rightists and northern liberals. Daily polls picked out a dangerous flaw in the first Carter campaign, his vagueness, and his advertisements quickly became very clear, just as the opposition were about to strike; and according to Caddell President Ford's polling had 'double or triple the reaction time to new voter moods'.[34] After the election Caddell advised Carter, again on the basis of his polls, to jettison some of the pomp of the Presidency, institute fireside chats, town meetings and so on; and he gave Carter protracted warning of trouble ahead.

The polling fed into Wirthlin's PINS system, without which that system could not operate, dictated the entirety of Reagan's 1980 campaign.[35] The strategy was predicated upon a need for Reagan to explain clearly and constantly exactly where he stood rather than play the more distant role that Sears, the manager of his 1976 campaign, had wanted, since polling revealed widespread ignorance about Reagan. Polling uncovered Reagan's critical deficiences: as Wirthlin told him: 'Governor, you are seen as dangerous and uncaring, and a potential warmonger'. There are countless other examples of the impact of polling on campaigns.[36] Thus Representative Helstoki, finding that 70 per cent of electors were against his wish to stop the bombing of Vietnam in 1966, simply dropped the issue, while the future Senator Brooke, then a senatorial candidate, reversed a dramatic decline in his popularity by condemning protest violence, and he became the first Black senator. Yet another election revealed great antagonism to Washington politicians, thus establishing a localist–populist theme for the campaign.

Polling has of course actually affected political events. Candidates may withdraw as a result of polling, as did Governor George Romney from the New Hampshire presidential primary. Polls also help stimulate campaign workers. Polling has especially strong influence in primary campaigns, yet Harris could at one time claim, 'No poll I have every been witness to has made the candidate a different man, has changed his position on an issue, has made him what he is not'.[37] Nimmo describes what he perceives as the vicious cycle of modern campaigning: that media exposure affects poll results, poll results affect fund-raising, fund-raising affects media exposure.

Polling has been employed in several imaginative strategic ways. After the 1968 election the Republicans used polling in key congressional districts (the cost of $400 000 was supported by the American Medical Political Action Committee). The polls suggested strategies for the key constituencies – the setting up of front committees, research, early candidate selection, gradual introduction and so on. Polling can also be used to determine the candidate most fitting for the type of constituency.

There are many instances where polling results should have influenced the campaign, but the myopia and disbelief of politicians prevented it. Thus the pollster Joseph Napolitan urged Hubert Humphrey to deviate from President Johnson's Vietnam policy; his advice was rejected. Carter again proved insensitive to polling once in office, and maladroit in turning its advice into political action and communication. Caddell's pollings, which delineated an intense but non-focussed national malaise, prompted Carter's televised 'crisis of confidence' speech which boosted his popularity by 11 per cent, but like so much in the Carter administration this proved to be empty symbolism, a tactical move not integrated with any overall strategic coherence. Hence there was no further working out of this critical theme in his period of office. But these are all rather dated examples, for politicians now exhibit a respect bordering on servility for the technology and this should perhaps alarm: they could become its prisoner, suspending that crucial exercise of political judgement which has been the test of statecraft down the years.

Without polling and computers, the concept of the perpetual campaign would be redundant, for it is predicated upon the counsel of polling data. Polling provides the raw intelligence and computers process it, politicians and their consultants proceed to interpret it in terms of policy initiatives and symbolic strategies, and this private use of polling remains the one most concealed from the public. But it enables politicians to appear in touch and to make elections last for ever.

LIMITATIONS OF POLLING

However, political polling is still a crude device with serious limitations, and little of the sophistication we associate with consumer market research. Often polls fail to measure the degree of commitment to a candidate, or whether the voter will turn out on the day, or the potential impact of issues; nor do they do much in the way of segmentation analysis – with whom, and when, the candidate is likely to have the most success – and specific issues may not have been considered by voters, while they may also have trouble ranking them in importance.

What of the accuracy of polls? According to Nimmo: 'If the sample is properly drawn it is possible to reduce the range of sampling errors so that in 99 out of 100 cases the results of a survey of 100 properly-selected adults will be within 4 per cent of accuracy. To cut the sample error in half, the size of the sample must be increased four times'.[38] Moreover there is always the possibility of sample error. Nor does a poll measure the emotional intensity with which views are held and internalised[39] – a factor if we wish to deduce who will actually turn out and vote. Many people today refuse to be interviewed or are elusive (the rate is 40–55 per cent for home polling and 25–35 per cent using the telephone); a further 20 per cent are evasive in their replies, and these figures illustrate the magnitude of the task of finding an accurate sample, since non-respondents could include critical segments of the target population.[40] Interviewers may be ignorant and seek to disguise the fact; hence, one-third of people had firm opinions of the (phantasmagorical) 1975 Public Affairs Act, and another poll claimed that 77 per cent of interviewees were unable to name the two countries engaged in the Salt II negotiations.[41] Further, the phrasing and numbering of the questions can virtually predetermine the response. Another problem is that 5–10 per cent are undecided and others may change their minds. And the interview 'is a contrived situation in which the respondent plays an unfamiliar role'.[42] At the primary level, the meaning of poll results may be particularly difficult to interpret.

Polling is also faddish. Shoals of pollsters, each offering a unique formula, descend on every election. They are the itinerant quacks, the medicine men, of America's campaigns and the market for political marketing is indeed large.

It is important to test out a questionnaire on a group for meaning, so that we know how people perceive the questions and, therefore, gain a more accurate poll. Polling has severe negatives: how the pollsters word the question is in fact critical, and very much an art, and differences in words and wording change data by a range between 10 and 40 per cent.[43] With reference to Great Britain, Butler and Kavanagh point out how different wordings of similar questions elicited different responses: for example, Labour's advantage on 'unemployment' (13 per cent) was higher than on 'jobs' (7 per cent).[44] Vital information could be missing, especially if the refusals coincide with important segments of the market; for example, those not answering the door could be precisely the ones most concerned about law and order. It is of course possible to get precisely the answer desired if the question is phrased in the right way; for instance a majority of people may want more spent on the old, the needy and so on, but a majority will also object to more taxes. Such polling could be used dishonestly for propaganda purposes and popular confusion about polling makes its unethical use relatively easy. However the political candidate in his private poll is concerned with eliciting the truth, to provide a realistic picture of his situation, and thus he should take care over the form and format of the questions.

Bias can easily infiltrate, and the order and sequence in which questions are given is important. On significant questions there may be a need for a check question to ensure that replies are the same, and if they are not an explanation is needed. Whether the voter actually turns out on the day is critical, for if he is not going to do so everything he says and thinks will be redundant, and in the United States even during a Presidential election half the people do not vote. And non-participation is much higher for local elections.

The potential impact of issues is also important: issues which have not come up in the campaign but might – what do the public think about them? Good potential issues for a candidate, or threatening ones, can be gauged in this way and the relevant exercises in damage limitation prepared. There is also the problem of how to treat the 'don't knows', for a high percentage of them can result in bias, so that the wording of the question is crucial here. Only judiciously designed questionnaires can mitigate the above problems; otherwise results can be misleading for the candidate seeking a focus for his campaign; for example people may be reluctant to admit that they do not intend to vote since this is perceived as socially irresponsible. Pollsters must therefore indicate indifference to the morality of non-voting if they are to obtain accurate response. Then there may also be problems of methodology. Gallup for example did not return when voters were not at home: instead he used the somewhat dubious method of weighing more heavily those found at home, at times abnormal for them. This is rather suspect.

The objective of polling is in part to identify the ticket splitters, often the voters who claim to be undecided during the election campaign itself; elections can be won or lost by the ticket splitters.[45] Polls can also be very deceitful; in 1966 Governor Romney on campaigning one day shook 265 hands, yet the pollsters found eight hundred people claiming to have experienced the gubernatorial grasp.[46] And polling results can communicate a false message: they easily give an illusion of permanence to what are in fact highly volatile data. Moreover political polling is often rather amateur, indeed fewer than 15 per cent of campaigns employ any type of scientific polling,[47] and most polling firms do not deal primarily with politics but with market research so that the subtleties of politics may elude them; bad practices have abounded in the past since politicians themselves were unskilled at judging what constitutes an effective poll.

Polling has other limitations and misapplications. There is of course the cost, for it is a major item in the campaigning budget: even when Nimmo was writing in 1970 a poll could easily cost $15 000 at $10 per interview.[48] This is one of the many reasons why campaign costs will continue to soar and why America's politics will become increasingly the plaything of America's millionaires; in November 1982 Mayor Koch lavished $100 000 on polling alone in his attempt at the New York governorship. Polling uses a large number of trained researchers, if it is any good. It is another marketing-induced price the politician has to sustain with consequences that will be by now very familiar in the transferral of dependence from parties to external financiers and lobbies and of executive power to other actors. It certainly represents a fragmentation of the old dependency, but also a transfer to entities less representative of the general will than a party was.

However, it is sometimes difficult to use polling as a strategic as distinct from a tactical instrument. The reasons are partly emotional:

swings and negatives in public opinion naturally make the politician anxious to reverse the position, and similarly he is anxious to capitalise on popularity. Polling gives a static picture in moving time, one formed by the latest events: it does not tell the politician about the situation eight months or two years hence. It tells him what he can do to make himself popular now, but not whether such an intiative will help win the election. Moreover it deals with the realm of immediate perception, that is, what people generally diagnose their problems as being. But such issues may not be 'real' in any historical sense, but peripheral: important problems may be missed both by the electors and the media who interpret for them. Polling, therefore, can never transcend popular wisdom.

Polls could sometimes be misused and misinterpreted, leading inevitably to demands for their control during elections. Butler and Kavanagh[49] point out how in Britain the *Daily Express* failed to distinguish sampling variations from genuine change; thus reports of large increases in the Conservative lead alternated with articles on an equally large decline.

Extensive polling has surely induced an obsession with short-term expediency, a playing to the gallery, and the polls give no credit for forward planning, anticipating future calamities, gaining efficiencies which are not trumpeted in the press. So the politics of theatre with its scenic tours and sensational language, its indulgent optimism and stage-managed sudden *coups de main*, really comes into its own age.

OTHER TECHNIQUES

Various technologies and techniques have been conjured up to make polling less art, more science. One method is to ask people to choose from imaginary parties with value-specific labels (such as 'free enterprise'); or there are 'open-ended' interviews; or people may be asked to rate politicians, or to rank problems according to urgency.[50] A further technique used is that of multidimensional scaling, which is a way of depicting the relative importance of components to a decision.[51] Multivariate statistics could be used to establish relationships between variables. The identification of needs would be a useful element to incorporate: attitudes and desires that interviewees may not formally admit to could be more clearly revealed by this. Polling could therefore add richly to the intelligence data available to the candidate, making his fine-tuning more effective, and pollsters will relay precise data on the intensity and location of support so that the candidate can take the necessary action; in Harrison's words, the aim will be to simulate and telescope an entire campaign. Patrick Caddell uses 'trust indices' to measure accurately the degree of voter alienation, on the premise that alienation is a key element in many elections.

It is possible that other techniques of marketing research will be annexed by candidates; polling will thus be supplemented. Motivation research has something to offer; hence in-depth interviewing could establish with much greater clarity the relative significance of issues and the precise nature of responses to candidates: one extreme is the fairly structured approach with predetermined opening questions followed by non-directive probes; the other is the psychoanalytic-type interview designed to explore the emotional context and symbolic meanings associated with ideas, words, candidates and so on. This method has now fallen into disrepute and at best simply suggests hypotheses. Panels akin to consumer discussion groups could better demonstrate how strongly issue positions were adhered to. They may be used to determine voting habits and shifts in voting, but doubts can always be cast on their representativeness: there is a problem of generalising from panel data since its members may develop more sensitivity to politics, and while longer-serving members permit longitudinal studies their behaviour may deviate increasingly from target group behaviour. There is the so-called 'Q-Method', which has the robust merit of cheapness.[52] This involves the detailed interrogation of a group representing segments of the electorate that are of strategic interest to the campaign; they are questioned at length on their attitudes to the candidate, his issue positions and so on, and their replies will illuminate his strengths and deficiencies.

In explaining political behaviour it may even be possible to set up controlled experiments, with the aim of controlling or eliminating 'interference'. 'Control' and 'experimental' groups are set up: analysis of variance may be used to check whether results could have arisen by chance – experiments can be highly corroborative but may still fail to distinguish cause from co-existence.

All these techniques will, in time, be adopted. The American voter will become a kind of microbe under a lens, with each contortion and fitful start observed by the men in grey suits. Amateurism in political campaigns is dying, and market research technology is becoming part of established political lore; people can be trained in it, even acquire it from manuals (for in America every new technique receives instant immortality in a simplified training manual). Polling will be as thoroughly organised as the intelligence operation of a military campaign.

Many surveys are concerned with measuring attitudes using various psychological scales. The 'semantic differential' is one such scale, a multiple-choice questionnaire that measures the meaning to the respondent of whatever is of interest. Thus in the Likert scale the respondent is asked about the extent to which he agrees with a statement on a five-point scale. Often the respondent is given a list of words, such as 'honest', 'cold', 'warm', 'trustworthy', and asked to rate the candidate according to these dimensions, to articulate the positives and negatives about the candidate; key statements, such as 'the candidate really cares about people like me' are evaluated.[53] Fred Currier of Market Opinion Research was one of those who employed the semantic differential. Hence in 1966 in Michigan he found that voters desired a middle-of-the-road candidate in the senatorial campaign: his candidate, a Republican (Robert Griffin) duly obliged and won.[54] And in 1968 the discovery that Americans attached importance to 'warmth' in their President, and perceived Richard Nixon as being without it, led to important changes in his campaign so that humorists were employed and television advertising was conceived to supply that vital heat.

CONCLUSIONS

Some benefits can be discerned from the evolution of polling. The politician will have at his disposal more complete data on what people are seeking – a map of the mental geography of each voting segment that is mobile, changing as their minds change, and this does at least facilitate the political interpretation of what people want. It would therefore be erroneous to dismiss polling as simply another debasing influence on the quality of American political culture, since it transmits to the politician information about what voters want with infinitely more refinement than, say, 'instinct' ever could. However much it leads to a tactical rather than strategic approach to the formation of public policy, its democratic credentials cannot be denied. In former times arbitrary and oppressive government was not necessarily a question of ill-will on the part of the governors. Distance and ignorance made their contributions to policies that alienated, and it follows that now, even if remedies lie only in the realm of symbolism, they are available for any groups in the strategic coalition that undergirds the party in power, and for some outside. The marketing approach, with its focus on a concept of permanent consumer satisfaction flowing from close identification of and attention to their wants, brings something of this flavour when internalised by politicians and applied to politics, for the voter becomes a consumer of political policy, his satisfactions traced and mapped out exactly as if he were being sold a commercial artefact.

However, such a process of constantly scrutinising electors to suggest policy (rather like the high priests of Rome contemplating entrails) takes as its model a somewhat passive voting nation, since initiatives do not emerge from the people, but are made in the people's name according to their investigated opinion. More traditional conceptions of democracy envisaged a more creative mass who would give rise to policy demands on their own initiative, but under marketing's regimen politics becomes a matter of identifying some facile, popular 'will'. In practice this will is changing and sometimes contradictory. But politics is not a product even if it has product-like characteristics: the danger of applying the marketing concept is that in treating politics exactly like a product a dependence on polling could subtract the persuasive and leadership function from politicians, leading to incoherence. Reliant on polling, political market research makes America a more mathematically representative democracy and also a more moribund one.

All methods and technologies, including polling, will mature and limitations will be transcended, for they are in their infancy and the political consulting firms that operate them are still a relatively new phenomenon. And such organisations will evolve a corporate lore of their own, with case studies and so on, and will do some learning from past errors. Nevertheless the exercise magnifies the ability of politicians to control their electorates, for via polling America's candidates possess a kind of blow-up of the elector's face, a gigantic physiognomy whose every nuance is analysed.

OTHER TOOLS

Telephone

Political marketing employs an assortment of other technologies, and again they illustrate how far politics borrows business methods and reinterprets them. Because of the political context and its constitutional implications such methods can attain a legitimacy; commercial telephone solicitation for example may be deemed intrusive, but when the cause is political may have a greater level of acceptance. The politicians have exploited every marketing medium, their aim always to achieve a heightened clarity of segmentation, but in thus paying dearly for the professionals they declare the cosy amateur redundant, and all these modes enable candidates to bypass the party, speeding it on its way not into retirement but possibly to a function more purely symbolic than hitherto.

Thus even the telephone has been annexed by America's political marketers, who use it for polling and canvassing. And fund-raising. Professional operators solicit pledges and play recordings of the candidate, and the sense is of actually speaking to him in the privacy of home. Some telephone campaigns have been notably successful, with McGovern's 1 400 000 calls in California, and Americans for Reagan raising seven million dollars by this device in 1980; Jimmy Carter used the telephone in that year's New Hampshire primary. The telephone was used extensively in the 1960 Nixon campaign, and in 1966 George Romney brought victory in a number of areas by a telephone operation.[55] On election day those who have not voted may be vigorously solicited by telephone, until they do.

As much planning can go into the telephone operation as into any other aspect of the marketing campaign, and the contents of the telephone call are standardised so that each recipient receives the same tailored message, and in the best-run campaigns the operators are professional: experience has shown that their use in preference to volunteers pays dividends. One Carter group found a 5–10 per cent greater turn-out when they used professional operators instead of their own. The operator will be given standard and possibly pre-tested replies to typical questions raised, and also the candidate's issue positions, and new and unanticipated questions will be relayed back so that an answer is available next time. Messages are crafted according to segment.

Moreover telephone messages can be changed daily to incorporate the candidate's reaction to the latest event, as can all the marketing mediums used by politicians – direct mail, television and the rest: they are therefore aptly married to the unpredictability of politics. If the 'product' is issue politics it is more evanescent than the products sold by conventional business, so that political consultants will look for the most malleable mediums to communicate their 'product's' characterististics.

The call itself will last between two and four minutes, with perhaps a minimum of ten voters addressed and thirty or so dialled every hour. The telephone is useful for raising money – for instance by approaching ex-donors, while known party supporters are also solicited – and it is on these occasions that a recording of the candidate might be played, and the taped message could even be made personal to include the recipient's name, for it is the personal note that political marketing constantly tries to attain. The potential target area is large since there are nearly sixty million telephones in the United States, and the cost of soliciting – often several times – an entire state by telephone would be $30 000. Hired expertise is leased to advise on this as on the other mediums, since their successful usage is a professional job.

The telephone is sometimes used in conjunction with direct mail: the mail can be sent to those who register uncertainty on the telephone, and also to get volunteers and contributions from amongst those who have expressed interest during the discussion, while mailing lists can also be created from the telephone campaign – segmented of course according to occupation, location and so on. Hence, in America, if the telephone rings it may not be some favourite aunt but a politician's lackey. Home, the refuge from a brash world, is no longer sacrosanct, and when the telephone rings the voice of the great man of the day may declaim his central message, as it has done on television, radio and through the letter-box.

Like much else in the zoology of political marketing the telephone does not exist only for the end of general persuasion but is targetted at the committed for the purposes of fund-raising and inspiration, so that at election time the politician is properly funded when he is at his most vulnerable, thus precommitting his legislative future to the lobbies that bind him, however much new knowledge and arguments may counsel a change of mind. So merchandised politics become a way of extending the power of faction at the expense of moderacy, and hampering centrifugal trends to broad and encompassing policies.

Yet telephone usage is not normally resented, and it works well if some initial marketing approach has already been made. There is always the possibility of course that some people will greet the telephone trespassers with irritation (especially true in the privacy-minded United Kingdom). A previous approach would appear crucial: and the relationship between politicians and politicised can then evolve in a sort of parody of friendship, and such acceptance may be explained by the fact that this alongside other tools of promotion, particularly direct mail, ministers to the individual's desire to feel needed and involved. Implicit in many marketing approaches is a subtle flattery: the individual is made to feel significant. Arguably the committed actually like to be solicited. We may view the process with cynicism, but it succeeds in giving to many a sense of worth – a society where the bonds of real community were long ago sundered, where all is transition, seems to be creating an electronic community: the 'electronic village' with its populations of relatively permanent celebrities. The familiar faces and voices are not those of our actual friends and neighbours (whom we know only dimly), but those we meet via telephone and screen.

The political operations of one firm, Mega-Dial, help create a sense of urgency that is useful to the persuader – 'Mega-Dial's mission is to highlight something'. All twenty-nine political candidates for whom it worked have won, though this may tell us more about the wealth of those candidates than the persuasiveness of Mega-Dial. But their technology is effective; each machine reaches over 500 homes a day and the firm possesses one thousand machines in total, so that it can reach half a million homes daily, while costs are lower than with human operators – the tape costs $1.09 compared with the $1.80 cost of the live call and the machines can make far more calls. A liberal group, People for the American Way, used telephones effectively in their successful campaign to stop Herbert Ellingwood being made Assistant Attorney General. A total of 100 000 people were sent telegrams, but 12 000 were contacted by Mega-Dial in addition: the response rate of this group was doubled. Telephones were much used in the 1986 campaign; computers dialled voters, who then listened to the voice of Ronald Reagan.

Telephone and the other political marketing devices do broaden the base of active popular democracy, for arguably they increase awareness of issues and spread political involvement beyond the hands of local power elites. But again, the massive cost of telephone campaigning helps to fortify American politics as a rich man's club, and many campaigns simply pick from a *smorgasbord* of marketing devices and hope that everything coheres, a morsel of telephone here, a piece of video there, so that a total campaign emerges with central messages reiterated through several marketing mediums.

If we perceive the politician as essentially a power-motivated extrovert, we know that marketing technology will proffer endless new ways to gratify his passion: he will be able to meet everyone, enter every home, a familiar figure in each community without ever having left the recording stuido. Videophone, the communication toy of the future, would be the ultimate prize. Here the statesman will address you personally, blazoning the good news of his candidacy, and technology will enable one of his myriad electronically-transmitted clones to answer most questions and attempt to assuage doubts.

Radio

In the search for precision selection of targets so necessary in political marketing campaigns, radio is an important ally, paid or unpaid. Again the marketing imperative is to circumvent the party and put over our man as an individual and not a party political symbol.

Radio is a passive medium lacking the aggression and investigative mission of television or the press, and offers many possibilities for tailoring the candidate; more of radio can be bought than of other mediums, and the focus is often more parochial, and although it may still be regarded as a superficial kind of communication it is less so perhaps than television.

Almost since its first beginnings radio has been employed as a political marketing device in the United States, but the more alert candidates are able in effect to advertise freely and they record their own comments on some issue of the moment, ring the station and play back; their gambit has an 80 per cent success rate. Reagan himself rose to prominence on the radio and has maintained it as a weapon in his artillery ever since. Such items of 'hot' news usually last between twenty and forty seconds: they can be sent via the telephone to different radio stations and the air-time is free. Unpaid, disguised marketing is necessarily more effective, since, masquerading as 'news', credulity will be greater than for a formal advertisement, while those who are remote and dispersed over broad territories can be solicited with a regard paid to their special interests that more extravagant tools of marketing could never supply.

Moreover the radio facilitates rapid response, with negative accusations quickly countered or even turned to advantage by a well-tuned riposte (as Ronald Reagan did in New Hampshire), while there is no long time period necessary to negotiate, test and produce advertising with this method of 'news feeding'. Political employment of radio shows how the political marketing approach favours some mediums. Clearly an attractive voice is also a useful attribute for radio, since there are no images to distract attention from vocal quality.

The importance of finely-segmented marketing mediums is clear, and different radio messages can be targetted to alternative kinds of listener: rural, young (pop music channels), housewife and so on. The major themes of the marketing campaign can be reinforced on radio so that there is in effect a cohesive, integrated media marketing assault with the same themes running throughout. The leading characteristic of the radio medium, and its chief attraction for the political marketer, is the constellation of different market segments that it comprehends, and numerous stations answer to every kind of taste, musical or otherwise. Cable television is only beginning to rival such refinement of segmentation. Since radio is a highly-segmented medium it is effective in the communication of issue positions and can get directly at the desired audience of the predisposed, doing so in a more overtly emotive way than the more general medium. It acts, therefore, as yet another force for fragmentation created by the conceptualisation of politics as a market, assaulting people in their ideological ghettoes and fortifying the prejudices that bind them there. It is a useful artefact in the perpetual campaign.

Nearly all stations in the United States are commercial, and radio marketing is cheaper than most mediums, so that it is a suitable vehicle for the local low-budget campaign, the communication tool for the pauper politician. Another consequence is that larger advertisements can also appear that give in-depth coverage, or the shorter advertisement at frequent intervals, while the multiplicity of small radio stations means that the focus on issues can be local.

Radio advertising is too easily dismissed. It can be of real significance. Prime spots, especially the morning and evening rush hours when drivers are tuned in to their radios, can command a potentially large audience, and specific market groups – salesmen, travellers, lorry drivers – often listen to the radio, so that it is the best way of reaching them. But radio is a semi-concentration medium. Its typical audiences are housewives and factory workers who use it for musical background – a kind of electronic wallpaper – and this gives radio some deficiency as a promotion medium, for it does not envelop its audience but engages them at a shallow level. Thus imaginative and unusual radio advertising can have disproportionate effect.

Americans are exposed to a substantial amount of advertising, so that they have ceased to be naive consumers of promotion, whether political or commercial. America is a 'promise' society and its advertising roars at people wherever they turn. For the tone of advertising is far more intense than in Europe, that of the hectoring, hard-selling 'man with a box'. Most American advertising attempts to shout through the barriers of cynicism deposited by the years, and political advertising is no exception, and of course, if a politician succeeds in presenting the piece as 'news' rather than advertising, he helps circumvent the barrier. The many radio stations have a greater need for material than television so that the possibilities of news manipulation are more numerous, with arranged interviews, 'documentary' pieces, publicity stunts and so on.

In 1968 the Nixon campaign used radio marketing for tactical moves, passages from his histrionic acceptance speech were used and the radio was also employed to make detailed pronouncements, a feat impossible of course on television, while as the candidate's plane flew over each region a specialised message was sent to its citizenry.[56] The local angle is important in political marketing in a way it never could be in conventional product advertising and this is a further point of distinction between the two formats. Radio is especially useful for the more provocative assault. And it is the more easily manipulated medium – talk shows, for instance, can be smothered with supportive calls.[57]

Newspapers

There is the controlled media, and there is the uncontrolled media that cannot be disciplined. Politicians can attempt to manage it, however, and many would perceive that as the most demanding of all the challenges facing the political merchandiser. Newspapers are politically significant not so much directly as through their effect on public opinion-forming agencies, news commentators, opinion leaders and the like; they create an orthodoxy which by being transmitted through others becomes definitive. While the alleged 'liberal bias' of the press can of course be short-circuited by the paid media, another alternative might also be to attempt to manage it. According to Nimmo, 'newspapers do influence the marginally interested voter and the typical reader will look at most – 80 per cent – of the pages that carry national advertising'.[58]

Politicians want the most favourable press interpretation; scene and speech will be composed with its needs in mind, a 'marketing' specifically to the press corps, and success here is also a function of expense. Journalists give interpretation as well as straight reporting – in fact there is no such thing, since description invariably involves selectivity, so news management is important. Thus candidates can concoct newsworthy stories and succour a languid press; their organisations can produce press kits, biographies and so on; hotels can be booked. In 1968 reporters of the Nixon campaign were treated to dazzling comforts, but only short interviews were granted so that a 'statesmanlike' image of the President could be crafted and managed.

Arterton describes at some length the kinds of distortion which the press can impose.[59] The 'horserace' preoccupation in particular can be misleading, yet the need for news makes it popular; a primary victory may be influenced by arcane factors, so that a candidate can rise almost by accident, while the areas an objective press would cover, such as issues, character and the like, get neglected.

Journalistic consensus also prevents depth and objectivity, for top journalists will define a scenario which becomes the received orthodoxy, the paradigm of the campaign. Its tyranny will usually go unchallenged. There is a habit, too, of inventing labels for candidates. These are a form of shorthand. But inertia ensures that they will remain, however misleading they might be. Polling is another source of journalistic confusion, for its limitations and the cautions of its authors are often ignored, margins of error are not mentioned, nor the extent of fluctuation in time.

The candidate will give special attention to certain journalists, and he will orchestrate competition among journalists for his favours. His statements will often be short and mildly exotic for the purposes of the news, and with journalists often dependent on candidates for the travel schedule that also can be a way of gaining influence over them. Such manipulation is important to the politician. Newspapers enjoy high credibility especially where news and commentary are perceived as issuing from an untainted source, so that the politician must sneak bias into an ostensibly non-partisan vehicle. The press can re-articulate impressions created elsewhere, pick issues, inflate them, toss them aside. Its interpretations matter and its mud is of the adhesive variety. Newspaper journalism is a source of aid – or injury – to a political campaign. The attitudes of columnists, headlines chosen, and their placement – all are significant.

Thus with Richard Nixon some parts of the press were overwhelmingly hostile and this cannot have helped his campaign. The anti-Nixon rhetoric was strong. Murray Kempton wrote:

> We are two nations of equal size . . . Richard Nixon's nation is white, Protestant, breathes clean air and advances towards middleage. Hubert Humphrey's nation is everything else, whatever is black – most of which breathes polluted air, pretty much what is young . . . There seems no place larger than Peoria from which [Nixon] has not been beaten back; he is the President of every place in this country which does not have a bookstore.[60]

The press can also work for a politician, as the British press did for Mrs Thatcher.[61] Press coverage was overwhelmingly pro-Conservative in 1983 and new levels of bathos were attained in the adulation of the Prime Minister: 'Surging down the runway at 145 miles an hour, I can feel Mrs Thatcher vibrating with crusading passion . . . She's an astonishing bird. A plane in herself.'

The American press is a local medium, for there are really no newspapers that are national in the European sense, and it helps to make local issues of extreme importance in the US politics. Moreover the press is by its very nature segmented according to demographic groups and through it the politician reaches the various coalitions in his constituency. Moreover the press is an actor in the perpetual campaign, and should be treated not as an adversary but as the most potent ally, well briefed and cosseted, and each policy needs a communications strategy of its own.

But candidates are often their own worst enemy.[62] Many fight unoriginal campaigns, for they exhibit 'a strong tendency to duplicate the ingredients of victory perceived in recent successes'. Sometimes they make the mistake of going into great detail about their ideas: the newsmen expose them without mercy. Candidates are also judged by criteria which they themselves, perhaps somewhat thoughtlessly, established; and they will be tried by them, whether or not these criteria are particularly meaningful, so that for instance victory by a certain date acquires a spurious significance. Candidates are also victims of factors beyond their control. For instance the large amount of travel 'erodes their ability to form strong coalitions during the election campaign'.

Politicians are amateurs; there is a limit to the extent to which they can be packaged and the totalitarian control marketing aspires to is impossible. Much still remains to chance and to the perhaps untutored skill of an individual: there are indeed limitations to the amount of packaging money can buy.

Candidate Leaflets

Candidate leaflets, sent through the doors, are often one of the campaign's expenses; they can also waste resources. While the literature may be an asset in conjunction with a visit from the candidate, on its own it creates scant impact and in a study of low-level elections[63] 'the gross cost for each unit of recognition was actually $13.45 when literature was directly mailed to the voters'. Personal contact was cheaper and more effective (mailed candidate leaflets are distinct from personalised direct mail). The leaflets alone made little impression on voter turn-out, voter preference and voter candidate recognition; indeed one study claims personal contact is four times as effective as direct mail.

Gimmicks

American campaigns are frequently awash with delicious gimmickry.[64] Thus in Florida a candidate walked constantly through a revolving door erected in the street, clad as a convict, while Mrs George Wallace sent thousands of prospective supporters a Christmas card asking that they send it to her husband along with a cheque, and not to be outdone Ms Bella Abzug sent specimen letters to supporters, urging them to copy and send them to friends. One candidate performed varieties of blue-collar jobs for his campaign: another began his television advertising one year before the election, while Mr George McGovern excelled everyone, sending supporters blank cheques in their name and urging their return, suitably embellished. American campaigning is also athletic, with most candidates seen performing some ludicrous feat of physical endurance, whereas in Europe the favoured political image used to be a sort of genial obesity. While conventional product marketing will sometimes also use the publicity stunt its political employment has far greater significance, given the more intensive journalistic focus, the greater need for recognition/identity and so on.

Political advertising certainly embroiders the concept of vulgarity. One piece pictured the conservative Senator Helms as a keystone cop, shining a torch at a married couple in bed. Public relations stunts always offer intriguing possibilities for the campaign: thus the Ben Kaplan agency organised a meeting between J. F. Kennedy and Southern protestant ministers to neutralise the matter of his Catholicism. People certainly go to inordinate lengths to get elected: one successful candidate in Alaska had: a television show; a newspaper; a book (*Jobs and more Jobs*); and a documentary 'special' near the election.

Much ingenuity has been put into attracting attention to a candidacy. In Pennsylvania Milton Shapp produced a half-hour documentary, 'The Man Against the Machine', which animated the chief theme of that campaign and brought into focus a hitherto obscure figure, and Spencer-Roberts sent thousands of formal invitations to meet Governor Rockefeller: by doing this they gained 12 000 volunteers for the campaign. These kinds of tactics were designed for the specialised needs of individual campaigns, however; they are not necessarily portable. John V. Lindsay's campaign created 122 neighbourhood storefront headquarters and Lindsay strode through these vicinities. Carter in contrast created his 'peanut brigades' of southern loyalists to evangelise for him. Governor Wallace, faced with a hostile press, sent pot-holders, displaying his rugged countenance, as a free gift to minority families (there was more than a touch of irony about this gesture).

Other gimmicks have included walking through a state in work clothes; 'work days'; appearing as a corpse in a student production and, as a bellhop, carrying an opponent's wife's luggage (Governor Bob Graham). 'Work days' can be made the occasion of political pronouncements. Another candidate traversed his state in a mock steam engine (a curious reincarnation of the whistle-stop tour). Mrs Philip Crane performed a belly dance and a candidate for the Senate was hospitalised after diving into the Hudson River. A candidate for the California governorship used his ordinariness as a gimmick; and, in the context of Californian politics, it was. So Evelle Younger advertised himself as 'normal, usual, unstrange'. And at 75, Senator Thurmond thought it prudent to bedeck his campaign with his 31-year-old wife and his children. As much thought and planning goes into these as into more conventional marketing approaches, since television and press provide free attention. Events seek to dramatise a central theme or message. They avoid some of the expenses of conventional marketing, humanise the politicians and deflate pomposity, making the opponent in contrast appear to wear a stuffed shirt. They dispel the boredom and antagonism felt by people.

Personal Contact

Personal selling in the commercial product world has long been reputed to be the most effective means of persuasion; it is also the traditional mode of political activism and as relevant now as ever it was, yet its modern effectiveness is hampered by the limited numbers of the committed campaign workers, the size of the target areas and the amateurism of the cadres.

At the primary level traditional means of campaigning can assume a particular importance. Thus in 1964, of Independents contacted by Republicans half voted for Goldwater, compared to 29 per cent of those not approached, and of Democrats approached 15 per cent voted for Goldwater as against 9 per cent of Democrats not contacted.[65] The personal elements can be particularly important in lower-level campaigns, referendum and issue campaigns: hence in a charter revision campaign one-third of those not contacted voted for the proponents, while 60 per cent of those contacted by mail did so and three-quarters of those who were asked personally; and according to Nimmo good precinct organisation could still boost the party's vote by an easily critical 5 per cent; ideally precinct work should be integrated with a media thrust.

9 Merchandising the Monarch: Reagan and the Presidential Elections

'The men who are entrusted with the direction of public affairs in the United States are frequently inferior, both in capacity and morality, to those whom an aristocracy would raise to power. But their interest is identified and confounded with that of the majority of their fellow-citizens. They may frequently be faithless, and frequently mistaken; but they will never systematically adopt a line of conduct hostile to the majority; and they cannot give a dangerous or exclusive tendency to the government.'

Alexis de Tocqueville, *Democracy in America*

The prerequisite of political success in America today is to conceive your election as a product marketing exercise. The marketing dynamic is not the only way to interpret elections – the play of orthodox political factors also colours and determines them – but as it explains the conceptual, tactical and technological approaches taken it is a useful one. Elections are spectacular, like a circus; they have their ringmasters and their acrobats. They are for the audience but not of them.

RICHARD NIXON

The 1968 Nixon campaign, so memorably described by Joe McGinnis in his book *The Selling of the President*,[1] used the latest in campaign technology then available and represented the first attempt to 'market' the candidate, in the sense that the entire campaign was conceived as a telemarketing strategy. The challenge was to market an insecure television performer[2] whose past carried the stigma of failure. The asset was a discredited incumbent party. McGinnis's book marked a watershed in public perceptions of politics, as people became acclimatised to the notion of political selling, and part of the successful application of the marketing genre is explained by public acquiescence in the process. Now advertising people were intimately

182

involved in campaign strategy itself, with much deliberate planning
for television and inattention to traditional campaigning. Given
Nixon's known past, it was the most successful example to date of
image surgery, and this campaign was therefore seminal in the sense
that it defined all the campaigns that were to come. Nixon's marketing was unimaginative: there was no element of spontaneity and no
creative drive. It was however a smooth and professionally organised
campaign:[3] and in the context of the climactic year 1968 this in itself
excited derision from many of the most articulate commentators.
Market research into perceptions laid bare the characteristics that
had to be changed: an aura of untrustworthiness had always been
attributed to him, and above all he was seen as cold in contrast to the
humanity of his opponent Hubert Humphrey, and the marketing task
was, at the least, to soften some of these perceptions. This was the
classic marketing approach, distilling weaknesses and providing
synthetic remedies. McGinnis sardonically quotes one of Nixon's
assistants observing a plastic flower in a shop: 'What impressed him
most, he (the assistant) said, was how skillfully something artificial
could be made'. Another commented: 'It's not the man we have to
change, but rather the received impression.' This is what marketing
executives might typically say about any product campaign: it is their
political context that makes them chilling.

The extent of this focus on television marketing, which distinguishes it from every campaign previously fought in America, is
explicable through Nixon's meditations on his 1960 defeat:[4] he began
to unlearn past political behaviour, and from media being his enemy,
it would become his friend.[5] Nixon recognised that he had to change
the product, that is, perceptions of personality, and his campaign was
self-consciously a marketing exercise. Is calling this 'marketing' just
applying a technical label to an intuitive process? No, for he actively
sought professional admen and communications experts.[6] Nixon the
intellectual consciously made the adjustment to the marketing
approach; Reagan and Carter grew up with it and owed all their
election careers to it.

Part of the marketing answer to the deficiency of this 'product' lay
in having Nixon interrogated by pre-selected panelists in front of
pre-selected audiences: '. . . the hypothesis [was] that Nixon could
appear to risk all by going live while in fact risking nothing by facing
the loose syntax and predictable, sloppy thrusts of amateurs'.[7]
Nixon's political erudition could be displayed to advantage in such a
setting; his emotions could be revealed as he reacted to the audience

and made himself master of the situation.[8] As subsequently with Reagan's talks facing the camera directly, the medium was being used in the way discovered to be the most beneficial to the candidate. Nixon could not act, but he could come to life before a sympathetic audience and this was the crucial discovery of his marketing packagers, while the campaign revealed that purchased marketing media could side-step press hostility, and the point was not lost on future proponents of views noxious to the liberal establishment. Similarly in the marketing of a product we select and stress its most attractive features: the essential thing is to keep out whatever can challenge the created impression, such as the impartial interrogator, and the image becomes a still pond that nothing must ripple. Afterwards five-minute advertisements were constructed from the panel discussions, and this 'live' concept created Nixon's version of the perpetual campaign while in office, just as Reagan carried over his face-to-camera method, and this shows the extent to which an image can be controlled: suggesting that it is critical to find the right context for the candidate, one which stimulates him to show feeling and be articulate, attractive and credible. In Nixon's case what was chosen was really live theatre. It was all stage-managed. So, bathed in false light, the illuminated mummeries of modern campaigning were performed, a pink radiance in a glowing studio, as natural as a goldfish bowl; volunteers meanwhile became less relevant.

Thus, as President, Nixon liked to face press and television with no props. One of Nixon's aides had noted: 'Television hurt you because you were not yourself', and Marshall McLuhan had observed how Nixon's piano playing would have helped him in 1960; now, his media men had discovered the right format for the projection of his personality.[9] Now television would constitute Nixon's real advantage, for without it '. . . he would not have a prayer of being elected because the press would not let him get through to the people'.[10] Marketing's search is for absolute control over projection, but this assumes of course that a politician possesses a core self that can be found and projected. Television could cosmeticise Nixon's deficiencies: cameras could turn away as he dried his perspiration ('I can't do that sincerity bit with the camera if he's sweating').[11] Nixon began to see modern politics as selling, and the career of one individual encompassed a move from old style parliamentarianism[12] to the new style at its most pronounced: his conversion was late but of the road to Damascus variety.

Such a merchandising approach to electors yields no insight into the candidate's skills of state-craft: the public were certainly sold a President whose reality was concealed from them, so that a talented neurotic was placed in the highest office in the land. His success was a serious indictment of all the 'politician product' media gimmickry. Another assistant, Roger Ailes, commented prophetically: 'This is the beginning of a whole new concept. This is it. This is the way they'll be elected for ever more. The next guys up will have to be performers'.[13] Script-writers could also improve Nixon by giving him more exciting language, and they did: all this came at high cost, and those who paid them would expect, and were to receive, their dividends during the Nixon administration. But how superficial were political promotion devices when they brought no debate or intellectual exchange, and this created a moribund election in which the conflict was external to the campaign.

The irony of the 1968 campaign was angrily noted by McGinnis:[14]

> We had seen the mules in the hot Atlanta street and heard the sobs of children inside the crowded church as they buried Martin Luther King. And watched Bobby Kennedy's life spill across the grey hotel kitchen floor, and taken the train ride and seen black men cry again, and we had cried with them. And now this Nixon came out of his country clubs which he had worked so hard to make and he waved his credit cards in our face.

The marketing approach had certainly reassured people, but with a falsely confident image of reality, that muffled alarming social change; for this genre simply reflects the image they desire back at people; it neither challenges, educates nor leads.

REAGAN'S ENTRY

In Ronald Reagan political market packaging found its own candidate, one whose career had groomed him for television politics, its ideal exponent and fleshly embodiment.[15] Reagan was selected by the business milieu who controlled politics in Southern California, and he operated in a state with few pre-existent loyalties,[16] whose high living standard meant that there was something to conserve. Significantly there was an element of external selection rather than internal drive in his early political career and, in a marketed politics, funders and ideologues will look for attractive and credible front men. For the *Washington Post* authors, 'It is a conceit of our system that anyone can be President and Reagan has taken this idea . . . quite literally'.[17] His achievement was to change the orthodox political style of the day.

Reagan had gone to Hollywood after working as a radio sports commentator and in the five years from 1937 he made 31 films.[18] Such a career was an ideal preparation for a political system in which communication was the key. This was a source of much negative comment, for an actor is a histrionic interpreter of a message whose originator is elsewhere: the powers called for are a subtlety and command of physical and vocal expression and some ability to interpret a role; as a range of skills these are impressive, but narrow. After the war his career began to move more from acting to advocacy: he was six times President of the Screen Actors Guild, and a liberal.[19] Thus while his formal political background may have been invisible he had a long history of quasi-political activity in public advocacy over and above the acting career.

The next phase, one of great significance, was as spokesman for the General Electric Corporation, and it was at this stage that he first became imbued with Republican values. He also gained television experience as presenter of a half-hour television series, 'General Electric Theatre'. He 'sold' General Electric's free enterprise philosophy.[20] But it was the Goldwater campaign that gave him his first taste of national politics, and as chairman of Goldwater's campaign in California he made a memorable televised speech that attracted one million dollars from viewers:[21] the themes, the rhetoric, were already worn and would be used again fondly for many years, like a battered but loved old jacket. Crawford gives a representative specimen: 'The Defence Department runs 269 supermarkets. They do a gross business of $730 million a year and lose $150 million'.[22] Reagan as orator illustrates the importance of tactical execution in communication; the political marketing concept cannot be scientifically implemented but intuitively interpreted.

REAGAN, 1966[23]

This television speech brought Reagan to the attention of rich Republican magnates in California who decided to run him for Governor in 1966. He was chosen because of his media communication abilities and ideological soundness: and for no other reason. Even then such communication criteria were crucially important.

California, rootless, a void for which it was necessary to devise forms to fill, was therefore open to garish novelty and had been the first place to experiment with political marketing.

Blumenthal has described the political climate of Southern California thus:[24]

> The representative thinker of Southern California was Walt Disney, as important to that region's history of ideas as Henry David Thoreau or Bronson Alcott were to New England . . . Disneyland was a totalitarian utopia for Middle Americans, a total environment efficiently organised in every aspect of its operation, offering itself as an idealisation of the laissez faire myth . . . Orange County contained the essential constituency longing for Ronald Reagan . . .

Right from the start, in his first campaign in California, communications methods were used to articulate the Reagan appeal. Reagan's advisers asked the Behaviour Science Corporation to categorise Californian problems and 'solutions' on card for their candidate: the press were consequently astonished at the knowledge of this novice.[25] For his election Reagan also relied on the consultants Spencer Roberts, claiming, 'I'd never run for office again without the help of professional managers like Spencer and Roberts'.[26] It was they who in large measure helped to create Candidate Reagan. The significance of this is that from the start Reagan used political consultants; his career was packaged as every other political one came to be. All over California Reagan committees came to life: Spencer Roberts advised a 'cool' Reagan, one who seemed indifferent to the barbs of his opponent Governor Brown.[27] His conservatism was neither promoted nor especially discernible when he was in power; all was mainstream. Reagan as a leader conscious of his 'market' would respond therefore to the conventional wisdom of the time as much as try to influence it, and conventional orthodoxies were then state welfarism, access to education and the pursuit of 'rights'.

There was of course a major liability: manifestly Reagan had no political experience. So he was packaged as a 'citizen politician', a concerned member of the public who could not recite glib answers but could bring to the job a basic man's warmth, discernment and sense of outrage, and this excused any errors he might make, lowering expectations without damaging esteem, so that any 'professional' touches could be admired as an unanticipated bonus.[28]

'Citizen politician': observe the genius of the marketing orientation where politics is conceived in 'product' terms and disadvantages become assets. This illustrates the way consultants think of 'placing' their candidate against an opponent, of setting off his deficiencies, they think conceptually, looking for themes to give a oneness to a campaign. And the political merchandisers use language to change our perceptions: thus the stumbling novice becomes the citizen politician.

In this campaign working people were reminded of Reagan's union past; and a theme – a Republican alternative to the Great Society – was created; it was called the Creative Society: in Spencer's words, 'Whatever Reagan wanted to do, it was creative. Shut down Berkeley? It was creative'.[29] Television advertising used his 'talking head'; this would give credibility to a candidate who needed it. The press was tightly controlled since Reagan had not at that stage learnt the easy control of temper, so that appearances were before select groups.[30] Marketing as an autocratic concept stresses control of all aspects of a fluid and competitive environment. Prominent Goldwater supporters were excluded from the campaign. Every speech was followed by a question and answer session, as an earnest of competence. Chagal[31] sums up the prototype Reagan oration, 'The Speech', thus: 'a twenty-minute orator's stew consisting of small-town protestant-safe jokes, bursts of passion against harmless targets, and lots of appeals to down-home patriotism'. The banality of his campaign was consistent with much that we have said about the effects of a conscious marketing approach to elections.

THE NINETEEN SEVENTIES

Reagan's strategists had, historically, placed reliance on polling. In commercial marketing we throw back in stylised form popular beliefs, we merchandise conventional wisdom so that people are led by their own reflection, dance to their own shadows. Similarly in politics, which discerns popular opinion through the medium of polling. His 1970 gubernatorial election strategy was shaped by attitude surveys, and the popular themes thus distilled were continually reiterated by Reagan: 'Public assistance should go to the needy and not the greedy', and so on. Reagan employed campaign simulations in 1970, and his computers would predict electorate reactions to the issue positions (given a mathematical weight) put into them; yet this device was still clumsy, with severe limitations due to the absence of up-to-the-minute information.

The polling guru Richard Wirthlin was able to distil the communications techniques that were best matched to Reagan's personality; for when speaking directly to the camera Reagan could command the attention of 80 per cent of his audience for thirty minutes, and when finally used in the North Carolina Republican primaries this method brought victory, with Reagan taking 52 delegates against 46; subsequently $1.5 million was raised on television, also by this means.[32] But even in 1976 Wirthlin still had limited influence on the Reagan team and the potential he offered was misunderstood.

Reagan always took a value-orientated approach to politics, values he believed in and whose assumption was genuine, not a political act. Thus while marketing describes a process it is not one which the Reagan team would have necessarily acknowledged, though as businessmen and as politicians his advisers had a predisposition to use them. For in important ways Reagan's methods when viewed as a marketing approach were limited in the extent to which they were 'consumer'-led. The sentiment then was real. Only its articulation was controlled, an exercise in cosmetics. Though the marketing concept is probably the most useful way to interpret his presidency it does not encapsulate the whole truth about him and the conceptualisation must not become a strait-jacket. In this and subsequent elections Reagan's political style was consolidated. It was not, however, a conventionally Republican style but became an iconoclastic right-wing idealism; Ford for example always scored more impressively with Republican voters.[33]

In 1980 Reagan proved a popular campaigner, but his ultimate success was far from predetermined. His speech to the Republican convention raised his lead from three points to fourteen. He began the campaign, with his customary sensitivity to symbolism, with a speech on Ellis Island and people listened to his often effective rhetoric: 'I will not apologise for our generation. We have known four wars and a Great Depression. No people who ever lived fought harder, paid a higher price for freedom, or did more to advance the dignity of man'.

NINETEEN EIGHTY[34]

Of Reagan's Democrat antagonists, Ted Kennedy stood se

discredited. Had his advisers had a more alert recognition of a marketing approach they could have sought long ago to exorcise Chappaquidick. Many of the elementary counsels of marketing were neglected, perhaps because of the arrogance consequent upon the inherited nature of his public status. From the very start the Kennedy campaign was complacent.[35] There was a paucity of polling and the belief was that Ted Kennedy could be carried from state to state, a somewhat obese icon eliciting the adoration of the faithful. Note the sectarian nature of the old approach, wonderful with the dedicated but exclusive: others do not feel a part of the show. By contrast, the marketing approach is inclusive. Kennedy had a curiously old-fashioned belief in the evangelising fervour of large public meetings.[36] Carter referred obliquely to doubts about Kennedy, and his communications approach did this by implication rather than direct criticism, which would alienate. He stressed those areas where he, Carter, had the positives of Kennedy's negatives, and his advertising carried forward the theme of his honesty, composure and domesticity;[37] pro-Carter types appeared being interviewed in the street, and Carter appeared – according to the latest counsel of polls – dovish or hawkish on defence.[38]

Much of Reagan's campaign communication in 1980 was not in fact aimed at his chief supporters. For their votes could be relied on and they only needed reassurance; they constituted 40 per cent of electors. The really critical area was the 15 per cent undecided, a group differentiated from the core supporters. Who were this 15 per cent, what kind of people were they? They were a suspicious group. They felt he lacked experience, was not erudite enough. As with commercial products the political artefact is modified according to the counsel of market research. So film depicted him at a desk in a library; or performing as governor of California, signing bills and so on.[39] Then they feared his martial instincts, calling forth a 'peace' advertisement to assuage them, which elaborated his peaceability; and his commercials were sometimes infused with an austere no-nonsense mood to banish any aura of Hollywood, for the critical 15 per cer͏͏ ͏usted him as an ex-actor. This shows the deficiency of ͏egy when it becomes enmeshed with a theory of ͏ that stresses image. For the lesson learned was not to ͏n's performance but simply to change his image in the ͏the market communication approach was a danger ͏rsued exclusively.

͏ss inherent in a marketing conceptualisation of

politics was shown in various ways. The Republicans wished to provoke the 'meanness factor' in Carter and to reveal his true self as they saw it, but whether such a 'mean' streak really existed is not our province to determine; our task is merely to observe that one was created by the Republicans to all intents and purposes as useful as if it were real. Reagan himself would not reply: others could undertake the abrasive parts of the campaign – such employment of surrogates was an increasingly used device in US political marketing. Carter himself made the mistake of direct attacks, a challenger's strategy and inappropriate for one holding presidential office.[40]

Carter's advertising faced a different task. It had to lower expectations as to what a president could actually achieve by emphasising how difficult the task was, yet Carter must also seem strong and tougher on defence: so now he appeared with construction workers, with the Secretary of Defence and so on and stress was laid on his naval background.[41] But you cannot alter a record. There is the fact of memory. A politician can expect too much from marketing: there are political facts which, thankfully, it cannot varnish, perceptions which cannot be changed. Moreover if political behaviour is too much influenced by polls there is a danger of seeming to vacillate and therefore be weak, as Carter so often did; government needs a guiding thematic approach. And, throughout this period, there were the long shadows of the hostage crisis.

One-third of Americans remained undecided until late on. Much of the early part of the campaign was spent simply introducing Reagan to an electorate for whom he was still something of a novelty; then he went on to the issues: 'peaceful' Reagan was the result, promising discussions with Russia on controlling nuclear proliferation. Then there was his 'blue woo', the attempt to seduce the blue-collar electorate, with advertisements depicting workers vowing a Republican vote. Reagan took up to 40 per cent of the blue-collar vote. Only near the end of the campaign did Reagan move tartly to the offensive: 'The symbol of this administration is a finger pointing at someone else' and so on.[42] A great assault was reserved for the last ten days: 40 per cent of the Reagan advertising budget was reserved for 16 per cent of the time, and near the end he was exceeding Carter in expenditure by a ratio of two and a half to one, while negative advertising against Carter now appeared to inspire loyal supporters. Newspaper advertising underpinned the themes of Reagan's television speech, one awash with vintage Reagan oratory.

The television debate with Carter was a critical event in the campaign. Reagan tailored his appeal to two swing groups, the undecideds and the women; 'peaceful' Reagan was much in evidence, and the geniality for which he became pre-eminent; Carter was cold and literal. More than any other factor the Carter–Reagan debate proved decisive. Reagan employed the 'thematic' approach and memorable phraseology: 'We don't have inflation because the people are living too well; we have inflation because the Government is living too well . . .' and 'Are you better off now than you were four years ago. . . ?' His histrionic abilities were put to good effect: the image contrasted sharply with his opponent, and in particular his thrust, 'there you go again', appeared to incorporate everything there was to say against Carter, and it impressed listeners. Wirthlin's post-debate poll revealed that fears of Reagan causing a war had declined from 44 per cent to 40 per cent, a critical margin, and suddenly Carter's position began to drop; it fell by 10 per cent. Reagan's campaign set out to conceal his inadequacies, and as before meetings with the press and their agendas were strictly superintended. Again therefore we see how perceptions of personality can be artfully managed: hence the persona of a 'knowledgeable' candidate.

Carter came to power as a media-created candidate but failed under scrutiny to sustain his original media performance. Media marketability was the key to the rise of modern presidents. It raises the question of whether a consequence of having an open market in politics rather than the restricted one that existed is the ascent of odd or seriously incompetent men; while televisuality must be a necessary political skill, the dangers of it posing as a sufficient one are apparent: Carter's problems, or Reagan's Irangate/Federal deficit imbroglio – is there an inevitability in the limited ability of the men thus selected?

The 1980 campaign was less a vote for Reagan than one against Carter. The campaign was dominated by an issue, Iran, but one which encapsulated a wider theme of the decline in American international prestige and power: campaign issues are usually symbolic of the broader anxiety. Reagan's candidacy expressed a strategic coalition of interests, essential if one is to win the US presidency; but it contained a strong core of ideological right-wingers. Since 1964 indeed elections had become increasingly ideological, although the numbers identifying themselves as Republican did not rise significantly in 1980;[43] the coalition comprised three elements – regional (West and South West), economic–ideological (a threatened middle class), religious–moral (fundamentalist),[44] though of course membership was in some degree overlapping. The segmentation ability of modern mediums assists in the build-up of coalitions, while Reagan's people had always thought in terms of them; and part of the coalition comprised disillusioned patriotic Democratic blue-collar voters.

Carter himself conducted a doomed campaign.[45] The media were against him and his meanness was the fourth most covered issue on the network news during September 1980, illustrating again the pre-eminence of image, while 'he depended for support on a media strategy perilously disconnected from policy';[46] his comprehension of the permanent campaign, of the linkages between policy and promotion, was inadequate. Like the British Labourites, Democrats had a naive conception of marketing and one which equated it entirely with advertising, with no regard to adjustments in the 'product' itself. Carter did have a conception of media-marketed politics, one broad enough to get him to the White House, but not deep enough to sustain him there.

In no way did the 1980 election indicate a permanent realignment; indeed in 1982 the Democrats regained twenty-six seats in the House and seven governorships.[47] But during this campaign electors remained uninformed in many key areas: how much did they really know about the new President and his capacities?

THE PERMANENT CAMPAIGN

Reagan saw more clearly than other Presidents that electioneering must be a continual process.[48] After the election therefore the utility of polling and computers was far from finished. Wirthlin ran the 'First Ninety Day Project' charged with giving the new regime firm direction; his computerised simulations would give guidance on strategy. In the permanent campaign the issues are like products, to be modified or discarded, or added to complete a particular range. An Office of Planning and Evaluation was created to sponsor proactive strategy rather than reactive tactics,[49] and the President's men were obsessed with the media, with issues rated on the amount of network news time they were given and polling used to gauge public sentiment; thus the need for and identity of Supreme Court Justice Sandra Day O'Connor was established through polling:[50] a symbolic strategy to close the 'gender gap' created by women's hostility to Reagan's supposed militarism. For a time the 'gap' fell from 12 per cent to 5 per cent.

This illustrates how far the political market approach was internal-ised by the new administration, for the essence of the marketing concept is that leadership comes ultimately from the market-place, and this weapon is effective in the gaining of temporary popularity. And polling revealed the vulnerability of the air traffic controllers, the point at which to intensify rhetoric, the place at which to deliver the ultimatum; polling also charted the rise in public alienation over El Salvador and Reagan's profile here was consequently reduced, with the economy made the central theme because it was both less divisive and more significant.[51] There were able communicators in the early days of the administration. Government was planned, actions and statements had a six-month preparation period and a set of rotating themes was in effect established: in the words of Carter's pollster Patrick Caddell, 'I could kiss them for using thematic approaches. They really do understand the importance of themes as the great projecting force of political management'.[52] This systema-tised approach could not last, for a business-strategic approach is ultimately ill-suited to the turbulence of the political world: it assumes a calmer environment.

Above all Reagan sought to woo and solicit the public, to 'market' his agenda, by direct televised appeals; in 1981 and 1982 he urged people to write to their Congressmen supporting his economic policies and his programmes were then passed with narrow margins. Given the legislature/executive division of the US constitution it made sense for the one to appeal to the power base of the other. Recent administrations had appeared to degenerate partly in con-sequence of media scrutiny since this was a phenomenon that many traditional politicians proved inept at handling. Reagan could handle it. There is a connection between his administration's long period of comparative success and its dedication to a view of government as an extended marketing exercise, to marketing itself the whole time, but here also lay the seeds of its failure in stressing communication to the detriment of administration.

However, if we argue that politics is to a high degree symbolic, a way of binding various disparate factions rather than a strictly administrative competence, then Reagan long fulfilled such an ideal. People felt that they were led by a person who experienced emotion in the same way and to the same intensity as they did, except that he expressed it more cogently. He delivered a quality ordinariness. He was an extraordinary ordinary man. In fact Reagan's style was highly democratic, the antithesis of elitist, involving as it did a gentle measure of self-deprecation: there was none of Mrs Thatcher's hauteur. He wielded power with a democratic twinkle in the eye.[53] All this was a lenitive to the outrage of those groups most negatively affected by his policies. It could be legitimately argued that such a reconciliatory role, achieved through mere words, postures and symbolic gestures, is in fact the central task of government, since society comprises a host of interests in aggressive competition and government has limited material scope to mollify them.

The new market-directed approach was partly responsible for one incident. The public relations strategists suggested that the shooting of Libyan jets would be the best way of sending signals to Gadaffi and the Kremlin, and reassuring a public worried about American impotence and yet wishing to avoid heavy military entanglement: so the deductions from polling/simulation suggested a deliberate human sacrifice.[54] Thus an incident was provoked, and the jets were shot down. Such an incident was also calculated to heighten public support for defence spending. There are shades here of 'mobocracy', and under an unstable President who can know what might arise? At one level people were manipulated, at another such manipulation was their own creation. A crisis can be created and stage-managed: potential for unscrupulous exploitation is implicit in the marketing approach to politics.

Focus groups, where a target group discusses some product, have long been a staple of consumer research. Reagan's team began to use them as a way of sustaining the perpetual campaign. They were employed to assess public opinion before the Geneva and Reykjavik summit, and before Reagan's State of the Union speeches.[55] Before the December 1987 summit, the idea was used to discuss what people wanted the summit to deliver and how its results could be best articulated to them, using words and phrases that a 'representative' group of them had concocted. The group suggested a number of major points that became important in planning the summit; it showed the extent of public ignorance and the lack of direct benefit to the United States seen to accrue from a deal on medium- and short-range nuclear missiles in Europe. However, the group saw importance in the treaty as the beginning of a reduction in intercontinental nuclear missiles, so that the theme adopted was 'First Stage for Peace' – hence the signing of the treaty before the end of the summit.

Marketed politics need credible performers, so that a central task is finding a mediable candidate. Thus another item of Reagan's skill was the quality of his rhetoric: he emphasised clear well-crafted English, sometimes with a memorable turn of phrase ('There you go again'; 'Are you better off now than you were four years ago?').[56] Points were buttressed by parables and by visual aids. The role of language is critical in history; in consumer advertising words are important, but politics can legitimately use a more exalted prose because of the high significance of that avocation (viz: Churchill). In fact Reagan's key weakness was the confusion he sometimes revealed under journalistic interrogation, and the marketing approach cannot do much about that; indeed journalists who ask the right questions are the best antidote to blandness. For Blumenthal, 'Reagan's coalition is personal. It is united around him, not his party. The methods he uses to maintain this coalition are the same that have destroyed partisanship. Reaganism creates Reaganites, not Republicans. By the same token Reaganism creates anti-Reaganites'.

THE 1984 ELECTIONS

In 1984 traditional Democrat slogans and issues were recycled and the liberal cohorts urged to action; but like liberal parties elsewhere they underrated a people's need for the patriotic appeal and misconstrued the enduring attraction of traditional values (of which Reagan deftly made himself the embodiment). Defence of the deprived can bore electorates. Moreover in the United States disillusion with liberalism had become a fairly permanent emotion. What this suggests is a deeply introspective party which had steadily lost touch with its traditional supporters and one sealed with the high polish of intellectual arrogance, for it assumed that its virtue was self-evident; the internal party culture became an exclusive one. Hence perhaps its initial reluctance to 'market' candidates and policies, for, in placing a premium on communications, politicians recognise that their truth is not self-evident.

During the 1984 election Republican emphasis was on co-ordination, with the setting of weekly themes and daily policy agreement: so the public heard and saw a coherent policy line. Visuals were used. Twenty-five million dollars were spent on advertising: the keynotes were patriotism and optimism. Scenes showed the sun setting on San Francisco bay; eager commuters; an embracing bride and groom; a small-town parade; the flag. More sinisterly, another film showed a rifleman and a large bear, with the message that some were tame and some dangerous – one could not be sure, and had to be as strong as the bear. In another, ordinary people derided Mondale's assertion that he would raise taxation. Such advertising stressed simplicity and repetition. Reagan could boast of tangible results. The poor had become poorer; but the fear had been of uncontrolled and uncontrollable costs incurred in making them comfortable.

Market-place politics call forth cosmetically appropriate themes: after Nixon 'honesty' was the criterion, after Carter 'strong and patriotic'. Electorates got exactly what they asked for and this is the great danger of market-place politics; they are preoccupied with the concerns of the moment and with particular character archetypes rather than that roundedness of political competence which the old, formalised party-arbitered system fostered.

Possibly one can even speak of a roundabout of political themes active in history, and periods of self-criticism alternate with moods of optimism, just as in the emotional chemistry of an individual. The political marketing skill is to identify and label the nation's mood. Caddell did this for Carter; but his advice was not carried over into political practice. Carter ignored this advice for two reasons related to the fact that he perceived marketing as a purely electoral activity: he failed to accept the diagnosis since it implied criticism, and he was too arrogant for that; and he lacked anyway the histrionic abilities to put over a cogent defence.

And so in 1984 the elections ushered in the last episode of the Reagan Raj. More than most of his predecessors Reagan recognised the symbolic aspect of the Presidency, one enhanced by a conscious communications approach, and his training as an actor gave him facility for expressing this: he perceived the Presidency as setting a tone and image that would elicit action. The key to his success was the recognition that the power of the Presidency lay not simply in a formal executive authority that was circumscribed anyway by constitution and Congress, but in the informal influence of personality and value-laden rhetoric. This leadership model will survive. His actions then were not just legislative; his achievement lay in changing values, minting a new currency of intellectual and popular dialogue, and this was his real accomplishment, to consolidate a value shift which his initial election perhaps did not really express. Moreover Reagan used the vociferous vested interests; Blumenthal quotes David Gergen: 'The president's strategists do not want him to lend more than rhetorical support to farouche New Right causes'.[57] Moral single issues for example were avoided during his Presidency as 'polarising'.

In a sense to make marketing a separate category in Ronald Reagan's case seems redundant; everything he did was an act of salesmanship. His European critics would assert that such emotions were based on foundations of *naïveté*, but what they neglect is the thirst America had for this type of leadership. Twenty years of trauma – the coalescence of Vietnam, Watergate and civil strife – engendered a need for leadership and affirmation; if Ronald Reagan did not exist, Americans would have invented him. This would explain that phenomenon, a septuagenarian's monopoly of the youth vote; youth is amenable to propaganda since it has little in the way of pre-existing standards and knowledge from which to form criteria, and they followed their wrinkled Pied Piper. Younger voters remembered no time in their lives when their country had a firm or great leader, and they strained to see these qualities in Ronald Reagan. Such an impression, however fanciful, was garlanded by grand media events on the passage to November. His style will be the model for successors; we may infer imitation but not similarity, for while others will be similarly equipped with all the apparatus of modern marketing technology the critical ability is to interpret feelingly the raw counsel of the polls, the magical, mesmeric play of word, tone and gesture.

His opponent's greatest problem was his personality. The Democrat failure was not to choose a communicator and they had used conventional but by now redundant political criteria; Mondale's stress, his 'un-cool', was perceptible ('the dull Norwegian'): his failure cannot simply be blamed on unpopular policies. There were many victims of recession who might have been seduced by a market appeal based on more state involvement and expansion and in the last great recession this is exactly what happened, while his endorsement came from groups who were not popular in the nation. With Mondale what were deficiencies would have been less so in a non-media marketing area. The criterion of political ability had simply changed.

REAGAN THE REVIVALIST

Reagan chose the role of revivalist, describing his performance as a 'great crusade' begun in 1980, offering Americans a 'sparkling vision of tomorrow, a belief that greatness lies ahead ... We've got everything before us'.[58] The crusader is a familiar figure in American culture and history, seen whenever there is an appetite for the breaking of a mould (for example, Teddy Roosevelt's 'Bull Moose' campaign). Subsequently Reagan dismissed the Democrats as 'that pack of pessimists roaming the land'. There was a yearning for vigorous innocence, a wish to shake off the despondency which began to penetrate the American psyche after 1968, a wish for hope uncluttered, for simple answers that would unite them with their forefathers. Revivalism proclaims a break with present failed solutions and unites implicitly the future and the heroic past, a distancing from the current confusions.

The future as a political marketed theme is exciting, and it contrasts with politicians who base their appeal on the past. If we see politics as a 'product' we recognise that it must be largely a matter of promise since we cannot really 'sell' the recent past, with all its disappointment. Politicians therefore sell hope.

A country oriented to change and future always has a predisposition towards leaders who offer a vision, and Reagan connected as he had always done with a key explanatory value of the society, its optimism. We have said that political style should connect with the key values of a culture: it is their projection. For you then enlist all the force of that cultural adherence and identification. As the anthropologist Mary Douglas has observed, conventional advertising often attempts to make this connection. The orthodox values of a society permeate consumer marketing: it is a conservative force, and at its centre is a stained-glass window portrayal of the nuclear family at play. This was also a role willed on Reagan to some extent by his own corps of enthusiasts and core ideological supporters; he was as much created as self-created.

But such feelings were sold by all the latest consumer advertising techniques. Thus the *New York Times* commented:[59] 'The emotional television sales pitch, already the major marketing weapon for soft drink, fragrance and beer advertisers, is bound to gain credibility and adherents as the result of the stunning examples that were used to start President Reagan's re-election campaign'. And Alvin Hempel, the Chairman of D'Arcy MacManus Masius, the advertising agency, said: 'Pure imagery by and large, it surrounds him with beautiful pictures, America. If you took some of the Reagan footage and put in some other voice-over and sound tracks, you could have the commercial for another product and vice-versa'.[60] It was merely an animated cliché. This is a good example of the transfusion of commercial techniques to political marketing, for 'emotion' was already the latest fad on Madison Avenue.

The Republican Party did not use merely one advertising agency to do its electoral promotion; they created an organisation – Tuesday Team Inc. – to co-ordinate the work of the agencies, and all the advertising was paid for by all Republican institutions. Legally, Tuesday Team were outside the campaign structure. Many senior advertising men were prominent in this campaign. The shadows here of 'CREEP' were not accidental, for both campaigns experienced a common need to go outside the traditional party structures and create more flexible and market-oriented vehicles.

Republican advertising did not concentrate on Reagan, but on Reaganism.[61] Thus the advertising was very precise in its focus and designed to work in conjunction with television news and current affairs reportage. The news would project Reagan's personality; his acting abilities would see to that. The advertising would then promote the broad values he had associated himself with:[62] the man himself was excluded. Political marketing faced the problem of how to meld straight advertising and news into a synthesis: this achieved it. The core theme was American renewal: 'The USA is getting better, prouder and stronger as witnessed by people raising the Stars and Stripes, buying a house, or going into a factory re-opened since the recession'.[63] There was a disconnection between the vagueness of advertising and the specificity of policy, and sceptics would say this shows the danger inherent in the 'marketed' approach where we stress image over substance.

DEMOCRATS IN TRAUMA

Reagan won 51.6 per cent of the votes cast. Etzioni distinguished, as did many commentators in this election, between themes and issues; the issues concern specific positions, programmes and differences and are followed only by the 'political nation', whereas themes appeal to large numbers of people with their broad focus, symbolism and emotiveness: 'the right themes allow him to mobilise masses of people and bring volunteers rushing to his campaign'.[64] Etzioni argued that the Democrats had wasted their time in an obsession with issues to the detriment of themes, and must evolve a new 'winning theme': 'The Democratic Party desperately needs a unifying and mobilising theme – something that has eluded it ever since the Great

Society ran out of public support'. Issues genuinely confuse people – a right answer is rarely self-evident and both sides appear to marshall telling statistics; issues automatically alienate many portions of the electorate when a strong stance is taken; they are technical, a specific benchmark, and for a highly pluralist society with increasingly less of core-shared cultural traits and values an issue-oriented policy is doomed.

Democrats failed to make the size of the deficit and the risks it threatened a going issue. Mondale had both an image and an issue problem. He relied on Roy Spence for much of his advertising: Spence invented 'Mondale Dares to be Cautious' – a profoundly insipid clarion call. The thematic approach in particular had been something they neglected, whereas the Reagan team made it the governing ideology of their whole campaign. There was a fundamental failure to perceive that a persuasion task was to be carried out. Parties must trim their ideologies to what the public wants in order to succeed: a demand-led kind of politics. Too often parties believe they have a sort of sacrosanct truth and that the public must long to incorporate itself into such an ideological autocracy. Moreover there was too much negativity in the Democratic Party: it appeared to have become what the right in the United States once was – an acrimonious coterie – this in a country where fun and optimism, however juvenile they appear to the jaded observer, are major values. But the power motive is a strong persuader for the unlearning of bad old habits, and subsequently Democrats began to discover much about political advertising.

In 1984 the Democrats began to re-annexe the traditionalist totems and symbols of Americana that had been taken by Republicans[65] – flag, law, religion, family – and endow them with a liberalistic interpretation; the aim was to deprive Reagan of his symbols and give them a more indulgent, less doctrinaire meaning. Patriotic symbols have a particular place in the iconography of American life – there is no national religion to act as a focus (unlike Ireland or Poland, say) no royalty, no traditional national culture in cooking or dancing; so symbols must fill the vacuum. Symbols provide a stylised message of national oneness and unity which little else can give in a pluralistic culture where even national institutions – the Pentagon, say, or even Medicare – are nationally divisive. Therefore it is natural that political marketing strategies in America will lay great stress on the symbolic.

Democrats were also mortgaging themselves to business interests.

By doing this of course business deftly prevents moves to cut down campaign spending and donations: it bribes both parties. A total of $3 million was contributed to the cost of the Democratic convention, and the Chevron company spent $105 000 on food and drink for Democrat delegates at a party.[66] This is at least some sort of answer to the critics of political marketing's equity.

The US Government paid $40 million to both Mondale and Reagan for their campaigns. Half of this would be spent on (mainly television) advertising and the rest on polling and so on, while parties were also allowed to raise money for legal and accounting costs and their national committees could contribute nearly $7 million.[67] Parties could also spend as much as they pleased on non-candidate generic party advertising. Mondale finances were drained by the primary battles ($40 million),[68] while the Republicans raised most of the twelve million dollars for the primaries in just three direct mail shots. There is, as we have seen, an intimate and organic connection between a party's ability to raise finance and its ability to market, and the Democrats paid a price for their archaic fund-raising practices in their poor electoral communication.

THE 1986 ELECTIONS

The Times described the nature of the Reagan appeal in 1986 in terms both condescending and impressive.[69] A 'fierce nationalism' would be in the air as bands played patriotic songs. And then the audience would be treated to '. . . the same speech, the same ridiculous jokes and anecdotes, the same upbeat Reagan telling people that nobody kicks America any more without paying a price'. *The Times* added: 'This immensely simple man connects so easily, so completely, with America's complex character and its deepest needs. Those who mock and deride him have to admit that he is a phenomenon, a man with a genius for the American occasion, playing heavily on sentimentality and American power. Without TV, none of it would work.' Further, 'Light on issues, the speech is heavy on imagery, sentiment and a heady nationalism'. *The Times* concluded that 'The Reagan image constantly overwhelms and conceals the issues' and added prophetically, 'Somebody said America is having too good a time'.

Reagan is instantly recognisable as a type, the home-town Rotarian. But he also transcends the type: he is a superior version of the norm. The Americanness of Reagan, his nativeness, even his *naïveté* connected him with his audiences. He fulfilled a key demand of the late twentieth-century hero, in that he was a stylised version of the common: a world where ordinary people possess most of the resources and the democratic power will place gilded versions of the average man on its pedestals. In all persuasion identity is important, and advertisers use people who are glamorous versions of ourselves – of what we would like to be, but not surpassing our aspirations – and we are flattered in the similarity. It was a mutual admiration society, Reagan reflecting to America an image of itself. The role of the President is as monarchic personifier of national virtues, for what else really personifies them?

The Times' correspondent noted '. . . you feel this mysterious communion with the American people'. But it also observed the meticulous organisation whose real purpose was to exercise control over the image projected – the orchestrated rallies; the journalists, sated with drink, hand-outs and reservations but prevented from asking the President questions; the subordination of all discussion to the interests of photo opportunities. The marketing approach aims for a rigidity of control to eliminate uncertainties and spontaneity, so it demands organisational skills of a high order, but what it seeks to extinguish is that which rendered politics interesting and gave insights to electors.

In 1986 the Republicans lost eight Senate seats and seven House seats, so that the House of Representatives divided only 52–48 per cent between Republicans and Democrats (though they did gain eight governorships). The new Democratic replacements were often conservative southern Democrats. Issues were local and the Democrats avoided criticising the main totems of Reaganism, and this shows how the Republicans had succeeded in shifting the centre-ground in US politics; as many now identified themselves as Republican as Democrat, with Republican majorities for those below age 27.

This campaign certainly confirmed the continuing supremacy of the money telemarketing nexus. *The Times* commented on this as the most noticeable feature of the campaign: '. . . this year they [the Republicans] have outspent the Democrats by five to one. This money has gone mainly on paid television advertising – now the principal means whereby the candidates influence the voters'.

The political marketing ethos may make for a contest of images rather than intellects, since specifics alienate. Thus: 'Neither Senator Cranston, a gaunt and wily 72-year-old campaign veteran, nor Zschau, a 46-year-old product of the entrepreneurial world high-tech, seems inclined to stoop to such a thing as debate about the issues. It is too easy to let their media managers do the work for them.'[70] The curious sameness of candidates and their views was also noted: 'Mr. Moore and Mr. Breaux are both congressmen; the Republican represents Baton Rouge, the Democrat Cajun country. Both hold similar conservative views. The main differences between them are their party labels and the amount of money at their disposal.'[71] Such blandness, inherent in the marketing approach to politics, was well satirised in the campaign propaganda of Mrs Harriett Woods, who asked, 'Why must a US senator look like this?', along with a sketch of the identikit senator ('impossibly white teeth, thick luxurious hair, jutting jaw') . . .'

OVERVIEW

So the power of image gathered momentum, towering over rational exposition. Political marketing is in its infancy and we should not assume that the new political facts it has created are irrevocable. It may be that the genre is sufficiently flexible to reverse the abuses it has itself created. As Sir Alfred Sherman has said of British politics: 'The old voluntary system worked well or badly by its own lights . . . The new system of policy entrepreneurship has its own internal logic. The real problem is how the two can mix'.[72]

In the ultimate, Reagan's political style was well matched to the special nature of the United States Presidency: 'Actions and words are thus much the same thing for the President. Commentators who apply to him the common distinction between those two turn out usually to be distinguishing between presidential words and the resulting action of other people.' Moreover, whatever his other faults, this was an aspect of the Presidency that Reagan well comprehended, holding twenty-six news conferences during his first presidency and making thirty-four speeches conveyed by one or more channels. He created a role of public spokesman, of benevolent tribune, a national moral awareness.

conscious 'marketing' of policy thus helped Reagan in the

paration of powers, it helped him to persuade

ive him legitimacy and to overcome opposition from

the media and vested interests by appeals to the court of public opinion;
- he enjoyed it;
- he recognised the significance of the perpetual campaign.

Reagan used largely though not exclusively the unpaid media to which his position gave access. For a surprisingly long time his approach worked well because of the brilliance of execution, but he was dependent on the existence of a competent staff.

Given the problems of pluralism in US society, such a 'marketed' communications style may be the type of leadership most appropriate to it. Diversity of religions, ethnic backgrounds and cultural traditions is increasing with the decline of the Anglo-Saxon core, and diversity also of social cause movements, life-styles, and regionalisms: how do you give unity and direction to a seeming anarchy, one which marketing exacerbates by its focussed appeals? Marketing may also provide the antidote in symbolic and inclusive communications strategies.

Did a less democratic society select better men? We may be overly romantic in conveying the impression of potential statesmen waiting discontentedly in the wings. Certainly American politics has been opened up to new 'talent' as a result of a market-arbitered, market-driven system. It is difficult if not impossible to imagine Reagan or even Carter rising to the top of a less communication-oriented polity: they are part of a merchandised political elite.

However, electronic democracy made for a lack of a sense of popular involvement in all these campaigns, so the depth of support was superficial; it was conditional only on continued success and was rapidly withdrawn – and how swift seemed the consequent demise. Observers have spoken legitimately of a 'dealignment' rather than a realignment in US politics and political marketing is the expression and the consequence of the creation of a politics of rented allegiance. No great movements were created under Carter and Reagan: 'mediability' is skin-deep. Republicans had a high profile in 1980 and 1984, but since its roots were in the light earth of media marketing, it could not last. For solidifying a movement urgent interest and a personal rapport are needed; neither existed, instead there was general discontent articulated electronically: a synthetic fickleness. Thus, while the strength of Reagan's marketing-oriented political approach was that it brought large numbers of Americans out of cynicism and malaise through the splendours of his tactical execution, the weakness was that this very approach re-created that malaise because it was predicated upon a communications concept that excluded vigilant administration. If Carter showed the limitations of the 'administrative' Presidential style, Reagan showed the problems of the communications mode. In earlier disasters Reagan escaped much of the blame by going quickly to the people with a relatively full account (on Beirut, for example). His later problems revealed both the tenuity of political reputation and the extent to which Reagan's was contingent upon a public perception of honesty.

Thus many key White House operatives conceptualised presidential government exclusively in terms of marketing communication. David Stockman claimed the 'Californians' were illiterate in policy,[73] their minds fixed on how well the president would come across on the seven o'clock news; *The Economist* added, 'Major, as well as minor, events have to happen to time: it is worth noting, perhaps, that [the] air attack on Libya was synchronised for 7pm, Eastern Standard Time, precisely.' Mr Michael Deaver, a life-time member of the California crowd, never, according to Mr Stockman, 'even feigned an interest in policy'. As a method of governing in the short term this worked well: a credible political philosophy could even be constructed from it – that with the onward pressure of political events government can only manage a responsive and fire-fighting approach, that strategy is impossible given the unpredictability of our future. This ignores the existence of protracted themes in politics – the deficit was certainly one – whose longevity and accumulating costs are predictable, and which require an act of confrontatory political leadership, a mobilisation of public will. A marketing conceptualisation of politics is simply no good at doing this, for, since political marketing is rooted in the identification of a promiscuous public opinion, it cannot look to the future. Arguably Reagan's 'perpetual campaign' had made for moves which while technically appealing in the short term illuminated no long-term strategy. These were piecemeal intiatives designed to keep cool a press ever willing to be critical, a scrutinising television and a very broad coalition of political support that could easily fragment. The marketing approach is predicated on a proactive rather than reactive politics, but great leadership must look to the long term and do unpopular things which are impossible if a market-directed approach is adopted.

10 A Licence to Export: The Spread of Political Marketing Methods to Britain

The British have a notion of political marketing as something done simply at election time and even then grudgingly. Political rhetoric is often exclusive rather than inclusive – ameliorative perhaps for those it aims at, but infuriating to those it does not. But Britain is as yet far from intending that marketing should be part of its political culture. The parties spent £6.15 million, a diminutive sum by America's standards, on local communication in 1983; according to R. J. Johnson it did influence the way some people voted.[1] The British notion of governing is an administrative and not a communications one, and what has already been done seems primitive by the standards of America's campaigns: indeed, it gives to elections a rather seedy aura. But many American methods would be unsuited to British conditions, for America is a 'sell' culture, a sustained act of promotion, and hucksterism is not merely a means but a social value.

BRITISH CRITICS OF POLITICAL MARKETING

In Britain the marketing of politics has been much debated publicly. Britons exhibit a great concern for its ethical implications, with many regarding it as a perversion of democracy. On the evidence of this book their fears might be justified. In 1986, the *New Statesman* was speaking for many when it asked:[2]

> How far does *image* making determine *policy* making? How far has our political process become captive to the demands of television, to the shaping of audience? To admit that no party which wishes to be in at the winning post can afford to ignore the agencies is not to endorse the trend.

Perhaps electorates are served best by a process of public debate and partisan criticism; ideas armed with words do battle. Such a process, say the sceptics, is being replaced by a gaudy parody of argument, not political theatre but political pantomime. Germaine Greer suggested:[3]

> Thatcher has more to lose by wearing the wrong colour, by showing a wattled upper arm or (imagine it) a half-inch of cleavage, or making a display of her husband's wealth, than she has by talking utter balderdash in the House or in the European parliament, or even on British television.

One perceptive critic of political marketing in Britain has been Sir Alfred Sherman.[4] He has suggested the corruption, present and potential, that it implies: 'I feared, too, that the new disposition was liable to reproduce the risks inherent when high earners were under the nominal control of low earners . . .'. Moreover he perceives the advent of marketing as sapping the intellectual vitality of politics since it becomes a thought-substitute. Speaking of Kinnock, he said, 'If only he could create new policies in the image of his image – it was seriously argued – victory might yet be within his grasp. Because political parties interact, the devaluation of ideas in one must affect their status in all.' Other aspects of political strategy would also suffer from the cosmetic: 'I feared, too, that the new manipulation technology would blunt the incentive to adduce, sharpen and propagate ideas'.

In perceiving the link between communication and policy he saw that the one could easily replace the other; marketers would acquire a policy-making role and fill it with their babble:

> I feared that a party which was far from united in its political and economic appreciation and objectives would be prone to leave advertisement to paper over differences. This would risk drawing advertisers into a political vacuum, where they might acquire a policy-making role by default. I feared a vulgarising process, whereby outsiders brought in for their skills in selling soap would go on selling soap.

He saw that marketing methods could ultimately undermine political leadership by inverting the leadership process:

> In the United States, polling has become an integral part of what is called policy entrepreneurship. It is used not primarily as a test of popularity, but as a basis for the elaboration of policy. This is not just a more scientific extension of the politician's traditional sense

of what the public wants, but a qualitatively new development. Followership replaces leadership.

He stresses the centrality of ideas rather than communication in the creation of the Thatcherite epic: 'Ideas were crucial: the skills of the hairdresser, the TV commercials producer or the night-club review compere were marginal.' For Sherman there is a clear conflict between political ideas and political marketing communication: focus on the one must necessarily tend to preclude the other.

Sherman's intellectual critique of political marketing was cogent. Much less so was that of Professor Lord Beloff.[5] He asserted: 'They are used to marketing products to which they have no personal commitment – Politics, on the contrary, demands total commitment because only those who are totally committed can take others along with them.' Now this is curious. 'Total' commitment may be an active bar to effective communication since our principles appear self-evident; moreover advertising copywriters usually have or develop some sympathy with the product they lyricise. This peer also asserts: 'Political polls are a poor guide to political choices either because of their complexity, their remoteness from daily life, or because they cannot measure intensity of commitment.' This is at best a half-truth. He added, with unabashed ethnocentricity: 'Nearly all attempts to graft American politics on to British institutions are misguided, and this is no exception.' For Beloff, 'Such devices – computerized records, direct mail, the 'telethon' soon if we can afford it – are irrelevant to a serious political party which has an organic personality and embodies a set of accepted values.'

As a species of unthinking reaction this would be hard to excel, since it is a critique based not on ethical grounds where political marketing is weakest, but on pragmatic grounds where the evidence – not least from the Conservatives themselves – is strongest, and if this then is a representative specimen of Tory thought at its highest, the party's amateur campaign in 1987 is not surprising, but a logical outcome of its internal culture. Lord Beloff went on to make an invidious comparison between the effectiveness of modern political marketing methods and those of the Primrose League in the nineteenth century.

Beloff felt that the Tory Party National Union should be the main source of political intelligence and campaign work, and this perhaps is his most extraordinary assertion, for to assume that party stalwarts can relay unbiassed, accurate information, to say that voters are really persuaded by people who knock on their door rather than the television campaign, is like advocating the use of horse cavalry in the age of mechanical warfare. Thus we may imagine the party workers, rank upon amateur antediluvian rank, going forth with their contagious loyalty, their little certainties and rehearsed dogmas, convincing the streets in a way which apparently television never can. He concluded his remarkable critique thus: 'Margaret Thatcher is not a bar of soap'. One certainly cannot disagree with this final sentiment. Seldom has the Tory Party had more loyal, or more useless, advice.

A LIMITED OPPORTUNITY

British parties were long reluctant to market their politics, not from priestly devotion to the sanctity of British politics but because they were too incurious to experiment. British reserve may recoil at the import of many of the techniques described but their politics will eventually integrate them just as their consumer marketing has done, while the Labour Party under Kinnock is open to the notion that ideas do not sell themselves but have to be persuasively articulated. Clearly the British parties could be far more effective at communicating with their publics than they actually are, and their slowness in doing so reflects a strange belief that politics should be somehow amateur: perhaps it is part of a wider cultural rejection of competitive values. Political marketing is an implicit threat to their traditions. Politics, perhaps like other areas of British life, is its own hermetically sealed world which has a limited commerce with the other professional worlds, so there are scant transfusions between the two: hence, politics has been slow to assume business methods. Partly also this reluctance to market reflects the continuity of large areas of traditional party allegiance and, as these begin to dissolve, marketing reveals its true potential.

However, the operation of political marketing in Britain is circumscribed by structural factors. There are the prohibitions of the law, perhaps the principal factor, for the individual candidate is limited to a low budget and television is forced into strict neutrality under equal-time rulings, and the consequences are far-reaching, since the candidate cannot simply bypass the party as he can in the United States. Another problem of the British system is the amount of territory that lies permanently in the hands of one or other of the main political parties, for in America more geography is opened up for real contest. The diminutive quantities of political marketing in

Britain also reflect the absence of significant local factors in the election campaign; this is not a federal system, and generally national issues constitute the electorate's criteria. In Britain the parties and the loyalties they command are stronger and most advertising is done on a national party basis: the candidate is usually a mere cipher for his party, not, as in America, a semi-independent operator running his own media campaign, a private politician. The fact that electioneering is so centralised leads to a poverty of local campaigning and the public meeting itself is, as in America, dead, while the average MP has about £5000–£6000 spent on his election, though such limits only come into play after the issue of the election writ.

Thus there is a large gulf in the operational character of political marketing in the two countries. The corrosion of big money politics is to some extent avoided in the United Kingdom and there is not yet the same trivialisation and gaucherie. Also in Britain the stress on image is less in evidence and there is good documentary and news coverage of issues, and television provides debating fora. These are enduring strengths. Perhaps also in the United States, with laxer equal-time laws, political advertising makes television companies less committed to extensive debate and documentary coverage, for why give free publicity for a perspective when its proponents are willing to pay for its promotion? Moreover political campaigning may create so much 'noise' that television companies feel they would merely irritate their viewers by providing further layers of coverage.

Nevertheless the political use of advertising has increased markedly in Britain; according to Ian Griffiths, 'Expenditure has risen by almost 100% in each of the past 3 years, notching up $7.4 million of rate and billings in newspapers and magazines last year.'[6] Pressure groups and other organisations which needed political weight began to turn to advertising; hence, during the miners' strike, the National Coal Board appealed through public media advertising to the public and to striking miners. Most memorably, the Greater London Council ran an extravagant campaign against its own abolition; before it began 45 per cent of Londoners were unaware of the intended abolition, and this figure was down to 21 per cent in six months.[7]

At one time the British public would never tolerate the trite salesmanship of insubstantial images, but this mood is changing. The Conservative Party has cautiously approved some at least of the things we have discussed. Labour now embraces them with fervour after a history of chaste disdain. The Conservatives appointed a

Director of Marketing, thereby endowing the concept with a formal status in their hierarchy, while their constituencies are using computers. And as in America television is the theatre in which politics are performed. The successful media packaging of the Conservative Party helped to ensure their first two terms of office and gimmickry, the media event and orchestrated party conferences are fast acquiring an American flavour.

The Social Democrat Party made some use of American political consultants after the 1983 General Election, the first British party to do so, hiring the liberal consulting firm Craver, Mathews and Smith, and their brief was to experiment with those direct mailing techniques that had proved so efficient in the United States: their target objective was a list of 100 000 donors with $3–4 million annual income. Their first test mailings yielded 45 000 donors.[8] Craver himself was careful to point to the important differences between British and American campaigning – fewer mailings would contain language that was 'more under-stated, with somewhat less hyperbole'.

As in the United States the decline of the party in Britain is significant in the rise of political marketing, for loyalties are much less automatic than they used to be and this results from many of the demographic and social trends observable in the United States of America. Such homogeneity is consequent upon the decline of the pre-existing cohesion that in the past would have prevented political marketing from being a really potent tool; conditions are maturing for the emergence of an American-style prime minister. Such an evolution should not surprise us, since the criteria we use to make political choices are necessarily superficial. Hence the art of politics becomes an exercise in the judicious manipulation of symbols, to which task the pseudo-science of marketing lends its nefarious lore.

WHAT BRITISH PARTIES COULD LEARN

Since they can store all kinds of data about local and national support, fund-raising, details of key swing areas and so on, and can regularly update campaign management data, computers could revolutionise British campaign management. Yet in 1983 the Labour Party possessed only one elderly model. In America computers have become an essential, the penknife in the kit-bag of every political campaign. Telephones could also be fruitfully used for fund-raising from the party faithful, but their wider employment could be deemed an offensive intrusion. Geodemographic propaganda techniques could also be valuable, since Britain's streets fall into much sharper categories with more predictable attitudes than do their American counterparts, and society is less mobile – I may for example inhabit a street peopled by Transylvanian microchip entrepreneurs, and polling will allegedly suggest the attitudes of all kindred areas.

Direct mailing techniques are another attractive resource and solicitation of central membership lists could replenish the fortunes of all political parties, counteracting Labour's constituency decay. The mail is a way of extending political association without political power to a reserved silent majority. The inference that there is not much money available for British parties reflects a failure of fund-raising technique and not an unavailability of funds, and direct mail would be a way of bringing big money into British politics while avoiding the taint of unions or business. Parties must have central computerised lists of members which they regularly keep informed and occasionally solicit. In the approach to the 1987 General Election five million young first-time voters received a letter from Mr Norman Tebbit, the sepulchral chairman of the Conservative Party, dealing with their (polling-validated) special concerns on jobs and training, and inviting comment on contemporary British problems. In autumn 1986 the Tories were recruiting 500 new members per week with direct mail and were aiming to select 16 million people in their 1987 mailings, including besides youth such groupings as shareholders in newly privatised companies, young householders and professionals.[9] While the scope is impressive, it is probable that such target groups are not specific enough for effective direct mail; moreover it is best used as a fund-raising device, whereas here the attempt is to use it as a cumbersome tool for more general persuasion, and many of those aimed at – such as the teachers – would probably not have been responsive enough to justify the communication effort.

Americans adore technique and exhibit an insatiable desire to organise and process everything; no area is without its overpaid technicians. Nor should Britons scoff at the American stress on training. For in Britain canvassers and candidates do not receive any training of any kind in electioneering; they are expected to learn by 'experience', which means they repeat the same errors: however, in the land of the gifted amateur, such a suggestion is unlikely to be welcomed.

THE 1979 GENERAL ELECTION

1979 was not of course the first time commercial advertisers had been involved in British politics. In fact they had played a prominent role from 1959, and political advertising goes back much further in time; even in 1903 the Conservatives had made a propaganda film, *John Bull*, on the subject of free trade. But 1979 is significant for the fact that the advertising was memorable, that it clarified the issues and that its significance entered the public consciousness.

In 1979 the strategy of Conservative propaganda was to force Prime Minister James Callaghan on the defensive before he actually called a general election. Never before had advertising been so important in a British election campaign, and although we cannot isolate this from the broader political effects it did sharpen arguments in favour of the Tories. The controversy over Saatchis' role generated considerable free publicity; it is claimed that Mr Callaghan postponed the elections from September to May as a result of the onslaught and intervening, of course, was the 'winter of discontent'. Saatchis' first poster featured a queue of unemployed and the caption 'Labour Isn't Working'.[10] A television advertisement claimed that the unemployed could form a line from Parliament to Glasgow, and another that 'Made in Britain meant it was the best in the world . . . today we are famous for discouraging people from getting to the top and not rewarding skill and talent. And because it pays people not to work, today less and less is made in Britain. In a word, Britain is going backwards' (at this point there was a picture of Big Ben with the hands going backwards quickly).[11] This expresses, in blunt language, what had almost become the conventional wisdom. Labour also faced a more right-wing electorate: in 1964 over half their supporters wanted more spent on social services and increased nationalisation and legal supports for the unions. But by 1979 only one-third of its voters desired such things.

THE 1983 GENERAL ELECTION

From our viewpoint the 1983 campaign is of limited interest, since pre-existing political factors determined the electorate's verdict and the campaign is relevant to us only in so far as it demonstrates the evolution of political marketing techniques in Britain today.

The Labour Party and many commentators[12] convinced themselves that public opinion was manipulated by advertisers in 1983. Such complaints imply in those who articulated them a low opinion of the gullibility of electors, while to say the intrusion of marketing was sinister implies an effective marketing product. For at a national level election promotions lacked flair. Slogans were insipid and meaningless. Alliance film was satiric in tone, ambiguous about policy, while Tory broadcasting showed optimistic images but remained excessively glib. Two-thirds of British voters said they had watched the party political broadcasts. Walter Cronkite dismissed the programmes as ranging from 'terrible to the barely tolerable'.[13] Both Labour and Conservative purchased newspaper advertising, the Tories taking full-page advertisements to denounce Labour extremists, ridicule Labour's unemployment policies and such. Labour also eccentrically took out an advertisement in *The Economist*.[14] The Tories were given a new symbol, a torch, by their head of marketing, a former director of Mars Chocolates. And they benefitted from press loyalty: thus George Gale with somewhat trite echoes of Shakespeare and the Elizabethan age:[15] 'The P.M. is the sun around which all other politicians orbit. They take their positions from her, they are her moons.'

Alliance advertising showed some imagination. A poster campaign depicted the other party leaders as characters from the *Wizard of Oz*, declaiming, 'If only I had a heart' (Mrs Thatcher), 'If only I had a brain' (Mr Foot), but the Alliance paid insufficient attention to the development of themes – too often they seemed to be merely interested in scoring debating points.[16] This kind of trivia shows the dangers of a humour so central that it detracts from necessary gravitas. Moreover commitment of their support was different, since their voters were often making an anti-two-party statement, a protest vote.

We may remark on the pathos of Labour's act: never again would they turn in such a performance since the marketing lesson was so severe. Their internal disputes were dissected by the campaign; their plans began to disintegrate under public scrutiny and the casual nature of their preparation was demonstrable. And Labour's manifesto proved its albatross. They simply took unfashionable minority positions on virtually all of the key issues. Their television advertising bore a rigid ideological stamp: it aimed at a minority audience, the under-privileged, and did not seek the broad constituency critical to political success. All their policies were unpopular, many strategically key interests were infuriated[17] and (this is an old danger with political parties) they came to perceive themselves as bearers of sacred texts, a secular priesthood: as with the Goldwater Republicans, compromise is betrayal.

In their choice of leader the parliamentary Labour Party gave a good example of the dangers of choosing on internal party criteria rather than 'mediability'. Michael Foot's self-indulgent campaign was idiosyncratic. Television coverage, the scene for instance of him singing the 'Red Flag', cast him as particularly fatuous and only when speaking to selected target groups was he effective; the length of his speeches made it difficult to use nuggets for media purposes and he would avoid contact with the radio and television journalists accompanying him on the campaign. Robert Fox wrote[18] 'he had thought that the issues needed only to be allowed to speak for themselves. The messages on unemployment and on the dangers of nuclear war were so vital that the nature of the medium by which it was to be conveyed scarcely merited a thought. In contrast to Mrs Thatcher's strictly superintended perambulations, Mr Foot visited seventy marginal seats.'

The Labour Party's marketing failures were diagnosed in an election post-mortem by Denis Healey.[19] He drew attention to their failure to appreciate the importance of media in concentrating on traditional methods. The party leaders should be put 'into settings which are cheerful, intimate, familiar, and photogenic'. His litany of complaints included:

1. Tories monitored every Labour broadcast, and concentrated their campaign against every vulnerable statement.
2. The Party's polling adviser and its advertising agent never met each other during the campaign.
3. The need to use graphics more often in press conferences.
4. The need for a short and vigorous manifesto.
5. The fatal decision to let policy development continue until the last minute.
6. The need for proper discussion of issues, slogans, phrases for key speeches, lines of argument, buzz words (such as 'one-sided nuclear disarmament').

This is a straight marketing evaluation, though of course he would never admit it; underlying all this is the theme that parties must cease to be introspective and recognise that they are in the business of advocacy, indeed of selling.

Labour was particularly antagonistic to polling: Aneurin Bevan had once told the pollsters: 'You are taking the poetry out of politics'. In the four years preceding the campaign Labour did no polling whatsoever, but once it began they were saturated with twice as many private polls as the Conservatives: and their news was always bad. Foot's belief and that of his close associates was that his declamatory oratory would arouse party activists who could then communicate such enthusiasm to the electorate – a naive supposition about voter decision making in a media age.

Polling certainly illuminated the strategy of the Conservatives: polls showed that Labour Party policy had scant credibility with the electorate and that there was no internalised commitment to the Alliance. Tory leaders could gauge how well their message was being communicated and polling told them what they really did need to hear: that electors did not make them the focus of blame for Britain's economic crisis; rather this was due to external causes and 'moral' factors.[20] Polling also warned the Tories how an assault on the Alliance could backfire. In the months leading up to the General Election 'the Conservatives took private opinion polls in key marginal constituencies to identify 'target' groups of voters as well as the most popular and unpopular issues. The results were fed into their new computer...'[21] The Conservatives engaged in qualitative research and in-depth discussion groups were videotaped, and they placed heavy reliance on big surveys – four were done – prepared ready for weekend strategy meetings; these used samples of 2000 people, and the Conservatives also commissioned six polls with samples of 1000.[22] 'Fast feedback' reports from AGB (Audits of Great Britain) were received by the Conservatives on most days of the week; a group of 200 opinion leaders was consulted in daily rotas of 40 and interrogated as to its reaction to the campaign on the salient issues, damaging statements, televisions coverage and so on.[23] Yet compared to Reagan's PINS system and even to the systems used by the Democrats, this was amateur and impressionistic; as a result it could even have been misleading. In this campaign private polls did not seek to probe individual images on behalf of the parties, nor did they seek to gauge the effectiveness of advertisements and broadcasts.

Certainly this was an issue-oriented campaign. The Tories and their advertising agency, Saatchis, made the decision to discredit the Labour manifesto: this was the pivot of Tory strategy and the agency advised an aggressive campaign. Saatchis' marketing triumph was a list of fourteen liberties allegedly surrendered with a Labour vote.

The strategic objective was not to convert new followers but to consolidate the groups that put them in power in 1979. They gained five points against Labour in the first week – a lead they maintained. They gave the agency £2.4 million and were also the beneficiaries of a substantial party organisation, with 357 full-time agents as opposed to Labour's 43, and they also experimented for the first time with direct mail for fund-raising and for targetting voters in key constituencies.

The Conservative manifesto itself was an anodyne document. Butler and Kavanagh record that 'so much of the Conservatives' detailed intentions remained as elusive at the end of the campaign as at the beginning'; it was surely a failure of the political opposition that this was the case. The party seemed adept at manufacturing platitudes but bereft of new ideas.

Mrs Thatcher gave simple basic messages and reiterated them. Her campaign was strongly charged with optimism, patriotism and other emotions. Hyperbole touched new levels of bathos: 'And what a prize we have to fight for: no less than the chance to banish from our land the dark divisive clouds of Marxist socialism . . .' and so on.

The emphasis in Mrs Thatcher's campaign trips, the centrefold of Tory strategy, was the media contexts which looked good on television, party rallies of delirious supporters, and crafted television interviews. The implicit message was of successful model industries that would return the country to the ranks of successful nations. America was an unarticulated presence in the Tory campaign. The party was given its own election song and a risible 'youth rally' where the Prime Minister made a Roman entrance before the 5000-strong audience. The important thing for Britain is not to forfeit some of the excellent television election scrutiny; the important task for America is to adopt something of that approach.

But any notion of the permanent campaign disappeared during the Conservatives' next period in office, when their communications were so inept that only nine per cent of Tory supporters knew that education expenditure had increased greatly, and only 22 per cent thought the same of health-welfare spending.

THE 1987 GENERAL ELECTION

It will become the conventional wisdom that the 1987 General Election marked the full migration of American political packaging techniques to Britain, and throughout the land pub bars murmured with the commonplace that politicians were being sold like a new brand of detergent.

How influential was political advertising in that election? Its effects may seldom be more than marginal: but then, elections are about margins. Undoubtedly it was a catalyst for the rejuvenation of Labour's image and contributed significantly to the seriousness of Labour's candidacy; as Labour found, marketing can help set the agenda of the campaign, eliciting responses from the press, opponents and the like, it can give high definition to a party's core arguments. Moreover televised political propaganda does bypass the interrogation of the media and presents an idealised image of personalities and programme. The direct influence of the broadcasts is not on most electors but on the 'political nation', the tribe of opinion formers who are actively interested in politics and are solicited for their advice by neighbours, workmates and the like. But surveys claimed that less than two per cent of all voters in 1987 believed they were influenced by press advertising or posters. The head of political research at Mori pointed out that Party Political Broadcasts had a 50 per cent desertion rate.

The 1987 Conservative campaign was not a disaster. But it was poor in relation to the resources at the party's disposal and the merits of its case, though in the event this hardly mattered, given the unsaleability of Labour's programme, but the outcome another time may be different. The Tories began their 1987 campaign without the communications men who had helped create the 1983 victory – Bell, Reece and Parkinson. A curious and theatrical sequence took place.[24] Young and Rubicam supplied Mrs Thatcher with secret information based on the 'VALs' system, while Saatchis remained the official party advisers, and later Mr Tim Bell of Campbell, Spink Ewald and Bell returned as the Conservative campaign flagged ('wobbly Thursday'). Now, with sharply etched advertising and the message 'Britain is great again, don't let Labour wreck it', their momentum returned. Each group had a different minister urging its case (Whitelaw, Tebbit, Lord Young); each claimed credit after the election victory. But at the same time such politicisation of advertising agencies is evidence of the significance that political marketing now assumes. Ministers in seeking to increase their power saw the sponsorship of an agency and its pet dogma as power sources; only Saatchis worked in public.

Mrs Thatcher took the results of Young and Rubicam research very seriously; this research assured her that the Westland affair was trivial, it pinpointed election concerns over leadership, education and health. Their VALs system classified consumers, not on the basis of class but as 'need-driven' (absence of choice), 'outer-directed' (those who respond to signals from others and number 70 per cent of the population), 'inner-directed' and 'integrated', and unlike Saatchis' research the Young and Rubicam work did not identify Mrs Thatcher as the prime liability. Lord Beloff said 'Many loyal Conservatives may well wish a plague on both [ad agencies]', and the editor of the *Sunday Telegraph* asked: 'Surely the great Conservative Party is not about to tear itself asunder over an issue so quintessentially vulgar and trivial as to whether to employ one advertising agency or another?'

There was indeed some fine propaganda in that election: as an image exercise Labour's 'Neil and Glenys' film pastiche was without peer in British politics. Yet the abiding impression remained one of tedium. The first Tory broadcast targetted exclusively its own suppor-ters and, while hope is the most persuasive election message, they neglected to articulate it, confining their creativity to negative attack. It would be tedious to disinter the failings of the Tory campaign, and one is left with an impression of gerontocratic flag-waving and the wearing of silly hats. There were many technical faults. Broadcasts were pedestrian and Central Office accepted Saatchis' advice uncriti-cally: they failed to present Mrs Thatcher as other than two-dimensional, unlike Labour's confectionery, and given the presiden-tial nature of modern British elections this was a serious error. Their complacent belief in a defensive campaign, the identification of the Alliance as a major target, were only challenged by the virility of Labour's assault.

Moreover the Socialists, young and incubated by television, have a shrewd understanding of promotion, as both the Labour campaign and municipal propaganda demonstrated; add to this the sermonising cant of the BBC and you get a Tory Party stupefied by its articulate enemies and mystified at its own success. In other elections the Conservatives may not have Mrs Thatcher; opposition parties may collaborate; Labour may jettison its liabilities; and above all new generations who have no remembrance of Labour in power will come to vote, and the Conservatives cannot then afford the indulgence of a Tsarist central bureaucracy in the age of telegenic socialism.

But most of Labour's advertising missed the point entirely. People feared not so much their explicit policies as their incompetence to govern and their inability to control their Visigoth left; and their disdain to reassure people on the nuclear issue epitomised the way they took their new zeal for packaging to an extreme and neglected the structural deficiencies of their product. And like the Alliance they discounted toughness as an electoral asset. Alliance advertising fortified every stereotype in its sanctimoniously vicarage way, congealing into a series of pedestrian monologues which, one imagines, only political scientists would watch.

Lyndon Johnson's old consultant Tony Schwartz claims that political advertising should 'surface the feelings' of voters about themselves and their society: yet the opposition's overly bleak portrayal of the Condition of England failed to do this. Indeed, there is something moribund about a political culture so obsessed with extremes of social despair, and the parties were fixated on the past even though all the American evidence suggests that a focus on the future as a theme is one of the most effective devices of political advocacy.

In general, party advertising strategists clung to attack rather than defence; there was no refutation: propagandists lacked the agility to defend their vulnerable areas, lending the curious appearance of a ballet of deaf mutes. Advertising could certainly have exploited the mobilising power of emotion more, and the parties ignored the proven persuasive effectiveness of themes in politics; they chose instead to concentrate on issues, which are less easily digested by electors, constructing their pseudo-rational artefacts. The Tories went some way towards a thematic approach, pointing to the indivisibility of social services and economic strengths, but they could have gone much further, stressing, for instance, the distinction between state *financing* of the welfare state, as against the bureaucratic excesses of state *management*.

Parties seemed indeed to have a highly amateur notion of the way voters decide. The objective of propaganda should be to put a few ideas in circulation, so that they become part of the popular orthodoxy – a point Goebbels understood well, with his strong belief in the power of conditioning. Instead they decanted for electors a mass of ill-focussed impressions.

It is fascinating to speculate on the tactics that the parties could have adopted. The Conservatives might have performed some image surgery on Mrs Thatcher and made her personality more intimate; and they could even have admitted that they did not get everything right in their eight years in office – a device that invariably succeeds in America. Labour, apart from its first film, exhibited little creativity to dramatise its point; why not use, for example, a rolling list of companies closed under the Conservatives (with, given the political discovery of classical music, Handel's 'Dead March from Saul')? Generally advertising assumed that all Britain's problems were within the competence of government to solve: it fortified a dependency syndrome. Politicians, like the courtiers of Lilliput, leapt and crept; they assured voters in their manikin vanity that the deeper flows of history could be tamed, by them alone, and the aggregate effect was probably to increase the sum of popular cynicism.

CONCLUSIONS

Despite its shortcomings the 1987 election defined the flavour of all successors: welcome then the whisper of image rather than the noise of argument. Increasingly British politicians will come to recognise that they are in a commercial selling job, not a debating marathon, and British elections will become a reflection of the American, just as their fast food eateries feebly imitate the transatlantic kind. How remote Mr Michael Foot seemed then – an old, eccentric vintage that came some time after Gladstone '86. But to those who regarded the manipulation as necromantic there was one point of reassurance. It was performed by mediocrities. Advertising executives, as this election showed, have little insight into the political product, so that the devious potential of packaged politics has yet to be realised in the United Kingdom.

Modern British political parties need to extend the role of whatever ancilliary marketing service they possess. For simply to entrust an advertising agency with the invention of a political promotion is naive: the agency is unlikely to number among its assets deep political skill and insight. The mission of the political salesman can never be easy, much in the marketing menagerie is excluded from election use and the scrutiny of media reportage creates a problem of saturation. Marketing may repel rather than seduce. Then there is the compression of time, a mere matter of weeks. These considerations introduce important questions as to the kind, tone, and intensity of marketing in British elections.

Marketing in elections does have an ethical dimension. Democracy must not degenerate into a mindless exchange of slogans that mask crude factional interests in strife against each other; for the foundation of electoral choice is not simply actual knowledge about the issues, but also how to interpret them; for those who are not part of any particular vested interest, this means that they will be spectators to a debate. The strongest case emerges in a lengthy act of mutual review and criticism. It is selling the government of a country, not soap, and these large issues merit full discussion. But if the British are going to do it, they should do it well, for otherwise they could get the worst of all worlds – a banality and insincere technology of manipulation that is imported, and an implementation whose tawdriness is indigenous. Even in America much of the political work is not so much effective marketing as expensive marketing; the content of American political advertising is every bit as inane as in Britain, it simply exists in greater abundance. The British will never go as far, but they cannot turn back the clock; television and admen are there, they are political facts, and parties must learn to live with and cajole them just as the oratory of their leaders manipulated the crowds of an earlier generation.

Gone, then, are the rubicund Tory knights of the shire, surely to some celestial green-leather bench, and their successors would be equally comfortable as IBM salesmen. Whatever the ethical misgivings, effective persuasion tools will be used if they exist, since the instinct (though not the rhetoric) of political parties is seldom to bear witness to enduring truth, but to win. Of course, in a sense, British politicians have always marketed themselves. Gladstone spoke from railway carriages. But such a gesture carries a guileless spontaneity which would bemuse the urbane technocrats of America's campaigns. And so as we leave the American candidate to his street war, armed with every novelty and bauble, a monosyllabic personality articulated by new technology, we wonder whether British politicians will be similarly defended in time to come? The task must be to distinguish what is worthy in political marketing, that sharpens debates and broadens involvement, from that which is cynically banal. British feelings on the subject mix the admiration and unease they experience so often in scrutiny of the American scene. Should parties accept the savoury narcotic offered by their amiable American friend? The promise of soap powder is less grime, but parties offer us a government: the consequences of choice are infinitely more profound, the means of promotion the same.

11 The Selling of the President 1988

BUSH THE UNDERDOG: THOSE BLUEFISH ARE DEAD MEAT

The Bush campaign began abysmally. This was not deliberate, but it was an invaluable asset in his merchandising. It meant that core Republican supporters and contributors were galvanised out of their apathy. It meant that the public wearied of the press baiting of Bush: he attracted the sympathy of the fighting underdog, an important symbol in American myth.

The position was bleak. Opinion polls suggested that Bush had the highest negatives of any Republican since Goldwater.[1] After the Atlanta Democratic convention 50 per cent of voters claimed to be voting for Dukakis and 33 per cent for Bush.[2] Then, his vote began to rise. How Bush and his consultants achieved their turnabout will ever rank as the superlative case of political merchandising.

At the beginning of August the Bush epitaph seemed already to have been written.:

> He tends to appear grim and unsmiling before the cameras, as though seized by an air of defeat.[3]

The contrast with Reagan was often noted:

> Too much of what he is saying sounds only like a rewarmed version of what came, more gloriously, before.[4]

By contrast people were talking about Dukakis showing the 'charisma of a winner'.[5] Many began to dismiss Bush. For Paul Weyrich Bush was bound to lose because 'You can't beat something with nothing'.[6] No one knew where he stood, or what he felt strongly about. Doonesbury depicted him as an invisible bubble. The communications objective was therefore clear: to define his position with blazing clarity, and to articulate his passion. The jokes about him – a man born with a silver foot in his mouth who reminded women of their first husband and always had a white-haired woman (his mother?) – at his side, were endless. His 'talent for just plain seeming silly'[7] made him a target of satire. One correspondent thus described Bushese:

Bush's vernacular has created its own little world: a place called 'Tension city' where George catches 'the dickens from friends' tells ocean bluefish they're 'dead meat' and searches for the 'vision thing' while trying to avoid stepping in deep doo-doo.[8]

For Frank Johnson[9]

Bushisms convey the kind of terror and panic to be found in the work of their author's fellow New Englander, Edgar Allan Poe. They are the kind of noise which the decent, upright patrician ends up babbling after he sets out for some great destination – in this case, the Presidency – only to find himself lost in evil-seeming countryside, and driven mad. First the dark-jowled assassin, Senator Dole, tries to thwart him. No sooner is that villain overcome, when Mr Bush looks like being cheated of reaching his goal by the sudden emergence, late in the story, of an implausible Greek dwarf.

In this supernatural universe, the texts supplied to the hero by his speechwriters take on a life of their own, where nothing is as it seems, and so rugs mysteriously become plugs. It is one of the earliest stories in American literature about possession by autocue. Also, his retainers keep involving him in ordeals – called 'photo opportunities', in which he has no idea what he is saying at all.

He concluded:

New Orleans, at the hottest time of its year, receives this most haunted figure in American fiction.

Running through all the ridicule at this stage was an obsession with George Bush's social class:[10]

Reagan is western boots and chopping wood to Bush's Lacoste shirts and tennis shoes . . .
[Reagan] makes all those in the lumpen electorate who also went to a mediocre college feel better. Then along comes George Bush, who is everything they're not – Greenwich, Andover, Yale, captain of the Yale baseball team, elitist clubman – and because he cannot be identified with any issues, people focus on the manners of his class.

Yet Bush was able to rise from this position of unique derision. In marketing similarity – the first basis of attraction – is often used to sell. There could be none of that here: Bush seemed to inhabit a private world that spoke its own peculiar hothouse preppie jargon.

He could not be democratised. Yet commentators erred in dismissing him as too elitist for the tastes of American democracy. The President of the United States is a monarch; an elite background gives credence to this role and echoes similarly patrician figures in American history. Moreover democratic publics do not detest inherited privilege. They feel ambivalent about it. Part of ambivalence is a feeling of attraction as well as rejection. In addition, personal style is not the exclusive basis of attraction: shared values are another and perhaps a more important one. All Bush had to do was to show he shared majority values and they would be with him, however distancing his style. The pundits did not understand this distinction. Bush's consultants did.

BUSH TURNAROUND

How was the Bush turnaround achieved? There had to be a 'new' Bush: the negative could be cosmeticised, new attributes of personality could be laid bare to counter them.

Bush had scored one notable hit early on with the Dan Rather incident: 'how would you like it if I judged your career by those seven minutes when you walked off the set in New York'. Like almost everything else in the campaign this was not spontaneous but the result of conscious packaging: a media ambush prepared by the political consultant Roger Ailes; and the beginning of a disciplined effort to change public perceptions.

The core of this effort was to emphasise shared values, with their emotive charge, as distinct from the managerial emphasis of Dukakis. Inevitably the result of such grand strategy would be that the Republican emerged as the more human candidate. Republicans chose symbolic acts to express their 'values', and emotive rhetoric; they underwrote this with a vehemently negative advertising campaign which sought to expose Dukakis as alienated from these values and by implication un-American, in that to be American is to laud such values. In the autumn campaign Bush successfully played two roles:

> He can, at the same time, appear as Dirty Harry the enforcer – his Texas persona – while also coming over as Bush the wistful advocate of a kinder, gentler nation.[11]

The touchstone for the strategy was a few obscure acts by Dukakis as

Governor of Massachusetts, which – paraded, inflated, decorated in savage colours – could be used to expose the 'real' (i.e. liberal) Dukakis, and damage his cultivated centrist image. The amazement of the campaign was Dukakis's failure to counterattack, and to a competitive society like the US this would be inexplicable.

Moreover any counterattack would have forced Dukakis to stress illiberalism, something he could not in conscience do, to participate in an auction as to who was the most hard right. Roger Ailes, in his usual way, expressed Republican strategy bluntly: 'That little computer heart from Massachusetts isn't going to know what hit him'.[12]

Partly the fight was at the level of speechifying rhetoric – the renowned, lush 'sound bites' that were articulated in some sort of memorable regional or social setting against a backdrop of delirious supporters. Thus Bush would speak 'at length of a problem of values in America and the need for self-discipline, courage, character, support for family and faith in God and one's self'.[13] Bush ridiculed the 'competence' unique selling proposition in his convention speech:

> a narrow ideal that makes trains run on time but doesn't know where they're going, the creed of the technocrat who makes sure the gears mesh but doesn't for a second understand the magic of the machine.[14]

He turned his reserve into an asset:

> I may sometimes be a little awkward but there's nothing self-conscious in my love of country. I am a quiet man, but I hear the quiet people others don't – the ones who raise the family, pay the taxes, meet the mortgage. I hear them and I am moved, and their concerns are mine.[15]

Now he was fighting and the door was yielding.

Complementing the rhetorical strategy was a more unbuttoned public posture: Americans are a relaxed people, primness annoys them, so to approximate their style more closely it was necessary to enact events such as when 'the would-be first couple broke out in a gushing display of "lovey-dovey" in a CBS television interview, right down to the Vice-President administering a sharp slap on Mrs Bush's derrière.'[16]

Then there was the purchased advertising. This echoed the themes of the sound bites, but it was coarser. Most outrageous of all was the Willie Horton commercial: the weekend release of this homicidal rapist, when he raped and wounded again, played on America's subterranean rage. It was a high risk strategy that worked, and rivals the 'Daisy spot' as the most famous political commercial of all time: legions of eerily silent prisoners were shown walking through a revolving door. This commercial hit American liberalism at its most vulnerable point: its ideologically conditioned inability to sound determined on crime, even though that is now a central choice criteria for American political consumers.

Then there was the 'Boston Harbor' commercial. Democrats have always been more believable on some of the 'quality of life' issues, particularly the environmental ones. To convict them here would seem to reduce much of their public posturing to cant and humbug. So film of noxious Boston harbour was repeatedly shown. This helped to challenge Dukakis's assumption of the moral highground: the remembrance of that image could make his sermonising tone seem merely ridiculous.

Then there were the symbolic appeals. Dukakis, on legal advice, had not assented to a bill committing teachers to the pledge of allegiance. This peripheral fact was made a Republican cause celèbre. It was ideal propaganda material. In a country as diverse as America the flag is an important unifier, an emblem of identity that commands intense emotional adherence: thus Dukakis's patriotism – and how could we have a President who was unpatriotic? – was questioned, the fact that he was only a second-generation immigrant darkly hinted. So Bush took to leading Republican audiences in pious theatrical pledges of mass allegiance, like a scandalised schoolmarm.

Bush had another, priceless, asset. He was – or could be made to seem – happy. He smiled, and seemed to relish living. To a nation that prizes its optimism this was wise. Dukakis by contrast often wore a look of accusation, and when he smiled it was more the worn, casual flash of an elevator operator than the projection of a man who has drunk richly of life, and found it fun: behind that look there seemed to lie an eternity of tiring days, of statistics studied, meetings chaired, memorandums written: of forever breathing the scentless air of bureaucratic culture.

THE RETREAT OF MICHAEL DUKAKIS

It is easy now to forget, so complete was the Republican villification of Dukakis, how strongly he once appeared. In part, this was due to the centricism of his message: never recently had a Democrat presidential candidate appeared so uninterested in ideology.

The communications objective of the Republicans was therefore to 'expose' this as a sham, to discover and merchandise the 'evidence' that really Dukakis was an unreconstructed liberal of the pattern American voters feared and had consistently rejected. The onus would be then on Dukakis to 'prove' his innocence of the charge, and thus be on the defensive.

The Dukakis strategy was vaguer: to appeal to 'competence', an appeal that it is intrinsically difficult to sell since it cannot be dramatised or made glamorous. According to the Dukakis thesis, Reaganite prosperity was an illusion created by borrowing[17]: a difficult theme to communicate, since prosperity for many was a fairly tangible thing. For 'competence' to work as a sales pitch, there has to be a considerable degree of consumer dissatisfaction: they had to be convinced (a) that there was gross incompetence and (b) that such incompetence was highly dysfunctional to their group interests. On neither point was Democrat propaganda sufficiently convincing.

The story of the Dukakis career is now well known – and 'career' is the apposite word, with its implications of an ordered, managerial approach to life. Dukakis made his administration of Massachusetts the selling patter. However, there were many doubts about whether the Massachusetts experience could be replicated elsewhere. Nor was the recent history of the state reassuring: in 1988 it had a large revenue shortfall.

Dukakis, as all the world now knows, had a fundamental problem. He bored people. Stories abounded about his pedantry – how, for example, he spent a vacation studying Swedish land use.[18] They told about his stinginess, the terraced house, the bargain hunting and changing of dollars[19] 'so that he does not have to leave too big a tip'.[20] Like George Bush, then, Dukakis had a problem in communicating a rounded personality. Observers remembered Mr Hart's words, that 'he liked people as a concept'.[21]

Clearly attractiveness as well as credibility is important in any communications process. Surely the failure of Dukakis to express this did mean something more than a lack of sympathy with the triteness of modern campaigning. Underpinning this failure, according to his political enemies, was a technician's view of life itself. Certainly modern Democrats have failed to make moral zeal exciting: the consequence of a party culture that has become privatised and introspective, that – conscious of its moral greatness – reproves others as it admires itself. It was the great achievement of Republicans in this campaign to allege such an element in Dukakis's make-up: how far different then from their hero: 'Kennedy [at least the buoyant, witty, graceful myth the public celebrates] was able to make altruism seem fun'.[22]

The major deficiency with Dukakis as a 'product' was his detachment. Americans are a passionate people. They show their emotions. they discuss them. Dukakis violated a cultural norm: in so doing he neglected the first principle of attractiveness, which is similarity. He was not 'similar' because he could not communicate outrage; Bush, dissimilar in background and style, united himself to people by affecting to share their emotions. That is why he came to be perceived as 'likeable'.

Are such criteria irrelevant? Communication skill must be the essence of the US presidency. The idea that administrative skill is an adequate substitute is erroneous: it is merely a desirable attribute, not a necessary one. The presidency is many roles – monarch, uncle, tribune of the people, high priest of national values, national totem – all of them have a common theme, the ability to project personality feelingly. Dukakis could do none of these things. He failed in the key job specification. His personality seemed to owe more to New England than sunlit vistas of Greece: his heritage more Cotton Mather than Demosthenes – or Melina Mercouri. A moralising, provincial damp seemed to have seeped into his soul: for all the world as if he would spring forth a wide white ruff and a high black hat.

This of course is merely the personality as it was projected, not necessarily as it really was, which is a very different thing. Moreover it was the personality as the Republicans wished us to see it, the overlay of their propaganda contributing mightily to the shaping of this perception. It was a perception which evolved through the campaign – that is to say, we began to receive a new interpretation of the known facts of the Dukakis personality. Originally then his frugal living seemed to signify an honest, self-disciplined character: later it seemed to suggest a ponderous dullness. His ethnicity appeared at first romantic: later just another empty political pose. By contrast, Bush made a journey in the opposite direction. This success cannot be attributed simply to the packagers. Whatever the panache of men like Roger Ailes, they must have responsive material to work with: moreover, humble material. For a consultant to successfully rework a candidate, the politician has to admit deficiency. Dukakis was just unwilling to change. Secondly, political packagers often claim that they simply allow the real man to speak, by enabling him to manage the artificial distortions of television. If they are right – and that is simply a matter of opinion – then the 'wimp' Bush was the distorted image, and 'likeable' Bush the proximate truth.

Above all else, it was the law and order issue which betrayed Dukakis. This is by tradition conservative territory: Dukakis like many Democrats chose to ignore it, or say of the causes of crime 'We all know them: the lack of jobs and opportunity'.[23] This led to the most pathetic memory of the whole campaign, Dukakis's bloodless response when asked if he would reconsider the death penalty were his own wife raped and murdered. As one observer commented, Dukakis's stance missed the fact that the law and order issue was less about keeping the streets safe, than about revenge.[24]

Then, in the words of one commentator, 'the body twitched'.[25] Dukakis Mark II was a reborn 'class war populist'.[26] Republicans were delighted. Their 'exposure' strategy had ostensibly succeeded.

PACKAGING FOR THE FREE MEDIA

Image management is an operation of quite remarkable subtlety. Completely unintentional nuances can easily be conveyed, and this is where the intuitive and tactical insights of the political consultants are most needed.

In the case of Quayle it almost seems to have been a case of life imitating art: apparently as a student he concluded after watching Redford's *The Candidate* that he was better looking than Redford and with the aid of consultants would excel in politics.[27] Quayle became an instant legend for his mediocrity – his startled doe expression, his answers 'waffle – a disjointed, meaningless and unknowledgeable ramble'.[28] Still, the packagers managed to silence him.

There was another reason why image should be central in this election: for the Reagan epoch had redefined our conception of presidential leadership; melodrama was now part of the job specification:

> The candidates were auditioning for the first time for the role of replacing Ronald Reagan each evening on the news for at least the next four years.[29]

Increasingly the election seemed to have become a game between rival political consultants. Contexts, the visual setting chosen to perform in, assumed a high importance.[30]

The 'Snoopy' incident, as well as displaying the amateurism of the Democrat team, also illustrates the difficulties of 'packaging' for the free media. For why precisely did this incident fail? The visual absurdity of a little man in a big hat has something to do with it: as has that of a civilian who has never raised a fist in anger assuming the paraphernalia of militarist aggression. But it is easy to see how, on paper, such an event would be attractive. It was an attempt to identify the candidate with defence concerns at the customary symbolic level. It failed because it was so obviously forced, for there was no conceivable connection between the candidate's characteristics as we had come to know them, and the costume and context to which he now had laid claim: the associations of the man and the setting were so contradictory that the contrast produced high mirth. The 'Snoopy' incident was described thus by Charles Bremner:

> On ABC News Sam Donaldson, the star reporter, relished the fun. 'Who is this?' Donaldson asked. 'Is it General Abrahams? Is it General Patton? No', he said, as the camera zoomed in to the Snoopy-like figure on top of the speeding tank, 'it is the governor of Massachusetts'.[31]

One Dukakis aide is supposed to have said:

> Here we are offering serious programmes in health care, college loans, the environment. Next week we do housing and you're talking about body language.

This remark encapsulates the reasons why the Democrats have lost recent Presidential elections.

By contrast, the packaging of Bush was often flawless: in the end all spontaneity was excised:

> His advisers now intend to keep him in a hermetic seal for the final three weeks. They plan not a single press conference. Every detail has been mapped out, including each day's photo-opportunity and one-line message for the voters.[32]

Such 'packaging' is currently the only way a candidate can manage. It may be too stilted for the life of a democracy: but its defenders would argue that given the piranha appetites of the American press, it is the only way to engage. Is it, as we suggest elsewhere, a necessary antidote to the adversarialism of the American press?

But even the Democrats had managed to package their convention, so strong were electorate expectations of a visually exciting political 'product' with a resounding message and contextual colour. Speeches were rehearsed by a speech consultant, with speakers on a dummy rostrum.[33] Reporters sat on the podium, delegates were relegated, 100 press assistants operated. Liberal motions were very firmly rejected.[34] Packaging – up to a point. There was a figure more difficult for merchandisers to control, Jesse Jackson. He plays a central role in this campaign, as much by his absence as by his presence. The tension between black and white was a 'hidden persuader' in the election.

TELEVISION COMMERCIALS

Television advertising established its significance early in the campaign, notably with Gephardt's abrasive commercials: his performance in New Hampshire, and success in South Dakota and Iowa, were partially attributed to them. The advertisements were aggressive, patriotic and simple, placed on sports and game shows: in one he made the subsequently notorious point of $48 000 Chryslers in South Korea and promised retaliation. Previously Gephardt had been written off, now, with pithy advertising, his candidacy was resuscitated.[35]

Purchased advertising was influential during the primaries. A New York Times – CBS news poll suggested that the television advertising contributed to 'dramatic shifts' in voter opinion at the end of the 'Super Tuesday' campaign, and election results revealed a marked connection between expenditure on television advertising and success.[36]

Campaign advertisements, portending the role they were to play in the general election, were responsible for the most inflammatory event of the primaries, Dole's retort to Bush 'stop lying about my record'. Dole was referring to Bush commercials suggesting he was ambivalent on the subject of tax rises, which was not a lie but was selective advocacy.[37]

However, advertising expenditures were not invariably a source of success; Albert Gore's advertisements 'invited damagingly close scrutiny of his trade policies', and his expenditure of over $200 000 on television in one week in Illinois purchased barely more than 5 per cent of the vote; concluded one observer: 'The muddled and opportunistic, using television to refashion their messages and images, have not won voter support'.[38]

Advertising on both sides during the general election interpreted the truth about the opponent flexibly, even if it did not exactly lie. Candidates, especially Bush, could remain 'nice', and the poison be carried by purchased persuasion which, being a commercial, somehow did not stigmatise the candidate who had sanctioned it. One-quarter of the electorate claimed to be influenced by the advertising, which was often repeated on the news. Moreover, there was the black propaganda, running across the campaign like a scrawl of obscene graffiti. In Illinois, pamphlets proclaimed that murderers, rapists and child molesters in Massachusetts would vote for Dukakis.[39] Maryland material referred to the 'Dukakis/Horton team'. They constructed a nightmare world which the central campaign could, of course, disown while harvesting the benefits.

Dukakis's advertising tried to avoid sounding liberal, and to humanise their man. Bland themes were picked. Thus Dukakis confided to viewers how much harder it is to be a young parent today: 'that's not a Democratic concern. That's not a Republican concern. That's a father's concern'. Dukakis's negative advertising focussed on the wrong victims, seeking to ridicule Bush's image makers, a target too esoteric for voters.

The political merit of Republican advertising, most especially on the Horton issue, was that it gave the debate flesh and bones: no longer could murder be an abstraction when perpetrators and victims were singled out. Was the tactic unethical? Massachusetts apparently was 'the only state to give weekend passes to first degree murderers facing life without parole'.[40] A cogent ethical defence can be made in that the release signified an entire corpus of attitudes to crime and punishment which many Americans reject, and that the attitudes of the future President were of central, not tangential, importance to voters. Was it, therefore, wrong of the Republicans to 'run' Willie Horton as a kind of anti-candidate? Many would say 'yes' on the grounds that the advertising constituted a covert racism – an argument the Republicans deny.

Another objective of the Bush purchased advertising was to expose Dukakis as a naive provincial. A still of Bush and Gorbachev was accompanied with the words 'This is no time to train somebody in how to meet with the Russians'.[41] Naturally, Bush's advertisers featured the martial Dukakis tank perambulation, illustrating the fast-responsive, hard hitting capacity of the purchased advertising: it added that Dukakis opposed 'virtually every defence system we developed . . . America can't afford that risk'.[42]

One Republican commercial was a straight lift from the Saatchi advertising for the British conservatives – the misery of life under the old regime (in this case Carter), with inflation, sneering foreigners, unemployment.[43]

Targetted advertising played a notable part in this campaign. Thus Bush's consultants dealt with the 'gender gap' by targetting specifically women voters. These advertisements repeated Bush's call for a kinder, gentler America – featuring his domesticity, cooking and petting his grandchildren – and were often shown on daytime soap operas, etc. By September the 'gender gap' had ceased to exist.[44] Jackson commercials went on exclusively black media, with anti-drug pro-Dukakis messages.[45] Dukakis was anti-gun in advertising on black radio, yet in Texas could denounce gun control in Bush's very distant past. Bush's daughter-in-law advertised to Hispanic voters.

GIVING AND SPENDING

It is significant that both the candidates who won their parties' nominations were blessed with masterful financial organisations. No Democratic candidate had been more cash laden; the reception that began the Dukakis campaign in 1987 garnered $2.2 million (three times the total for any previous Democratic event). By March 1981 the campaign chest was $20 million, twice that of any party rival: thus Dukakis was in a position to invest heavily in television advertising. There is no better illustration of the intimate connection between financial organisation and campaign success.[46]

It was estimated that a total of $400 million would be spent in the 1988 election, with the winner spending around $75 million. Television advertisements themselves could easily cost $500 000 per week for those pursuing national or major state office in the later stages of their campaigns. An individual poll surveying a state could cost $30 000 and direct mailing came at 50 cents per shot. Dukakis spent some $70 million on television commercials. Final nominees would get $46.75 million apiece from the federal government. Additionally each state had spending limits for primaries – limits which all the candidates managed to pervert in ingenious ways, such as by buying time on television channels beamed from other states.[47]

During this election season pressure group activity was as strong as ever: but conservative forces were no longer dominant. Others had learnt the same tune. The AFL–CIO purchased a $13 million advertising campaign, an exercise in image surgery for unions; and commercials of the garment workers referred to the national trade imbalance. Corporate America also strode directly into the election, with Kodak hiring political consultants to help make manufacturing industry an issue, and Drexel Burnham Lambert incorporating election images – housing, child care, factory closings – into its advertising.[48]

Then there were the PACS. At the congressional level they had now become thoroughly bonded to incumbents – which meant the Democratic party. Of the top fifty receivers of PAC money by midsummer, 48 were incumbents. Only five were Republicans. By this stage they had given $66 million to congressional incumbents over eighteen months, an increase of nearly 30 per cent over the 1986 campaign season.[49]

ORGANISATION

At the organisational level, the Dukakis campaign was amateur and, for a long time, complacent. They closed their California office in June. Their key personnel were 'high minded neophytes'.[50]

This demonstrates that the Democrats are still not up to the business-like demands of merchandised political communication. Their party culture is still too introspective and besotted with dated individualism. By contrast, the Republicans, being more of a managerial culture, are better suited to the marketing-led, market-arbitered style of modern campaigning.

COMPETENCE VERSUS VALUES

For John O'Sullivan 'attitudes and the values they express *are* the real issues, far more so than the technical economic arguments that the media affect to respect'.[51] O'Sullivan's point is fundamental to the modern presidential campaign, yet the Democrats had still not grasped it or – as the Snoopy–tank affair showed – understood it at only a superficial level. And according to the pollster Richard Wirthlin:

> You move people's votes through emotion, and the best way to give an emotional cut to your message is through talking about

values. Bush has to do that. He has to touch the values of family, self-esteem, hope, opportunity, security![52]

Things we care about have meaning for us and reflect our values. We want them to be endorsed by others, particularly the powerful. This is because

- values give our life inspiration and point – a position to defend, to hold precious
- it is difficult to uphold things that have meaning unless others support us
- the more others support, the greater the meaningfulness of our lives.

Politicians cannot reaffirm all the particular things that mean something to each voter. But pronouncements can or do come to symbolise a particular stance that is interpreted to be for or against a particular set of values. Politicians who openly affirm our values express their identification with us and indirectly affirm and enhance the importance and meaningfulness of our lives. In this election, there was real ambiguity about the future performance and policies of the candidates. Even late on, one-third of prospective voters remained swingable:[53] as Yankelevich[54] pointed out, 'if a conflict-ridden decision is postponeable, most people will postpone it as long as possible'. Whenever there is ambiguity like this, decision-makers fall back on symbolism.

Just as the consumer looks for indicators of likely future performance of a product, the electorate looks for signs that appear significant. Such signs are symbols. The Bush campaign was run on symbols – the flag, Horton, Boston Harbour, etc. If the country was in a bad state it is unlikely that this would have worked.

Dukakis put too much exclusive stress on economic and technical matters. This does not exploit emotions unless accompanied by pictures of soup kitchens, ghostly regiments of the unemployed, etc. A candidate must present a vision that appeals to people's self-image. If both candidates ignore these but instead stress topics like the standard of living, they are really competing on price – and will rent allegiance only until a better promise is made. Also, many voters are frightened by anyone who promises great changes in times of prosperity. Continuity means predictability. If a candidate can also parade the symbols of the things people cherish, the reaction is more emotional support. Bush was the leader here even though personally his own attractiveness and credibility were not high.

WHY ARE AMERICAN PRESIDENTIAL CANDIDATES SO BORING?

Why are American Presidential candidates – indeed, American politicians – so boring? The question is not a trivial one: excitement, given the leadership and symbolic pseudo-monarch functions of the US Presidency, is not a frivolous thing to demand. By 'boring' I mean that a man is inarticulate, unable to express a vision, and provincial – he cannot think in the large, and his political consciousness hums with the minor concerns of the moment and the locality. This campaign saw two boring individuals emerge from a field of forgettable candidates.

How, then, does a country with so much talent, and which spends big sums on public elections, manage to produce such mediocrity; and why out of so many candidates – there are countless elective offices in the US – do such depressing ones rise to the top? Partly we must blame the sheer strength of the democratic ethos itself. For America's self-concept is one of a homogeneous society that mistrusts privilege: its popular heroes are simply the norm writ large, gigantic reflections of the little guy, in politics as in Hollywood. De Tocqueville saw the outcome of American democracy as being enormous pressure for equality: in modern democratic societies we have no heroes because we extinguish the conditions necessary for heroism to exist.

This pressure for conformity necessarily helps prevent interesting leaders emerging, because to be interesting is to say something different, and therefore to challenge and offend. Such pressure is attributable also to the extraordinary power of pressure groups and other groupings in US public life. Partly this is historic – a society which had to assimilate diverse cultures and regional forces developed an especially strong sensitivity to group interests. Today their weight is reinforced by PACs. One-third of campaign finance comes from them. Individual candidates have to build up their own individual coalitions and avoid offending those such as the National Rifle Association, whose enmity means political extinction.

All this makes for policies which are pitched towards the centre. Non-ideological politics are inherently tedious because there is no great substratum of emotion and intellectual critique: and while one may admire the practised ease with which US politicians can ostensibly jettison any baggage of ideology, one must also wonder whether such cosmeticry conceals a hidden agenda, and is therefore undemocratic. In such a political climate, matters for argument become

peripheral or merely symbolic, such as the row about Dukakis's veto
of a bill to make the pledge of allegiance compulsory in schools.
Much is common ground, Republicans offering 'barbecue dreams of
no taxes, job protection and crackdowns on crime'[55] and Democrats
likewise, each party accusing the other of being soft on major items in
the current litany. This election saw the coronation of the bland
platitude as the central artefact of American campaigning. Dukakis
made a call for 'decent and affordable housing for every family', and
a 'new era of greatness', etc.: plaster bric à brac besides the great
rhetorical monoliths of US history.

This is a centricism not only of ideals, but also of personal style.
Dukakis vaunted his drip-dry shirts, subway travel and home-grown
vegetables: he was the white coated psychiatrist who would listen
sympathetically to America's babble about its nightmares and
neuroses. If Dukakis did not exist the Democrats would have
invented him. Both candidates were representative American types –
Bush the gushing, naive preppy, Dukakis the urbane technocrat, a
political Mr Spock.

Moreover American campaigns are costly, since they are predicated on purchased media persuasion, and it is almost essential to be
rich to stand. By making wealth the criteria of entry we artificially
limit the pool of potential talent from which politics draws. Dukakis
spent $200 000 on his first week's advertising in New York. Some,
such as Senator Quayle with his $110 million fortune, or Pierre du
Pont, will have inherited wealth. Many, however, have made it
themselves in business, the product of a lifetime devoted to the
anxieties of making money, and consequently they have not had the
time to cultivate the broader graces of personality, to reading, study
or cultural pursuits. There is no necessary connection between
business and political skill, they are different in kind, yet in America
the one is a prerequisite of the other.

Candidates also face massive press security. Journalists hover over
the candidate and scrounge for every youthful peccadillo. Given the
extent of electronic scrutiny today every utterance of the candidate is
also recorded for all time. Senator Biden's distortion of his career at a
very minor public meeting was recorded by C-Span, the congressional network. All this makes it difficult to develop as a politician or
change one's mind since the record is graven in stone, and as
experiment is almost a requirement of being an interesting personality this process may well deter the best from entering public life. Hart
and Biden may be no great loss, but who in any given population

could survive such surveillance? Only someone extraordinarily boring, which is exactly what they got.

So a process of public humiliation is now an integral part of the
American electoral system. This is reinforced by the prominence of
negative advertising.

If such vilification were merely political it would be tolerable, but it
is more usually personal, concentrating on impressionistic characteristics irrelevant to any job specification. Criticisms of Bush were often
unrelated to perceived competence, simply to the nature of the image
projected, so suddenly Mrs Bush's white hair becomes a political fact,
irrelevant physiological detail assumes importance. The political
response is therefore to create an inflammable image. The politician
is sealed in a waxwork pose, an icon brought before the party faithful,
and amidst all this his individuality is lost.

American campaigns are now constructed almost exclusively for
television. The average American spends three hours per night viewing,
and political events must compete with other forms of entertainment.
At the Democrat convention 'visibility whips'[56] roamed the hall and
'bite patrols' – baseball hatted teams of speech writers – were on hand;
demonstrators were relegated to the 'protest pen', a car park. It is not
surprising that politicians come to resemble the actors with whom they
compete for air time, and that indeed sometimes they are actors. The
American election process is now designed to 'produce professional
campaigners and amateur presidents'; in the words of J. M. Burns,
America has 'the worst top leadership recruitment system in the
democratic societies of the world'.

Much of the harm is done by a conscious conceptualisation of
American campaigning as an exercise in product marketing. It is a
demand-led kind of politics in which real leadership is impossible.
Consultants' invisible hand is behind almost everything we see in
American politics. Senator Quayle was chosen on their advice, the
ultimate exercise in identikit politics, a plastic mannequin who filled
the specifications charted by market research. On the advice of their
consultants American politicians struggled to be charismatic: Dukakis's laboured ethnicity, Bush's sudden predilection for chromium
diners and the company of truck drivers. Consultants would be better
advised to work within and not against the limits of the candidate's
personality.

Finally, the veneration of market values tends to devalue the
perceived worth of public service so that the best seek distinction
elsewhere, in the professions and business. A country that places the

commercial ethos on a pedestal will have little tolerance for the stillness and reflection and erudition that enable leadership to reach its classical forms: a Roosevelt, for example, now seems the leisured creation of a bygone age. Ultimately great leaders cannot emerge when politicians are expected simply to reflect, not direct or modify, popular will, and where truth is assumed to be what the majority of people think. In Andrew Bonar Law's words, 'I must follow them, I am their leader'.

CONCLUSIONS

On the basis of this campaign the advice for any future presidential candidate is as follows:

(1) The candidate should connect with majority values. He does not need to have been born in a log cabin: he must show, however, that he experiences common emotion with uncommon intensity. So he will play on whatever suburban anxieties happen to be uppermost, especially fear of disorder and delinquency, and he needs to project a fierce patriotism.

(2) Such concern about values should not be merely enunciated through traditional speeches, but also via symbolic appeals, which can both avoid polarising issues such as abortion, and make a notation in the elector's mind such as mere argument never can. The memorable image, significant setting or symbolic rite will therefore articulate the values the candidate has laid claim to.

(3) In general a point-scoring debating style is ill-suited to the needs of modern campaigning. But if debate means less, rhetoric means more: a kinder, gentler sound bite.

(4) Candidates must conceive the campaign in strategic marketing terms, with full integration of advertising and free media. An entirely consumerist approach is adopted, with prior market research discovering the winning themes and candidates listening reverently to their packagers.

(5) This campaign also established the importance of a sureness of touch with the free media, and therefore the need for a pedantic attention to the visual. However, the point needs qualification: the staged symbolic event can backfire.

(6) The candidate should purchase wholesale a negative strategy, especially if personally somewhat vacuous, creating fear and propos-

ing himself as the antidote. He must press the emotive buttons, particularly anger. He will expose his opponents' key vulnerabilities, pervert them, magnify them. Underlying the overt strategy will be the covert strategy involving black propaganda. Voters will claim to deride the negativity, but they will listen.

(7) The candidate who is villified must counter-attack eloquently and even brutally. He must have every conceivable aspect of his record manicured for the agnostic light of public scrutiny. In one sense a campaign is a simulated anticipation of the political confrontations of the real world, national and international, and whatever we might mean by strength, the candidate must communicate the signals that indicate strength.

(8) In all this, the role of the consultant becomes critical. Therefore novices, academics, etc., should be jettisoned from the campaign. Candidates should only employ seasoned campaigners, those at the top of their trade.

None of this style is however any replacement for the substance of moral worth, intellectual depth and a demeanour most sublime. Stature cannot be manufactured, but will it ever return to transcend the exhaustions and triviality of the campaign trail? America's problem is the imagining that it once experienced a golden age. And indeed, from time to time in the history of the Republic giants have ascended the stage, so that their successors, tedious and grey, seem toiling lilliputians beside the past masters. Americans suffer a bereavement syndrome, the remembrance of great ones who came and, seizing their bewitched partner, took it on a grand and terrible journey.

12 An Ethical Conundrum?

'In aristocratic nations, the body of the nobles and the wealthy are in themselves natural associations, which check the abuses of power. In countries where such associations do not exist, if private individuals cannot create an artificial and temporary substitute for them, I can see no permanent protection against the most galling tyranny; and a great people may be oppressed with impunity by a small faction, or by a single individual.'

Alexis de Tocqueville, *Democracy in America*

'Thus, not only does democracy make every man forget his ancestors, but it hides his descendants and separates his contemporaries from him; it throws him back forever upon himself alone, and threatens in the end to confine him entirely within the solitude of his own heart.'

Alexis de Tocqueville, *Democracy in America*

And so, during his frequently occurring elections, the American citizen does not stride abroad in sturdy liberty, rather he is a dazed man under siege, and through letter-box, telephone, television, doorbell (eventually, we are reliably assured, his home computer) the empty smiles of his politicians pursue him. Politics will ooze through every fissure. Soap powder, at least, confines its vulgar brightness to the screen.

Popular apathy nourishes the phenomenon of political marketing, its prominence reflects not the strong bonds of communities but their demise, and the supremacy of visual over literary media. Political marketing is an American phenomenon and all major political phenomena tell something about the host culture. But it certainly points up the disaggregation in contemporary society.

POLITICAL FRAGMENTATION

A number of underlying social currents promise a more fragmented US political culture. There is the crisis of authority in modern

243

democracies which all western governments face in some degree, the issue of the legitimacy of rules and the lack of a common, internalised sense of responsibility to obey them unless coercion or cajolery are present, particularly so in urban America. Moreover the United States faces a greater problem of pluralism than Europe, and the associated demands posed by the thinning of the common culture: ethnic, regional, class, age, and religious divergence certainly, but also the clamourings of different value/issue grouping and the stridency of the various family/sexuality/gender debates.

Yet a society needs some core identity to achieve a modicum of order and efficiency in the conduct of its affairs. In the United States such an identity was once achieved by a common language, super-ordinate and various nationalising political and legal institutions, the public school system, and through 'patriotism' and its articulation through rites and symbols: for all immigrants the implicit mandate was to assimilate themselves into a new American identity. Yet it has sometimes seemed that this core identity has faded, that 'American-ism' is being strained by the various fragmentary pressures. While many celebrate pluralism as a social ideal, others have become aware of the costs posed by its increasingly sharp definition. Often political marketing strengthens these divisive pressures, it articulates differences cogently and ignores areas of sameness; viewing or reading it, one would conclude that the United States had regressed to pseudo-tribalism with electronic incantations and warpaint.

The multiplication of media outlets is also a force for political fragmentation. The marketing approach heightens this by taking advantage of their potential for selecting targets. 'Television in its first age was primarily nationalising in its effects on political culture',[1] but commentators fear the 'single greatest danger lurking within the new media – the danger that their political use will result in a fragmentation of the body politic'.[2] Some political scientists have also pointed up a central irony about the new media: it should in theory provide a much richer stream of information to voters; in practice it could reduce the supply of information since much of the political audience is an inadvertent one and refinement of targeting reduces such inadvertence.[3]

The very openness of the parties also contributes to US political disaggregation, especially since marketing methods can be used to take advantage of this openness. The problem of an open nominating system replacing party machines is illustrated at the extreme by the 1986 Illinois Democratic primary victories of supporters of Mr

Lyndon Larouche on a 28 per cent turnout. *The Economist* thus described the new *status quo*:[4]

> Particularly in the 1960s and 1970s, the ties attaching congressmen to their parties became ever more elastic as they grew less dependent on party money, better skilled at taking the credit for federal grants to their districts, more adept at polling their constituents' views. Congressmen became independent agents. The party reforms, aimed at greater democracy, merely weakened the authority of the party regulars.

The Economist added:

> In such circumstances, the traditional role attributed to political parties – that of constraining the reconciling interest groups' demands, and promoting responsible candidates – was bound to become less effective. It was further eroded by the growth of single-issue organisations (many negative in their aims) and of their little treasuries, the political action committees. Increasingly, activists had only narrow concerns and made only temporary coalitions. The smooth flow of party supremacy had given way to the abrasive anarchy of granulated politics.

And finally: 'The disintegration of American parties has now gone so far that oddballs, rapscallions, poltroons and worse can pop up as easily as evangelists or ingenues. They probably will'.

While this is a telling summation of the qualitative changes in US politics, it fails to do adequate justice to the market-driven and marketing-led dynamo that underlies these changes. For without incorporating the key role of marketing in their explanation, they make no sense.

THE IRRELEVANT MAJORITY

Nor do electors necessarily feel more at ease with the sensitised leadership that is the ostensible gift of merchandised politics, for by definition members of single-issue groups seldom feel part of the political mainstream since their demands are too extreme to be mollified, and the majority itself feels crowded out by single-issue causes. Constant surrender to pressure groups by government could diminish the quality of life, with the emergence of an interest-dominated politics in which the majority get an inferior deal, so groups shepherd their own legislation against the proven verdict of public opinion. This is a responsiveness not necessarily to the majority but to those who feel most intensely. Here is cause for concern. Majority opinion on almost anything is tentative; it is those most emotionally aroused who lead public opinion, raise the money, articulate the issues, so society of the future will be shaped not by the most representative passion but by the strongest, a dictatorship of the vociferous. This has been true of any age, but never before orchestrated as now. Thus sex education in schools, which may arguably be seen as ideological, is universally taught, but transmission of notions of divinely inspired moral precepts are illegal. A liberal totalitarianism interpreted its agenda in terms of individual interest group rights rather than any superordinate public duty. The right responded in kind. Constitutional arrangements and the convergence of a market-driven, marketing-articulated political system with social pluralism increased these fissiparous tendencies.

Hence the potential problem with the emergent pressure group political system is that, for the return of marginal satisfaction for the opinionated, the great segments of society – middle-class, blue-collar and so on – witness no period where a consolidated attempt is made to satisfy their needs. The very architecture of the US constitution, with its checks and balances, encourages this by preventing the absolute dominion of one party. Moreover the demise of parties may produce a rising alienation, since all-embracing structures will have ceased to function popularly: this is an inherent risk of political systems that accord high legitimacy to vested interest.

All this can lead to a sense of irrelevance as people no longer feel responsible for politicians' actions: that what is done in their name is without their sanction. Will they continue to obey laws where political decisions were seen to be arrived at bizarrely, since confidence in the legitimacy of laws is ever the basis of political authority? A key issue then is how far democracies should willingly subordinate themselves to the power of pressure groups.

THE EFFECTS OF POLITICAL MARKETING

Other effects of the universality of a marketing conception of the electoral process can be summarised as follows:

1. Arguably political marketing conveys a spurious idea of the

political process and the ease with which 'solutions' can be traded and implemented.

2. Where commercial motivation becomes paramount in politics the danger is that disquiet is exploited by business means for profit with the growth of false 'issues', ones selected on the irrelevant criteria of their dramatic appeal.

3. The marketing imperative helps to create a society resistant to change – a rather un-American phenomenon. Vested interests of all kinds are becoming obstacles by their ability to purchase political shares, making a country whose historic mandate was acquired through its flexibility become increasingly impervious to change. Impedimenta are created every time the demands of a vested interest are gratified, so that the future is put into a strait-jacket and only real crisis will be able to prevail against the fortified heights of subsidy, special interest, tariff and concession. It restricts the capacity of the US political machine to make decisions.

4. There have also been consequences for America's international role in contradictory and incoherent policy. We may envisage then a continued international disenchantment with the United States, with other countries attributing to perfidy or incompetence what is not only a consequence of men and politics but of systems, the fragmented and marketing-derived policy-making process, so that theoretically one branch of government may even offer a country a defensive alliance and another may impose a tariff on its trade and therefore alienate it.

5. The growth of the marketing approach combined with the emergence of provincial media has led some to speak about a 'renaissance of localism'[5] in American politics, and they are right: the aggregate effect is to fortify local awareness, but possibly at the cost of national consensus-building. People prefer local news foremost, according to market research commissioned by newspapers. But, in the words of one commentator, some new technologies threaten our common data base,[6] in contrast to the now somewhat antique national media that promoted a shared political vocabulary and homogeneous opinion.

6. Usage – or abusage – of these marketing methods will make for a lack of political leadership in society and a lack of political courage, since they take as their reference point a servile rather than a directorial attitude to public opinion. The importance of an independent and bold journalist cadre with a commitment to

standards cannot be underestimated: it is, indeed, a barrier against the rising bathos.

7. The coalescence of electronic media and the marketing impera-
    tive have from the first undermined those interrelated character-
    istics of traditional politics, discussion, bargaining and secrecy.
    Conventions ceased to be fora for discussion when they were first
    thrown open to television in the early fifties. Political discussion
    is repetitive, obscure and inconclusive; the demands of television
    are exactly the opposite: speed, fun, a story and hard news.
    Hitherto conventions had embodied a long bargaining process.
    This went. And similarly with caucuses: television prefers open
    and direct primaries, for it is essentially a dramatic medium, so
    the media/marketing nexus has re-defined key institutions of
    American democracy, always in the direction of excitement and
    away from prosaic caution.

8. Political marketing will spread internationally, for all govern-
    ments feel a need to legitimate their rule and influence the
    uneducated. A new breed of international consultants may arise.
    Awareness of the centrality of media marketing could help to
    make governments more accommodating – even more democra-
    tic – and use of political marketing techniques will become an
    issue in the politics of other countries, more so than they have
    done in the United States which is more acclimatised to the
    marketing ethos. Israel, a country of three million people, spent
    $9 million on its 1981 election; ten million Venezuelans were
    more extravagant, spending $250 million in 1983; significantly, all
    these campaigns employed American consultants.

9. Given the dividends political action has so far brought them
    businesses will continue to invest in American politics. The
    consultants themselves will continue to grow wealthy from the
    political marketing game, descending on each big election like a
    bevy of bluebottles. Thus one commentator described 1980
    beginning 'as a mating ritual between the leading candidates and
    the leading consultants' (it is however possible to envisage the
    larger consulting firms leaving the political market because of the
    unpredictability of its business).

TOWARDS POPULISM

Is the alliance of the marketing conception and media technology creating a new kind of democracy, perhaps a broader 'political nation'? The twentieth-century American story had been one of continuous pressure for more democracy, a broadening-down of civic participation, and the permeation of the marketing concept with its locus in consumer orientation has enhanced this trend by giving it a practical as well as an ethical justification. This populist notion of democracy has been an identifiable current in American politics throughout the Republic and the referendum, initiative and primary election movements can be seen squarely in this tradition.[7] But now for the first time the new direct technology makes feasible a usurpation of the delegative function of legislatures, since an epoch of mass referenda is now possible, though fanciful, with democracy evolving (or regressing) from the simple assent of the majority to the participation of that majority in decision making.

There are risks in such marketing-sanctioned movement towards a plebiscitary democracy.[8] Public opinion is sometimes volatile, sometimes it can touch extremes; also people do necessarily mean what they tell pollsters, so that most would certainly claim to wish to execute murderers and castrate rapists, but if individually given the responsibility of passing sentence their response might not be so robust. There is also something problematic about the permanent campaign, for it could lead to the abandonment of any strategic content to politics, in its eagerness to appease could create 'mobocracy', and thus Roland Perry's claim that the Libyan jets were shot down by opinion polls could have been the beginning of a novel and ominous direction in American politics.[9]

Under such auspices the legislator becomes increasingly, not exactly a delegate, but a conduit for the feelings of powerful national lobbies and local interest groups, so that their agenda becomes his. For Schumpeter,[10] for example, such a change would be highly regrettable: to him, popular will was nothing but 'an indeterminate bundle of vague impulses loosely playing about given slogans and mistaken impressions'. Similarly with Dahl[11] in 'A Preface to Democratic Theory', who stresses the significance of ensuring that 'the deciding of issues by the electorate [is] secondary to the elections of the men who are to do the deciding'. Therefore under such interpretations voting becomes the pivotal act, and leadership the central function, whereas marketing notions stress responsiveness. But Abramson is unhappy with the elite model of democracy: 'The interest of individuals becomes less something government represents and more something it mobilises, potentially even manipulates.

Wherein is the democracy?'

The debate on the political uses of new communications technology has been vigorous but incomplete, since while political scientists perceive an ideologically driven movement towards greater voter participation in political decisions, they neglect the pressure of the marketing approach for such involvement. The menace or benevolence of new media employed by political communicators has been summarised thus: '. . . it depends on which conception of democracy appeals to us. One's evaluation of the electoral consequences of the new media depends on whether you are a proponent of individualist, pluralist or citizenship democracy'.[12] 'Teledemocracy', the fraternity of political idealism and political marketing, is most inimical to what we might call the elitist theory of democracy, which would give paramountcy to the mediating and deliberative influence of wise and informed legislators.[13] Both the populist and corporatist views would be more favourable.

Abramson develops what is surely the key point: '. . . it is the underlying but undisclosed presence of a dispute about the meaning of democracy that leads people so often to invest the technology itself with the quality of good or evil'.[14]

AN ALTERNATIVE VIEW

It is perhaps easy to dramatise the mischief political marketing implies and exaggerate the effectiveness of advertising, for the traditional political skills are far from being superseded; political processes are inherently propagandist: they always were. What, for example, was Prime Minister Gladstone's polemic on Turkey's Bulgarian attrocities in 1875–6, but political propaganda to discredit the Turkophile policies of his Tory opponents?

There are those who question the novelty of political marketing, and would argue that only the technology is new. Thus stratospheric campaign expenditures are not as modern as they might appear: the 'robber barons' spent perhaps $10 million to defeat Bryan in the eighteen nineties ($138 million today).[15] Negative advertising has a reverend pedigree: Jefferson was called an atheist, the father of a black mistress's children and so on; J. Q. Adams was accused of procuring American girls for the Tsar. In the thirties, the US Post Office labelled an anti-FDR Republican political stamp 'scurrilous, libellous, and unfit for mailing'.[16] Moreover segmentation, the crafting of different messages to different groups, was a political fashion long before marketing made it a business science. Teddy Roosevelt was able to say different things to different towns and regions via the whistle-stop; John Kennedy kept political analysis notebooks which carefully segmented towns.[17] Pseudo-plebeian antecedents have always been important: supporters of the aristocratic Benjamin Harrison carried model log cabins.[18]

Perhaps also we should not so easily overestimate public credulity, for exposure to electronic persuasion has arguably left people wary. Commercial advertising finds the persuasion task a challenge to the extent that it needs constantly to experiment in order to be effective. People do have some notions of political rectitude and equity, they will reject what is oversold, and moreover political judgement always will be an important factor: they can never cosmeticise that out of existence. Thus it is possible to be overtly pessimistic. A sediment of public scepticism may accumulate as it has done with other consumer advertising, so that political marketers will increasingly need ingenuity to overcome it, and perhaps the entire phenomenon represents merely a necessary adjustment of society's political institutions to the electronic age just as the invention of the printing press demanded change; indeed it is surprising how long this adjustment has taken and that even now major politicians can be inept at handling the media.

But the role of money in democratic election campaigns must always be controversial. How 'pure' is it necessary for democracy to be? Everything in this book will be anathema to the purist school, who would regard political marketing as embodying an un-American elitism. Others would argue that it is no great departure from the central trends of the past: that America has a tradition of giving disproportionate power to organised interest groups, one made necessary by the historical imperative to reconcile and assimilate divergent groups quickly.

And strong parties did harm at times. There is the point about new blood, the opening up of exclusive political oligarchies; as Sherman, commenting on British political marketing, has remarked:[19]

This in itself has a good side as well as a bad one. Do we wish to be ruled by professional politicians who began as student politicians and progressed as research assistants and special assistants before eventually making it into the Commons and up the ladder, always toeing the line, without ever living in the real world? The system is unlikely to produce Peels, Gladstones, Disraelis, Salisburies – or Thatchers.

In illustration of this openness of the American system, *The Economist* has thus described the political emergence of Ben Nighthorse Campbell, Cheyenne Indian and Colarado Democratic candidate:

> Mr Campbell got into politics almost by mistake. During the 1982 election bad weather grounded his light aircraft at Durango airport. With nothing else to do, he wandered into a Democratic gathering, and emerged as the candidate for the State legislature.[20]

The political adoption of the marketing orientation makes politicians deferential to public opinion. Reaganite foreign adventurism for example never forfeited the basic support of Americans until 'Irangate'. Grenada was invaded; but this was an invasion supported by US people and by the islanders, and while money and training went to Nicaraguan Contras the threat of direct intervention was never more than rhetoric, and then there was the broadly popular Libyan raid; excluding Beirut, few American lives were lost in military operations. Until 'Irangate' control of public response was often flawless: polls and computers would have judged the moment of timing and degree of commitment, communication support would be worked out; compared with Reagan's immediate predecessors this may be seen as vindication.

Political marketing could also sharpen its focus. Constituencies could include the 'new collar' workers, and the ecologically minded baby boomers, who might constitute a source of money for political campaigns attempting to tap their residual idealism. They need leadership, issues and movements to enlist in. But political marketing may not be fulfilling its potential since it is aimed at a normative identikit, thus minority groups could adapt all these techniques and methods – and are in fact doing so.

Networks and foundations and advertisers do have power to improve the quality of political dialogue in the United States; there is nothing immutable about a situation when money flows in the other direction could be a corrective to the excesses described. Americans may be slow in diagnosing a problem, that is perhaps inevitable in a highly pluralist democratic system, but once having done so they commmit an urgency to its solution, and their failure fully to recognise the problem associated with the marketing conceptualisation of politics is in part attributable to an informal conspiracy of silence among their politicians.

Moreover there could be a reaction against the pretensions of political marketing and in favour of 'truth' – rather like the return to natural foods, cleansed of false colour and syrups and monosodium glutamate; the 'anti-marketing' electoral stance will become frequent, just like the own-label and non-boast square-deal brands in commerce. Citizens' movements like Common Cause will arise to combat the phenomenon, though their success will be limited; marketing is a permanent participant on the scene, transforming American politics for good or ill.

Nor does the prevalence of merchandised politics necessarily indicate an immature political civilisation. The decline of the active volunteer, for example, may be a product of our own self-engrossment, but it also reflects a heightened political sophistication in which partisanship becomes more difficult.

A POLITICAL CULTURE TRANSFORMED

The term 'democracy' is subject to myriad permutations – there is no aboriginal democracy for everyone to copy, no definitive archtype. Democracy is a system of popular representative power, and since it cannot be defined more precisely its inherent vagueness necessarily leads to debate as to what its venerable architects really intended. Decisions are made in the name of the people, but by no means necessarily in their opinion: there are degrees in the directness of the power electorates actually possess, for theirs is a delegated authority.

What criteria then should we apply in evaluating the various democratic systems? Perhaps the test should be not how significantly representative systems are but whether they lead to good government, whether they adequately ventilate the grievances of groups external to the majority (as the 'democracy' of Ulster, for example, failed to do). There is risk of course that this argument becomes circular – the test of good government may be its continued popularity, which in turn rests on its representativeness and responsiveness. The test of a good government therefore – if indeed in history any such paragon can be said to have existed – would be public esteem, but also preparedness for confrontation and controversy such as the Reagan administration sought to elude in its frivolous attitude to deficits; and it would plan for a future as well as react to a present (an activity that democratic systems seldom reward, as with Baldwin's problems over British rearmament policies in the nineteen thirties). Such a test would not endorse the marketing-articulated political system, faulting it, rather, for an inherent fickleness and opportunism.

Also political marketing methods arrived at a relatively stable period in US history: depression, war, McCarthyism were in the past. Yet in such an open system another crisis may create potential for a demagogue with no pre-existing base to amplify his message, provided only that he has money, for there is less political process and system through which a parish Mussolini could be extinguished. An organised group could gain political power in the United States, and possibly pervert it. It is easy to forget the novelty of parliamentary democracy, that votes for women occurred within the maturity of many still living, and we cannot well predict how this democracy will evolve, whether in stable and just ways, and what the long-term impact of new communications will be. We have given the picture as it is, perhaps not such a bad one. The picture as it could be may be dark, as we look to the future with the eagerness and superstition with which seamen once faced the oceans.

But the United States is now more than just a democratic system in which marketing occurs. For that system itself has not become a market-place, and conforms to such a definition in every respect. Politics does not merely use the technologies of marketing. Office is fought for in a market-place as a marketing exercise. This point is crucial. While many areas of modern life also use technologies borrowed from marketing, the context in which they work is not market-arbitered as the political one has become. Politics has become a market-place because there is intense competition, a monetary price, a currency (legislative favours) and target markets (voters and funders) and because disquietude is exploited and packaged by businesses (consultants) for commercial ends (profit). In the aggregate these amount to a market dynamic; one that sanctifies individual wilfulness at the expense of public responsibility. The success of the gun lobby remains, of itself, an indictment of market interest-arbitered policy and the political concept which underpins it; there may be little scope for responsibility in an impregnable universe of individual want, and a political consciousness that hums with the melodies of narcissism. This connects with the larger issues of the workability of the US constitution and particularly of the US Presidency, and while the final answer to such questions is beyond the scope of this book, the market-driven nature of the political regimen must be part of that answer.

We might usefully compare the quality of leadership thrown up by this market-mediated system with the calibre generated by more elitist systems: such a comparison raises doubts. Under such a regimen what will happen to political integrity, if ever it existed? An unbalanced and promiscuous politics is the outcome, a chaos to which only brilliance could give guiding shape. Media communications sponsors a world in which men come to know a little about a lot, one dominated by personalities rather than ideas, and it therefore encourages politicians to bathe supine in the mainstream, to craft vacuities when there is an unrecognised need for vigorous and so necessarily divisive leadership. Media-marketed politics affect the personnel and personality of legislatures, the kind of people who seek office: they foster the dangerous illusion that those with the common touch are most suited to interpret the common good. Those unwilling to merchandise themselves will be debarred from the political process, and some good people will be excluded by the casting directors of media politics, or indeed self-excluded: to be sold like deodorant may be too high a price for the best man and the intellectual to pay. It is really a recipe for having grinning mediocrity dominate the apparatus of US government, and you might say that the significance of Carter's election was that an incompetent was foisted by the media onto American voters. Packaging candidates for the media can inhibit genuine creativity, for when every motion is calculated the candidate becomes a lifeless mannequin with a plaster smile. American politicians are cloned – bland, packaged, antiseptic. Their last eccentric, the pipe-smoking Representative Millicent Fenwick, failed to win election to the Senate. The market segments rule, and in the effort to charm one is reminded of Lloyd George's remark on another politician, that like a cushion he always bore the impression of the last man who sat on him.

We have tended to discuss political marketing in terms of its effects on particular campaigns; what, though, of its cumulative social influence? In commercial advertising the individual campaign has scant impact on society, but advertising in the aggregate deeply influences contemporary culture by promoting a set of idealised images and certain values, and similarly in seeking to evaluate the significance of political advertising the need is to measure the consolidated influence of all campaigns, not just the individual. Where everything is marketed, where nothing commands disinterested respect, the effect is that citizens perceive themselves adrift in a universe of sensory bombardment where no quality appears unblazoned and politics is robbed of its aboriginal mystique: from such a diminution ill consequences could flow.

How inevitable is the phenomenon of political marketing, can we frustrate it and indeed would we wish to? It is difficult to predict the extent of public pressures to end the marketing–money nexus, and disquiet must be distinguished from that lethal abhorrence which on occasion ushers in an epoch of reform. Movements to limit spending are bound to be resisted by those who derive most from it: the majority of current members of Congress. The lush growth of political marketing is really uncontrollable since all those who legislate benefit, and there appears to exist an informal conspiracy not to make it an issue. The eighteenth-century House of Commons with its weak party control and bribery is a good model of what could happen to the US legislature, as independent congressmen loyal only to their district inhibit attempts to reduce state spending.

Our final picture gives an image of political culture transformed by the wholesale adoption of the marketing incubus. The hallmarks of such a culture will be: politicians independent of party but dependent on pressure groups; real power of decision accumulated by grey men, bureaucrat and consultant; administrative actions lacking cohesive policy, being rather a *smorgasbord* of initiatives to appease divergent interests; politics becoming more symbolic theatre as true power is siphoned off elsewhere; an indifferent and disloyal electorate; a 'political nation' of vociferous single-issue single-candidate supporters; a freemasonry of moneyed vested interests asserting exorbitant political power. We suggest that this perspective is something new, a vision of a political civilisation different in kind from that which until recently existed in America, even though many of its details remain constant.

We end with a vision – what ought elections to be like? While there is danger in straying into the somnambulant realms of speculation and idealism, in the perfect election citizens would receive from press and media high-quality information, as non-partisan as possible, and from their politicians a lucid debate: marketing would be peripheral, the relish, as it were, on the salami.

Politics will not, however, cease to be entertaining as a result of the entry of the new, the maverick and the buccaneer. No soap opera mannequin, no Hollywood idol, would now ignore the prospect of Washington as the garden of their senescence. American politics has gained in glamour what it has lost in credibility. And the sleek shall inherit the earth.

Notes and References

1 Introduction: The Electronic Soapbox

1. Hunt, Shelby D., 'The Nature and Scope of Marketing', *Journal of Marketing*, vol. 40, July 1976, pp. 17–28.
2. Kotler, Philip, 'A Generic Concept of Marketing', *Journal of Marketing*, vol. 36, April 1972, pp. 45–6.
3. Ibid.
4. Hunt, 'Nature and Scope'.
5. Ibid.
6. Ibid.
7. Ibid.
8. Kotler, 'Generic Concept'.
9. Hunt, 'Nature and Scope'.
10. Ibid.
11. Kotler, 'Generic Concept'.
12. Hunt, 'Nature and Scope'.
13. Kotler, Philip, 'Voter marketing – Attracting Votes', *Marketing for Non-profit Organisations*, ch. 20 (Englewood Cliffs: Prentice Hall, 1982).
14. Ibid.
15. This summary of evaluations of democracy by the classical political philosophers is drawn from the *Dictionary of the History of Ideas* (New York: Charles Scribner's Sons, 1968), chapter on 'Democracy', by Stephen R. Graubard.
16. McGinnis, Joe, *The Selling of the President, 1968* (New York: Trident Press Inc., 1969).
17. Graubard, *Dictionary of the History of Ideas*.
18. Alexis de Tocqueville, *Democracy in America*, Trans. Henry Reeve (New York: Simon & Schuster, 1964).
19. Ibid.
20. Ibid.
21. Ibid.
22. Hewitt, Bill, Martin, Bradley and Faraso, Kim, 'Enter the Image Makers', *Newsweek*, 14 December 1987.
23. McKay, David, *American Politics and Society* (Oxford: Martin Robertson, 1983).
24. Sellers, Patricia, 'The Selling of the President in '88', *Fortune*, 21 December 1987.
25. Ibid.
26. Ibid.
27. 'How to become President of the United States', *The Economist*, 26 December 1987.

2 Big Lies, Little Lies: The Story of Propaganda

1. Chakotin, Serge, *The Rape of the Masses: The Psychology of Totalitarian Political Propaganda* (New York: Haskell House Publishers, 1971).
2. In Good, C.A., *British Eloquence* (New York: Harper and Brothers, 1884) pp. 292–311.
3. Philippe, Robert, *Political Graphics, Art as a Weapon* (Oxford: Phaidon Press, 1982).
4. Ibid.
5. Ibid.
6. Chakotin, *The Rape of the Masses*.
7. Philippe, *Political Graphics*.
8. Melder, Keith, 'The Birth of Modern Campaigning', *Campaigns and Elections*, Summer 1985.
9. Ibid.
10. Ibid.
11. Ibid.
12. Ibid.
13. 'The glorious past that never was', *The Economist*, 26 Dec. 1987, pp. 49–52.
14. Chakotin, *The Rape of the Masses*.
15. Ibid.
16. Ibid.
17. See Mack Smith, Denis, *Mussolini* (London: Weidenfeld & Nicolson, 1981).
18. Adolf Hitler, *Mein Kampf* (Boston: Houghton Miflin, 1943).
19. Ibid.
20. Chakotin, *The Rape of the Masses*.
21. Goebbels, Joseph, *The Diaries of Dr. Joseph Goebbels*, Trans. Fred Taylor (London: Hamish Hamilton, 1982).
22. See Herstein, Robert Edwin, *The War That Hitler Won* (London: Hamish Hamilton, 1982).
23. Fox, Stephen, *The Mirror Makers* (New York: Vantage Books, pp. 306–13).
24. Ibid.
25. Ibid.
26. Ibid.
27. Ibid.
28. *The Economist*, 26 Dec. 1987.
29. Blumenthal, Sidney, *The Permanent Campaign* (New York: Simon & Schuster, 1984).
30. Ibid.
31. Ibid.
32. Fox, *Mirror Makers*.
33. Ibid.
34. *The Economist*, 26 Dec. 1987.
35. Fox, *Mirror Makers*.
36. Ibid.

37.   Blumenthal, *Permanent Campaign*.

Further Reading

Ellul, Jacques, *Propaganda* (New York: Alfred A. Knopf, 1965).
Boorstin's comment is quoted in Keith Melder, 'The Birth of Modern Campaigning', *Campaigns and Elections*, Summer 1985.
MacNeil, Robert, *The People Machine* (London: Eyre & Spottiswoode, 1968) for use of radio in 1924 and 1928, p. 127, and purchased advertising in 1936 and 1940; on FDR's use of radio, p. 131 and Dewey's use of television in 1948 and 1950.
Praonisy, Nicholas and Spring, F.W., *Propaganda, Politics and Film, 1918–1945* (London: Macmillan, 1982).
Shirer, William L., *The Rise and Fall of the Third Reich* (London: Secker and Warburg, 1960).

3   Only in America

1.   Nevins, Alan and Commager, Henry Steele, *A Pocket History of the United States* (New York: Pocket Books, 1976).
2.   McKay, David, *American Politics and Society* (Oxford: Martin Robertson, 1983).
3.   Ibid.
4.   De Tocqueville's insights into the early nineteenth-century American character are still pertinent. See de Tocqueville, Thomas, *Democracy in America*, Trans. Henry Reeve (Washington Square Press, 1964).
5.   For an account of the operation of machine politics, see Burnham, Walter Dean, *The Current Crisis in American Politics* (New York: Oxford University Press, 1982) p. 143.
6.   For discussions of the 'new right' and its political packaging see Crawford, Alan (*Thunder on the Right*, New York: Pantheon Books, 1980). Also see Saloma, John S., *Ominous Politics* (New York: Hill and Wang, 1984).
7.   For an account of direct mail and the 'new right' see Sabato, Larry, *The Rise of Political Consultants: New Ways of Winning Elections* (New York: Basic Books, 1981).
8.   McKay, *American Politics*.
9.   Ibid.
10.   Ibid.
11.   For an account of how Americans shunned a negative, pessimistic credo, see Theodore H. White, *The Making of the President, 1964* (London: Jonathan Cape, 1965) ch. 11.
12.   For information on the decline in party loyalty, see Crotty, William J. and Jacobson, Gary C., *American Parties in Decline* (Boston and Toronto: Little, Brown and Co., 1980).
13.   For Kennedy's consciousness of the role of image see Hodgson, Godfrey, *All Things To All Men* (Harmondsworth: Penguin Books, 1984) p. 174.

14. McKay, *American Politics.*
15. Blumenthal, Sidney, *The Permanent Campaign* (New York: Simon & Schuster, 1982).
16. McKay, *American Politics.*
17. Ibid.
18. Crotty, William J. and Jacobson, Gary C., *American Parties in Decline* (Boston and Toronto: Little, Brown and Co., 1980).
19. Crawford, Alan, *Thunder on the Right* (New York: Pantheon Books, 1980).
20. Ibid.
21. Ibid.
22. Ibid.
23. Ibid.

Further Reading

For further reading on the US political system see:

Denenberg, R.V., *Understanding American Politics* (London: Fontana Books, 1984).
Nicholas, H.G., *The Nature of American Politics* (Oxford University Press, 1980).
Vile, M.S.C., *Politics in the U.S.A.* (London: Hutchinson, 1982).

For decline in party allegiance see:

Graber, Doris A., *Mass Media and American Politics* (Congressional Quarterly Press, Washington, 1984) p. 180.
Hodgson, Godfrey, *All things to all men* (Penguin Books, 1984) Chapter Five.
Polsby and Wildavsky, *Presidential Elections*, p. 159 (Charles Scribner's Sons New York, 1976).

4 Television

1. Griese, N.H., 'Rosser Reeves and the 1952 Eisenhower TV Spot Blitz', *Journal of Advertising*, vol. 4, no. 4, Fall 1975, pp. 34–8.
2. McGinnis, Joe, *The Selling of the President, 1968* (New York: Trident Press, 1969).
3. Ibid.
4. Ibid.
5. Seymour-Ure, Colin, *The American President: Power and Communication* (London: Macmillan, 1982).
6. Ibid.
7. Ibid.
8. Ibid.
9. Ibid.
10. Crotty, William J. and Jacobson, Gary C., *American Parties in Decline* (Boston and Toronto: Little Brown and Co., 1980).
11. Ibid.

12. Ibid.
13. Ibid.
14. Reviewed by author, offices of Mr David Sawyer.
15. Sabato, Larry, *The Rise of Political Consultants: New Ways of Winning Elections* (New York: Basic Books, 1981).
16. Ibid.
17. Blumenthal, Sidney, *The Permanent Campaign* (New York: Simon & Schuster, 1982).
18. Nimmo, Dan, *The Political Persuaders* (Englewood Cliffs: Prentice-Hall, 1970).
19. Sabato, *New Ways of Winning*.
20. Ibid.
21. Diamond, E. and Bates, S., *New York*, 1 October 1984.
22. Nimmo, *Political Persuaders*.
23. Ibid.
24. Ibid.
25. Perry, James M., *The New Politics* (London: Weidenfeld & Nicolson, 1968), pp. 116–17.
26. Diamond and Bates, *New York*, 1 October 1984.
27. Ibid.
28. Blumenthal, *Permanent Campaign*.
29. Nimmo, *Political Persuaders*.
30. These examples from Edwin Diamond and Stephen Bates, 'Hot Spots', *New York*, 15 Feb. 1988.
31. *The Times*, 7 March 1988.
32. Nimmo, *Political Persuaders*.
33. Ibid.
34. Ibid.
35. Ibid.
36. Ibid.
37. Blumenthal, *Permanent Campaign*.
38. Ibid.
39. Ibid.
40. Nimmo, *Political Persuaders*.
41. Blumenthal, *Permanent Campaign*.
42. Ibid.
43. Nimmo, *Political Persuaders*.
44. Sabato, *New Ways of Winning*.
45. Ibid.
46. Blumenthal, *Permanent Campaign*.
47. *Project on New Communication Technologies, Public Policy and Democratic Values*, Harvard University, Dec. 1985, ch. 4: Abramson, Jeffrey, 'Democratic Theory and Communications Technology'.
48. *New York Times*, 31 May 1981.
49. Sabato, *New Ways of Winning*.
50. Rothschild, Michael, 'Political Advertising: A Neglected Policy Issue In Marketing', *Journal of Marketing Research*, vol. 15, no. 1, Feb. 1978.
51. Soley, L.S. and Read, L.N., 'Promotional Expenditure in US Congres-

sional Elections', *Journal of Marketing and Public Policy*, vol. 1, Quotes, Atkin and Heald (1976), Mulder (1979), and Palda (1975).

52. Humke, R.G., Schmitt, R.L. and Grupp, S.J., 'Candidates, Issues and Party in Newspaper Political Advertisements', *Journalism Quarterly*, Autumn 1975, p. 10.
53. Atwood, L.E. and Sanders, K.R., 'Perception of Information Sources and Likelihood of Split Ticket Voting', *Journalism Quarterly*, Autumn 1975.
54. See Sabato, *New Ways of Winning*.
55. Ibid.
56. *Campaigns and Elections*, vol. 7, no. 4, Nov.–Dec. 1986.
57. *The Times*, 3 Nov. 1986, 'Senate control lies with US farm vote'.
58. Ibid.
59. 'Commercials and Real People', by Robert Jones, *New York Times*, 18 Feb. 1986.
60. Ibid.
61. Ibid.
62. Nimmo, *Political Persuaders*.
63. Ibid.
64. *The Times*, 4 Nov. 1986, 'Democrats look for lame-duck Reagan'.
65. Charles Guggenheim, *New York Times*, 'For Accountability in Political Ads'.
66. Abramson, *Project*.
67. Ibid., ch. 2, 'What's New About the New Media', by Garry Orren.
68. Ibid.
69. Ibid.
70. Abramson, *Project*.
71. Paley, W.C. and Moffet, S., 'The New Electronic Media Instant Action and Reaction', *Campaigns and Elections*, vol. 4, no. 4, Winter 1984.
72. Orren, 'What's New'.
73. Ibid.
74. Ibid.
75. Ranney, Austin, *Channels of Power* (New York: Basic Books, 1983).
76. Orren, 'What's New'.
77. Ibid.
78. Ibid.
79. Ibid.
80. Ibid.
81. Ibid.
82. Ibid.
83. Ibid.
84. Ibid.
85. Arterton, Christopher, 'Communications Technology and Governance', Dec. 1985, in *Project on New Communications Technologies*.
86. Orren, 'What's New'.
87. Ibid.
88. Ibid.
89. Ibid.

90. *Project on New Communications Technologies*, 1985.
91. Orren, 'What's New'.
92. Ibid.
93. Ibid.
94. Sabato, *New Ways of Winning*.
95. Crotty and Jacobson, *Parties in Decline*.
96. Ibid.
97. Ibid.
98. Ranney, *Channels of Power*.
99. Nimmo, *Political Persuaders*.
100. Ibid.
101. Bluementhal, *Permanent Campaign*.
102. McKay, David, *American Politics and Society* (Oxford: Martin Robertson, 1983).
103. Crotty and Jacobson, *Parties in Decline*.
104. Seymour-Ure, *The American President*.
105. Blumenthal, *Permanent Campaign*, ch. 11.
106. Crotty and Jacobson, *Parties in Decline*.
107. Ibid.
108. Kristol, Irving, *Two Cheers for Capitalism* (New York: Basic Books, 1978).
109. Crotty and Jacobson, *Parties in Decline*.
110. Nimmo, *Political Persuaders*.

Further Reading

Atkinson, Max, *Our Masters' Voices* (London: Methuen, 1984), for discussion of range and subtlety of television's demands; of the differences between a live and a televised performance style, and how oratory is ill-suited to television (pp. 175–6).
Bakshian, Aram, *Winning the White House* (Bolton: Ross Anderson Publications, 1984), for discussion of Mondale's use of satellite (p. 94).
Barber, James David, *The Pulse of Politics* (New York: W. W. Norton, 1980) for discussion of candidate gaffes, particularly Carter and 'ethnic purity' (pp. 194–9).
Flanigan, William M., *Political Behaviour of the American Electorate* (Boston: Allyn and Bacon, 1968, 1977), for discussion of how Kennedy defused the issue of his catholicism.
Hodgson, Godfrey, *All things to all men* (Harmondsworth: Penguin Books, 1984) for description of Lyndon Johnson's difficulties with television (p. 176).
MacNeil, Robert, *The People Machine* (London: Eyre and Spottiswoode, 1968) for viewpoint on the triviality of television (pp. 35, 41); blandness of television news (pp. 39, 60); lack of serious social documentary coverage (pp. 81, 82); inability to explore the 'why' factor (p. 57); television as escapism (pp. 13, 14); news as entertainment (p. 21); Nixon–Kennedy debates (pp. 168–72); Nixon's telethon (p. 198); Kennedy's campaign film (p. 200); anti-Goldwater commercials (pp. 207, 208).
Saldich, Anne Rowley, *Electronic Democracy* (New York: Praeger, 1979) for assertions about the political effects of television: claims that it hinders

reasoned discussion (p. 42), weakens parties and conventions (p. 43) and makes democracy more cynical (p. 40).
White, Theodore H. *The Making of the President 1964* (London: Jonathan Cape, 1965), for description of the Goldwater campaign's non-mediable ranting aggression, its excellence at the administration level but poverty in the area of speechwriters, media men and so on.

5   The Peevish Penmen: Direct Mail and US Elections

1. For a specialist discussion, see 'Direct Mail Political Fund Raising', by Brian Haggerty, *Public Relations Journal*, March 1979, vol. 35, no. 3, pp. 10–12. For a general discussion of advertising, see Sandage, C.M. and Fryburger, U., *Advertising Theory and Practice* (Homewood, Illinois, Richard D. Irwin Inc., 1975) pp. 509–12.
2. 'Politics by Mail', by Paul C. Harris, *Wharton Magazine*, Fall 1982, pp. 16, 18, 19.
3. 'Playing Politics by Mail', by James D. Snyder, *Sales and Marketing Management*, 5 July 1982, pp. 44–6.
4. See *Campaigns and Elections*, March–April 1986.
5. For a helpful recent examination of advertising with relevance for direct mail, see Kaufman, Louis, *Essentials of Advertising* (New York: Harcourt Brace Jovanovitch, 1980) especially ch. 12.
6. For a general overview of the political impact of direct mail, see Sabato, Larry, *The Rise of Political Consultants: New Ways Of Winning Elections* (New York: Basic Books, 1981) pp. 220–58.
7. On these points, see 'Direct Mail Fundraising Roundtable: The Pros Speak', *Campaigns and Elections*, Fall 1980; also 'How the Republicans and personalized direct response won the U.S.A.', *ZIP*, October 1981, vol. 4, no. 8, pp. 88–92.
8. 'The 1982 Elections', *Campaigns and Elections*, Winter 1983, vol. 3, no. 4.
9. 'Direct Mail Fundraising Roundtable: The Pros Speak', *Campaigns and Elections*, Fall 1980.
10. Fenno, R., *Homestyle: House Members in their Districts* (Denver, Colorado: Little Inc., 1978).
11. 'Catalyst for dollars and issues is role of mail', by Ralph Whitehead Jr, *Fundraising Management*, July 1983, pp. 52–3.
12. 'Playing politics by mail', by James D. Snyder, *Sales and Marketing Management*, 5 July 1982, pp. 44–6.
13. Dunn, S.W. and Barban, A.M., *Advertising: its Role in Modern Marketing* (Minsdale, Illinois: The Dryden Press, 1978).
14. 'Computers and direct mail are being married on the hill to keep incumbents in office', by Irwin B. Arieff, *Congressional Quarterly World Report*, 21 July 1979, pp. 1445–8.
15. 'Democrat won in Michigan with TV-less ad campaign', by Fred Danzig, *Advertising Age*, 25 Feb. 1974, vol. 45, no. 6, p. 4.
16. For details see 'Costly fund raising: direct mail bids do not ensure pot

of gold', by Larry Light, *Congressional Quarterly World Report*, vol. 40, pp. 2714–15.
17. Larry Light, *C.Q.W.R.*, vol. 40.
18. Larry Light, *C.Q.W.R.*, vol. 40.
19. Clark, E., 'The Lists Business', *Marketing (U.K.)*, December 1981, p. 25.
20. 'Politics by Mail: A New Platform', by Paul C. Harris, *Wharton Magazine*, Fall 1982.
21. Aldige, J.C., 'Political Mail Will Raise Money for Image Makers', *Fundraising Management*, March 1980, pp. 26–31.

6 The Monopoly of Midas Congress and Political Action Committees

1. McKay, David, *American Politics and Society* (Oxford: Martin Robertson, 1983).
2. Oakes, John B., 'The Pac-Man's Game: Eating Legislators', *New York Times*, 6 Sept. 1984.
3. 'How to become President of the United States', *The Economist*, 26 Dec. 1987.
4. Clymer, Adam, '84 PACs gave more to Senate Winners', *New York Times*, 6 Jan. 1985.
5. Ibid.
6. Lipsom, J., '2 N.Y. Reps Among Top "Pac-Men"', *New York Post*, 4 Jan. 1985.
7. Oakes, 'Pac-Man's Game'.
8. Ibid.
9. Berke, Richard L., 'Study Links Contributions To How Lawmakers Voted', *New York Times*, 30 Dec. 1987.
10. Ibid.
11. Kaplan, John, 'That's How the Money Changes Hands', *New York Times Book Review*, 27 Jan. 1985, pp. 9, 10.
12. *Campaigns and Elections*, Feb. 1982.
13. Adam Clymer, '84 PACs'.
14. Ibid.
15. McKay, *American Politics*, ch. 6.
16. *New York Times*, 28 Oct. 1987.
17. Ibid.
18. *New York Times*, Advertisement for Common Cause, 7 April 1987.
19. *New York Times*, 28 Oct. 1987.
20. Common Cause, *New York Times* advertisement.
21. Ibid.
22. *Insight*, 13 April 1987.
23. Binyon, Michael, 'Democrats left behind in record spending on television campaigns', *The Times*, 31 Oct. 1986.
24. Ibid.
25. Berke, Richard L., 'Spending Limit up 14% for Primaries', *New York Times*, 6 February 1988.

26. Oakes, 'Pac-Man's Game'.
27. Ordovensky, Pat, 'Realtors, doctors, teachers top list of big givers', *New York Times*, 1984.
28. Oakes, 'Pac-Man's Game'.
29. *USA Today*, 1 Nov. 1984.
30. Ibid.
31. Ibid.
32. Oakes, 'Pac-Man's Game'.
33. Sabato, Larry, *The Rise of Political Consultants: New Ways of Winning Elections* (New York: Basic Books, 1981).
34. Brannan, Brad, 'Nacpac in the 80's', *Campaigns and Elections*, Winter 1983.
35. Ibid.
36. Ibid.
37. Brad Brannan, 'Nacpac role in the 1980 Senate elections', *Campaigns and Elections*, Spring 1982.
38. *New York Times*, 13 April 1986.
39. Charles Bremner, *New York Times*, 28 October 1987, 'Guns for all crusade prospers in US'.
40. Ibid.
41. Ibid.
42. *New York Times*, 27 December 1976.
43. Michael Binyon, 'Reagan faces cool welcome on prairies', *The Times*, 29 September 1986.
44. Ibid.
45. Ibid.
46. 'Corporate PACs', by D. R. Kendall, *Campaigns and Elections*, Spring 1980, p. 55.
47. Ibid.
48. *New York Times*, 6 Nov. 1984, 'Democrats Gain in Business PAC Funds', by Adam Clymer.
49. Ibid.
50. Ibid.
51. *New York Times*, 6 Nov. 1984.
52. McKay, *American Politics*.
53. 'Democrats Rebuilding', *Campaigns and Elections*, Spring 1982, p. 58.
54. Ibid.
55. Bonitati, Robert F., 'Labor Political Clout in the '80s: The New Strategies', *Campaigns and Elections*, Fall 1980.
56. Ibid.
57. Adam Clymer, *New York Times*, 6 Nov. 1984.
58. The *New York Times*, 6 Nov. 1984, 'Democrats Gain in Business PAC Funds', by Adam Clymer.
59. Ibid.
60. Clymer, Adam, ''84 PAC's gave more to Senate Winners', *New York Times*, 6 January 1985.
61. Grigg, John, 'America's Flawed Democracy', *The Times* 4 Nov. 1986.
62. McKay, *American Politics*.
63. Richard Berke, *New York Times*, 30 December 1987.

64. *Insight*, 13 April 1987.
65. Ibid.
66. *New York Times*, 21 April 1986, 'Lobbying by Ex-Reagan Aides Leads to Calls for New Rules'.
67. *Time*, 3 March 1986, 'Peddling Influence'.
68. Arterton, Christopher, 'Communications Technology and Governance', *Project on New Communications Technology*, ch. 5, Harvard J.F.K. School, 1985.
69. *New York Times*, 21 April 1986.
70. Arterton, 'Communications Technology'.
71. *Time*, 3 March 1986, 'Peddling Influence'.
72. *New York Times*, 21 October 1985, 'Lobbyists line-up the power on arms for Jordan'.
73. *Time*, 'Peddling Influence'.
74. *New York Times*, 21 April 1986.
75. *Time*, 'Peddling Influence'.
76. Oakes, John B. 'The PAC-Man's Game: Eating Legislators', *New York Times*, 6 September 1984.
77. Ibid.
78. Ibid.
79. Ibid.
80. Kaplan, 'That's How'.
81. Ibid.
82. Ibid.
83. Oakes, 'Pac-Man's Game'.
84. *The Economist*, 26 Dec. 1987.
85. Professor John C. Pittenger, *New York Times*, 25 March 1985.
86. *The Economist*, 21 December 1985.

Further Reading

Fritschler, A.L. and Ross, B.M., *How Washington Works* (Cambridge, Mass.: Ballinger, 1987) for discussion of lobbyists (ch. 5) and PAC rules (Appendix E).
Twentieth Century Fund, *What Price PAC?*1984; this supplies data, outlines PAC strategies and suggests possible reforms.

7 High Priesthood, Low Priesthood: The Role of Political Consultants

1. Sabato, Larry. *The Rise of Political Consultants: New Ways of Winning Elections* (New York: Basic Books, 1981).
2. Ibid.
3. Blumenthal, Sidney, *The Permanent Campaign* (New York: Simon & Schuster, 1984) ch. 4.
4. Blumenthal, *Permanent Campaign*.
5. Sabato, op. cit.
6. Ibid.

268   *Notes and References*

7. Ibid.
8. Ibid.
9. See Saloma, John S., *Ominous Politics: The New Conservative Labyrinth* (New York: Hill and Wang, 1984).
10. Author's interview with Joe White, New York, January 1987.
11. Peele, Gillian, 'Campaign Consultants', *Electoral Studies 1:3*, December 1982, pp. 355–62.
12. Nimmo, Dan, *The Political Persuaders* (Englewood Cliffs: Prentice-Hall, 1970).
13. Ibid.
14. Blumenthal, *Permanent Campaign*, ch. 10.
15. Ibid.
16. Sabato, *New Ways of Winning*.
17. Ibid.
18. Peele, 'Campaign Consultants'.
19. Saloma, *Ominous Politics*.
20. Ibid.
21. Blumenthal, *Permanent Campaign*.
22. Ibid.
23. Author's interview with David Sawyer, January 1987.
24. Author's interview with Joseph Napolitan, January 1987.
25. Author's interview with Roger Ailes, January 1987.
26. Author's interview with James Severin, January 1987.
27. Author's interview with Video Base International, January 1987.
28. Author's interview with David Garth, January 1987.
29. Blumenthal, *Permanent Campaign*.
30. Ibid.
31. Ibid.
32. Ibid.
33. Author's interview with Tony Schwartz, January 1987.
34. Blumenthal, *Permanent Campaign*.
35. Chagal, David, *The New Kingmakers* (New York: Harcourt Brace Jovanovich, 1981) ch. 9.
36. Ibid.
37. Ibid.
38. Author's interview with Joe White, January 1987.

Further Reading

Denton, R.E. and Woodard, Gary C., *Political Communication in America* (New York: Praeger, 1985), ch. 3 on the professionalisation of political communication.
Schwartz, Tony, *Media the Second God* (New York: Anchor Books, 1983) for his theories on political communication and description of how commercials work.

8 Washington's Space Cadets: The Centrality of Polling, Computer and Other Technologies in US Politics Today

1. Stein, Art, 'The Powerful New Machine On The Political Scene', *Business Week*, 5 November 1984.
2. Ibid.
3. Ibid.
4. Burnham, David, 'When an Ethnic Name Makes a Voter Fair Game', *New York Times*, 17 April 1984.
5. Ibid.
6. Ibid.
7. *The Economist*, 1 September 1984.
8. 'Reagan's Campaign Adds Strategy Role to use of Computer', *New York Times*, 22 April 1984.
9. Ibid.
10. Ibid.
11. Ibid.
12. Art Stein, 'Powerful New Machine'.
13. *The Economist*, 1 September 1984.
14. *New York Times* 22 April 1984.
15. Ibid.
16. Ibid.
17. 'Small Computers Open Politics to Citizens with Little Money', *New York Times*, 15 February 1984.
18. Ibid.
19. Ibid.
20. Ibid.
21. *New York Times*, 15 February 1984.
22. Art Stein, 'Powerful New Machine'.
23. Ibid.
24. Nimmo, Dan, *The Political Persuaders* (New Jersey: Prentice-Hall, 1970).
25. Blumenthal, Sidney, *The Permanent Campaign* (New York: Simon & Schuster, 1984) ch. 4.
26. Nimmo, *Political Persuaders*.
27. Ibid.
28. Sabato, Larry, *The Rise of Political Consultants, New Ways of Winning Elections* (New York: Basic Books, 1981).
29. See O'Shaughnessy, John, *Competitive and Strategic Marketing* (London: George Allen & Unwin, 1984).
30. Nimmo, *Political Persuaders*.
31. Ibid.
32. Blumenthal, *Permanent Campaign*.
33. Perry, Roland, *The Programming of the President* (London: Aurum Press, 1984).
34. Ibid.
35. Ibid.
36. Nimmo, *Political Persuaders*.
37. Ibid.

270 *Notes and References*

38. Ibid.
39. Sabato, *New Ways of Winning.*
40. Ibid.
41. Ibid.
42. Nimmo, *Political Persuaders.*
43. Perry, James M., *The New Politics* (London: Weidenfeld and Nicolson, 1968).
44. Butler, David and Kavanagh, Dennis, *The British General Election of 1987* (London: Macmillan, 1984).
45. Perry, James M., *New Politics.*
46. Ibid.
47. Chagal, David, *The New Kingmakers* (New York: Harcourt Brace Jovanovich, 1981).
48. Nimmo, *Political Persuaders.*
49. Butler and Kavanagh, *Election 1987.*
50. Sabato, *New Ways of Winning.*
51. Ibid.
52. Ibid.
53. Blumenthal, *Permanent Campaign.*
54. Nimmo, *Political Persuaders.*
55. Ibid.
56. Ibid.
57. Ibid.
58. Ibid.
59. Arterton, F. Christopher, *Media Politics: The News Strategies of Presidential Campaigns* (Lexington, Mass.: D. C. Heath, 1984).
60. McGinnis, Joe, *The Selling of the President, 1968* (New York: Trident Press, 1969).
61. Butler and Kavanagh, *Election 1987.*
62. Arterton, *The News Strategies.*
63. Ibid.
64. For details of gimmickry see Sabato, *New Ways of Winning.*
65. Nimmo, *Political Persuaders.*

Further Reading

Bakshian, Aram, *Winning the White House* (Bolton: Ross Anderson Publications, 1984) on how Wirthlin would provide updated polling data every two weeks, pp. 90, 91; on gender gap, pp. 91–3; and on the great importance of newspapers, pp. 95, 96.

Graber, Doris A., *Mass Media and American Politics* (Washington: Congressional Quarterly Press, 1984) for account of muck-raking journalism, ch. 8.

Harrison, T. 'Impact Polling: Feedback for a Winning Strategy', *Campaigns and Elections*, Spring 1980.

MacNeil, Robert, *The People Machine* (London: Eyre and Spottiswoode, 1968) on Kennedy making the first political use of computers.

Teer, F. and Spence J.D., *Political Opinion Polls* (London: Hutchinson, 1973) especially ch. 2 on methods.

White, Theodore H., *The Making of the President 1960* (London: Jonathan Cape, 1962) for discussion of J. F. Kennedy's management of the press, p. 339.

9 Merchandising the Monarch: Reagan and the Presidential Elections

1. These pages refer extensively to McGinnis, Joe, *The Selling of the President, 1968* (New York: Trident Press, 1969).
2. See MacNeil, Robert, *The People Machine* (London: Eyre and Spottis-woode, 1970) for account of Nixon's lack of televisual appeal (p. 138).
3. See English, David, *Divided They Stand* (London: Michael Joseph, 1969).
4. MacNeil, *People Machine*.
5. See White, Theodore, H., *The Making of the President, 1960* (London: Jonathan Cape, 1962) on how Nixon ignored his advertising advisers (p. 312).
6. Ibid.
7. McGinnis, *Selling the President*.
8. Ibid.
9. Ibid.
10. Ibid.
11. Ibid.
12. For account of Nixon's debating style contrasted with Kennedy's image management, see White, *Making the President*, p. 287.
13. McGinnis, *Selling the President*.
14. Ibid.
15. See MacNeil, *People Machine*, for account of Reagan's early packaging (pp. 142, 143).
16. Ibid., p. 143.
17. *The Washington Post, The Pursuit of the Presidency 1980* (New York: Berkeley Books, 1980).
18. Ibid.
19. Ibid.
20. Ibid.
21. Ibid.
22. Ibid.
23. See MacNeil, *People Machine*, for account of Reagan's campaign.
24. Blumenthal, Sidney, *The Permanent Campaign* (New York: Simon & Schuster, 1982).
25. Nimmo, Dan, *The Political Persuaders* (Englewood Cliffs, New Jersey: Prentice-Hall, 1970).
26. Perry, James, *The New Politics* (London: Weidenfeld and Nicolson, 1968).
27. Ibid.
28. Ibid.
29. Nimmo, *Political Persuaders*.
30. Ibid.
31. Chagal, David, *The New Kingmakers* (New York: Harcourt Brace Jovanovich, 1981).
32. Perry, *New Politics*.
33. Chagal, *New Kingmakers*.

34. For an account of the 1980 Presidential Campaign see Wayne, Stephen J., *The Road to the White House* (New York: St. Martin's Press, 1980) and also the *Washington Post, Pursuit of the Presidency*.
35. Chagal, *New Kingmakers*.
36. For an account of Kennedy in 1980 see Drew, Elizabeth, *Portrait of an Election* (New York: Simon & Schuster, 1981) p. 161.
37. Chagal, *New Kingmakers*.
38. Ibid.
39. Ibid.
40. Ibid.
41. Ibid.
42. Ibid.
43. McKay, David, *American Politics and Society* (Oxford: Martin Robertson, 1983).
44. Ibid.
45. See Drew, *Portrait*, for an account of the Carter campaign.
46. Blumenthal, *Permanent Campaign*.
47. McKay, *American Politics*.
48. For an account of Reagan's Presidential Leadership see Sandoz and Cecil (eds), *Election 84* (New York: Mentor Books, 1985) ch. 3.
49. Blumenthal, *Permanent Campaign*.
50. Ibid.
51. Ibid.
52. Ibid.
53. See Atkinson, Max, *Our Masters' Voices* (London: Methuen, 1984) for an account of Reagan's conversational style and its suitability for television, pp. 166, 167.
54. Perry, *New Politics*.
55. Report, *International Herald Tribune*, 24 Nov. 1987.
56. Blumenthal, *Permanent Campaign*.
57. Ibid.
58. 'The American Dream Behind Reagan Vote', *The Daily Telegraph*, 4 Sept. 1984.
59. Philip M. Dougherty, 'Reagan's Emotional Campaign', *New York Times*, 8 Nov. 1987.
60. Ibid.
61. McElvaine, Robert S., 'Liberals Go Back to the Flag', *New York Times*, 2 Sept. 1984.
62. Ibid.
63. Ibid.
64. Amitai Etzioni, 'The Democrats Need a Unifying Theme', *New York Times*, 5 Oct. 1984.
65. McElvaine, 'Liberals'.
66. 'The Price Of Starting The Presidential Race', *Marketing Week*, 28 Aug. 1984.
67. Ibid.
68. 'Campaign', 24 Aug. 1984, p. 11.
69. 'An Eagle in his element', *The Times*, 3 Nov. 1986.
70. *Daily Telegraph*, 28 Oct. 1986.

71. *The Economist*, Autumn 1986
72. Sir Alfred Sherman, 'The Ad-Man Cometh', *Guardian*, June 1987.
73. *The Economist*, 19 April 1986.

Further Reading

Denton, R.E. and Woodard, Gary C., *Political Communication in America* (New York: Praeger, 1985) for mention of political symbols, p. 34 and symbolic nature of presidency, ch. 7.
Seymour Ure, Colin, *The American President: Power and Communication* (London: Macmillan, 1982).

10 A Licence to Export: The Spread of Political Marketing Methods to Britain

1. Johnson, R.J., 'Political Advertising and the Geography of Voting in England at the 1983 General Election', *International Journal of Advertising*, vol. 4, no. 1, 1985.
2. 'The War of the Agencies', *New Statesman*, 22 August 1986.
3. *New Society*, 16 August 1985, 'Nanny of the Nation', pp. 234–5.
4. Sir Alfred Sherman 'The Ad-man Cometh', *Guardian*, June 1987.
5. Max Beloff, 'Fire the ad men and put the money up front', *The Times*, 30 August 1987.
6. 'Political advertising booms in Britain. . . .', Ian Griffiths, *The Times*, 16 April 1985.
7. Ibid.
8. Ibid.
9. *The Times*, 24 Nov. 1986.
10. Magnet, Myron, 'What Makes Saatchi Grow', *Fortune*, 19 March 1984.
11. Ibid.
12. Claim of Michael Cockerell, *Listener* June 1983, 'The Marketing of Margaret'.
13. Butler, David and Kavanagh, Dennis, *The British General Election of 1983* (London: Macmillan, 1984).
14. Ibid.
15. Ibid.
16. Ibid.
17. Ibid.
18. Robert Fox, *Listener*, 16 June 1983, 'He was out-Saatchied at every turn'.
19. 'Healey on why Labour lost', by Donald Macintyre, *The Sunday Times*, 11 September 1983.
20. Butler, David and Kavanagh, Dennis, *The British General Election of 1983* (London: Macmillan, 1984).
21. Ibid.
22. Ibid.
23. Ibid.
24. Butler, David and Kavanagh, Dennis, *The British General Election of 1987* (London: Macmillan, 1988), pp. 251.

Further Reading

Atkinson, Max, *Our Masters' Voices* (London: Methuen, 1984) for account of Mrs Thatcher's voice change and re-packaging, pp. 113–15; and on Foot's rhetoric as being geared to a pre-television age, p. 166.

Butler, David and Kavanagh, Dennis, *The British General Election of 1987* (London: Macmillan, 1988) for account of 1987, especially ch. 7 on broadcasting.

Kleinman, Philip, *The Saatchi and Saatchi Story* (London: Butler and Tanner, 1987) for account of the rise of the Saatchis, especially ch. 3.

Tyler, Rodney, *Campaign* (London: Grafton Books, 1987) for 1987 account.

11   The Selling of the President 1988

1.   *Sunday Times*, 14 August 1988.
2.   *Time*, 8 August 1988.
3.   *The Times*, 14 August 1988.
4.   Michael Binyon, *The Times*, 9 August 1988.
5.   Michael Binyon, *The Times*, 17 February 1988.
6.   *Economist*, 2 July 1988.
7.   *Newsweek*, 1 August 1988.
8.   *Newsweek*, 22 August 1988.
9.   *Sunday Telegraph*, 14 August 1988.
10. Gail Sheely, *Sunday Times*, 14 August 1988.
11. *New York Times*, 29 September 1988.
12. *Newsweek*, 22 August 1988.
13. *The Times*, 9 August 1988.
14. *The Times*, 20 August 1988.
15. *The Times*, 29 August 1988.
16. *The Times*, 10 August 1988.
17. Charles Bremner, *The Times*, 18 October 1988.
18. *Sunday Times*, 21 February 1988.
19. Ibid.
20. *The Times*, 17 February 1988.
21. Michael White, *Guardian*, 7 November 1988.
22. Joe Klein, *Sunday Times*, 9 October 1988.
23. Joe Klein, *New York*, 24 October 1988.
24. Simon Hoggart, *Observer*, 16 October 1988.
25. David Blundy, *Sunday Telegraph*, 6 November 1988.
26. *Economist*, 29 October 1988.
27. Charles Bremner, *The Times*, 14 October 1988.
28. Christopher Thomas, *The Times*, 26 September 1988.
29. John Buckley, *New York Times*, 29 September 1988.
30. Bremner, *The Times*, 18 October 1988.
31. Ibid.
32. Simon Hoggart, *Observer*, 16 October 1988.
33. *Newsweek*, 1 August 1988.
34. *Economist*, 23 July 1988.
35. Andrew Rosenthal, *New York Times*, 26 February 1988.

36. M. O'Neil, *New York Times*, 9 April 1988.
37. *Sunday Times*, 21 February 1988.
38. *The Times*, 11 April 1988.
39. *Economist*, 29 October 1988.
40. Joe Klein, *New York Times*, 24 October 1988.
41. *New York Times*, 19 October 1988.
42. Ibid.
43. *The Times*, 16 August 1988.
44. Hoggart, *Observer*, 16 October 1988.
45. William Safire, *New York Times*, 13 October 1988.
46. Richard L. Berke, *New York Times*, 21 March 1988.
47. *The Times*, 17 February 1988.
48. *New York Times*, 21 May 1988.
49. *New York Times*, 20 October 1988.
50. Hoggart, *Observer*, 16 October 1988.
51. *Sunday Telegraph*, 6 October 1988.
52. *Newsweek*, 22 August 1988.
53. *New York Times*, 20 October 1988.
54. *New York Times*, 7 October 1988.
55. *Newsweek*, 1 August 1988.
56. Ibid.

12 An Ethical Conundrum?

1. Abramson, Jeffrey, 'The New Media and Democratic Participation', *Project on New Communication Technologies, Public Policy and Democratic Values*, ch. 6, Harvard University John F. Kennedy School of Government, December 1985.
2. Ibid.
3. Ibid.
4. *The Economist*, 29 March 1986.
5. Orren, Garry, 'Elections and The Media', *Project on New Communication Technologies*, ch. 4, Dec. 1985.
6. Ibid.
7. Abramson, 'The New Media', ch. 3.
8. Abramson, 'The New Media', ch. 6.
9. Perry, Roland, 'The Programming of The President' (London: Aurum Press, 1983).
10. Abramson, 'The New Media', ch. 3.
11. Ibid.
12. Ibid.
13. Ibid.
14. Abramson, 'The New Media', ch. 6.
15. 'The glorious past that never was', *The Economist*, 26 Dec. 1987.
16. Ibid.
17. Ibid.
18. Ibid.
19. Sir Alfred Sherman, 'The Ad-Man Cometh', *Guardian*, 1987.

20.   *The Economist*, 11–17 Oct. 1986, p. 13.

Further Reading

Denton, R.E. and Woodard, Gary C., *Political Communication in America* (New York: Praeger, 1985) for discussion of politics and the crisis of authority, pp. 331–3.

Robert MacNeil, *The People Machine* (London: Eyre and Spottiswoode, 1968) for discussion of the redesign of conventions for television, pp. 109, 110.

Index

277